# The Financial Crisis in Bible Prophecy

## T. H. Aka

Coldwater, Michigan 49036
www.remnantpublications.com

Copyright © 2013 by T. H. Aka
All Rights Reserved

Printed in the USA

Published by Remnant Publications, Inc.
649 E. Chicago Road
Coldwater, MI 49036
517-279-1304
www.remnantpublications.com

Unless otherwise noted, Scripture quotations are taken from The Holy Bible, King James Version.

Scripture quotations marked (NKJV) are from the New King James Version®. Copyright © 1982 by Thomas Nelson, Inc. Used by permission. All rights reserved.

Cover designed by David Berthiaume
Copy editing by Debi Tesser
Text designed by Greg Solie • AltamontGraphics.com

ISBN: 978-1-937718-75-6

# Table of Contents

Dedication . . . . . . . . . . . . . . . . . . . . . . . . . . . . . . . . . . . . . . . . . . . . . . . . . . 4

Introduction . . . . . . . . . . . . . . . . . . . . . . . . . . . . . . . . . . . . . . . . . . . . . . 5

Chapter 1   2008—The Awakening . . . . . . . . . . . . . . . . . . . . . . . . . . . . 13

Chapter 2   Habakkuk 2—The Debt Default . . . . . . . . . . . . . . . . . . . . . 21

Chapter 3   A Measure of Wheat for a Penny—Hyperinflation . . . . . . . . 39

Chapter 4   The Gospel Bubble? . . . . . . . . . . . . . . . . . . . . . . . . . . . . . . . . 49

Chapter 5   Too Big to Fail . . . . . . . . . . . . . . . . . . . . . . . . . . . . . . . . . . . . 61

Chapter 6   The Salvation Option . . . . . . . . . . . . . . . . . . . . . . . . . . . . . . 79

Chapter 7   The Bride, the Builders, and the Crisis . . . . . . . . . . . . . . . . . . 89

Chapter 8   Laodicea and the Root of All Evil . . . . . . . . . . . . . . . . . . . . 101

Chapter 9   The Panic of 1873—A Prelude to a Sunday Law . . . . . . . . . . 115

Chapter 10  The Food Crisis . . . . . . . . . . . . . . . . . . . . . . . . . . . . . . . . . . 127

Chapter 11  Unions and Monopolies . . . . . . . . . . . . . . . . . . . . . . . . . . . 141

Chapter 12  Spoke Like a Dragon . . . . . . . . . . . . . . . . . . . . . . . . . . . . . . 153

Chapter 13  Slaves and Souls of Men . . . . . . . . . . . . . . . . . . . . . . . . . . . 171

Chapter 14  Lovers of Pleasure . . . . . . . . . . . . . . . . . . . . . . . . . . . . . . . . 183

Chapter 15  Joseph and His Two Coats . . . . . . . . . . . . . . . . . . . . . . . . . . 191

Chapter 16  The Law of the Medes and Persians Which Altereth Not . . . . 197

Chapter 17  Approaching the Jordan Again . . . . . . . . . . . . . . . . . . . . . . 217

# Dedication

My father, Pastor Koei Aka, has been my example through his 42 years of ministry in the Seventh-day Adventist Church. My mother has been my steadfast support throughout my life. I dedicate this book to them.

# Introduction

The Apple iPhone 5 was launched on September 21, 2012, as thousands lined up at Best Buy and Apple stores to be one of the first to own the device. More than five million iPhone 5s were sold in the first three days, setting a record pace for the sale of a new Smartphone. Faster, more apps, better camera, and better screen resolution were all selling features of the new iPhone 5. One analyst expected that the sales of iPhone 5s in the first three months of sales could be as high as 41 million units.

On September 4, 2012, the US Department of Agriculture announced a new record; 46.7 million Americans were using "food stamps" or receiving some form of government aid in order to purchase food. The estimated annual cost for the food stamp program is about $75 billion. This figure has doubled in the past four years. Fourteen percent of American's cannot put food on the table for themselves and their families without the aid of the government. The CEO of Wal-Mart noted the increase in shoppers on the last night of every month. Dozens of shoppers would come in to the store late in the evening and shop for essentials and wait for the stroke of midnight when their "benefit cards" were "reloaded" for the month. Wal-Mart has increased its staffing on these month-end nights to serve these customers.

Yet, sales at stores like Tiffany's, Coach, and Saks Fifth Avenue have seen strong growth since 2010. Luxury item sales grew 13% and 10% in 2010 and 2012 respectively, and they are expected to continue to rise by about 6% to 7% a year, including clothing, jewelry, cars, vacations, and houses, compared to the less than 2% rate for the general economy. Luxury product sales are strong globally, with robust sales growth particularly in China and India. Still, the Americans, predominantly the younger generation, are spending more on luxury goods, even with the economic uncertainty surrounding the world. Whether spending $4 million on a Manhattan condo, $80,000 on a BMW, or $5,000 on a Rolex, the wealthy continue to spend freely.

Most Americans aren't in that tax bracket and live on a much more restricted budget. Still they like to live in comfort, trying to live like the rich and famous by hosting parties, taking luxurious holidays, generously furnishing their home, and buying the latest technological gadgets. Middle class consumers continue to spend on goods and services. Think about the iPhone 5. The phones are only $199, but the service plan is $150 per month for 10 gigabytes of data and unlimited calling for the family or $1,800 per year. The satellite TV is $39 per month times three TVs, one for upstairs, downstairs, and the basement for a monthly cost of $120, or $1,440 per year. Home internet averages $60 per month, or $720 per year. Just those items come to $330 per month, or almost $4,000 per year. These costs were nonexistent when the baby boomers were growing up.

Add $600 for two car payments, $400 for insurance, $800 for mortgage or rent, $200 for utilities, $1,000 for groceries, and $200 on gas for a total monthly cost of $3,530. For the average American family who earns $44,000 per year or $3,666 per month, it leaves very little if anything for clothing, entertainment, maintenance, or any other incidentals. Heaven forbid that anyone gets ill and needs costly medical care. Major repairs on the house or car could send the household budget into chaos. Any of these items are paid for by credit in the hope that there will be better times tomorrow to pay off the debt.

The middle class remains the largest segment of the population in developed nations, but their numbers are declining as these nations are increasingly becoming polarized into groups of the rich and the poor. The gap between the rich and poor, "the haves and have nots," continues to widen, even as an increasing number in the middle fall toward the lower strata. Many in the middle are often unaware that they have fallen so far behind that they are effectively among the poor, even if statistically, they are not.

Demographics also play a large part in this transformation of our society's economics. As greater numbers of the baby boomers retire, they become reliant on Social Security and pay fewer taxes adding to an already unsustainable cost. The Social Security Administration has estimated that they will run out of funds by 2025, given the current rate of income and spending. Social aid and entitlement programs continue to be a large part of the annual costs of the government funded by deficit spending.

Understanding these three social strata gives us a window into the financial state of the government. Looking at government spending and policies in the context of these three social strata helps to explain the priorities of the government and where the future may be headed.

In looking at those who are on the lower end of the wealth scale, about half of the government budget, $1.8 trillion, goes toward "social assistance" programs. This includes Social Security, Medicare/Medicaid, and food stamps. The number of persons who are aided by these programs continues to increase and will likely see a dramatic increase as more of the baby boomers reach the age of retirement.

On the other end of the spectrum, there are the wealthy who hold about three-quarters of the nation's wealth, and who pay a large portion of the taxes. They pay a disproportionate share of the taxes collected by the government, but they also hold a disproportionate share of the wealth, in stocks, bonds, precious metals, and real estate. They benefit from the government policies that, in effect, support their wealth. Policies like low interest and quantitative easing indirectly support the stock market and thereby support the wealthy. Over the past four years, trillions of dollars have been used to stabilize the financial institutions and prop up the stock markets, largely to the benefit of the wealthy. Even defense spending, to a large extent, benefits the wealthy, who own the majority of the stocks in defense-related companies.

Then we are left with the group in the middle—the middle class. They still form the largest part of the workforce, pay a fair share of taxes, but they generally do not benefit from government spending as the other two groups. Yes, there are infrastructure spending programs, educational aid, and of course government jobs that help the middle class. These include both direct employment by federal, state, and municipal governments as well as government agencies and publicly funded institutions like schools, health care, and the military.

Spending on the middle class tends to be in the tens of billions, which, though significant, is starkly less than the trillions of dollars spent on the other two classes, social programs, or bailing out the financial system. The middle class continues to be squeezed through higher costs, fewer jobs, lower pay, and more taxes. The squeeze on the middle class will continue and the battles will intensify between the workers with the labor unions and the governments that pay them.

When we look at government spending, we begin to see its annual budget, just like a family budget has been locked into programs of spending that can't be avoided. There is $850 billion in Medicare/Medicaid, $820 billion on Social Security, $150 billion on agriculture (of which $75 billion is food stamps), $130 billion on veterans, $100 billion on education, $80 billion on transportation (roads), and of course $160 billion on the interest cost of debt. Still, this is only a partial list, and it doesn't include the money spent on making everyone feel safe. The cost for that is $800 billion on defense, including homeland security and foreign aid. The total amount of government spending each year is about $3.5 trillion. Though some of these costs are labeled as discretionary spending, they happen every year, year after year. Yet the government, just like many average American households, can't make ends meet, and it needs to borrow money to pay its bills.

Here are the simple numbers for the federal finances. The US economy is about $15 trillion in size. The government spends about $3.5 trillion, but only collects about $2.5 trillion in taxes. It has to "borrow" more than $1 trillion each year. In the past four years, from 2008 to 2012, the government has "borrowed" more than $1 trillion per year. The amount of debt owed by the US is now about $16 trillion. The debt to gross domestic product (GDP) ratio has surpassed 100%, or in other words, the US owes more than it produces in a year, which adds to the debt at the pace of about 6% a year. The average growth of the economy, as measured by GDP, is about 4.4% year. Even in the best of times, GDP growth is 6% to 7%. The economy cannot keep pace with the amount of debt that is being amassed, even if it was firing on all cylinders. Sadly, the economy is far from robust growth, but is rather anemic today and looks to be weak for years to come. At the current pace, by 2020 the nation could be facing a debt of $23 trillion.

So just who is lending the money to the government? China and Japan are the largest creditors of the US, but those countries have been scaling back the level of investments of late. Other nations are looking to make bilateral trade agreements, particularly in oil, to avoid the use of the US dollar, further reducing the demand for US dollars and US Treasury debt. At record low interest rates, savers and investors are less interested in putting their money into US bills, notes, and bonds.

On September 13, 2012, Ben Bernanke launched the third round of the quantitative easing program (QE3) by the US Federal Reserve (the Fed). This is actually the fourth major program that the Fed launched to try to bring the country out of an economic slump and restore prosperity. It was touted as an all-out effort to bring economic growth back to the nation, using jobs growth as the yardstick for the program's success. The stock market saw it as another boom with the additional money that the Fed will pump into the financial institutions. But the benefits from each of the successive quantitative easing programs appear to be of a smaller magnitude and shorter in duration. Economists question the effectiveness of this latest program of QE3. Still, the Fed has created an open-ended program that allows it to continue the program indefinitely and fund the borrowing needs of the government.

QE3 may be the only tool that the government has left to fund the deficit that the US government runs year after year. It is also necessary to keep interest rates low. If interest rates were allowed to rise in a free market, the cost of debt would quickly drown any economic growth, the debt would become unsustainable, and no further debt could be issued. This would be the same scenario as the European nations, such as Greece, Ireland, Portugal, and Spain are now facing.

At the beginning of September 2012, the European Central Bank (ECB) announced their outright monetary transactions program which, like QE3, was intended to ease the financial burden on European nations struggling with debt. This was the third program in less than a year for the ECB to alleviate the European debt crisis. Each of the past programs proved to be less effective than the previous one and none have been able to pull the economy out of the malaise. Europe is trying to deal with its debt problems, which have advanced past a critical stage. Like the US, the Europeans have been trying to fund their deficit for years, but they have now reached an unsustainable level.

Japan has similar circumstances, but it has been able to keep its debt problems contained within the country. Due to the large amounts of exports, they have been able to keep their currency strong and fund their own debts, but they too are fast approaching a critical stage where they will no longer be able to borrow money. Their aging population and declining workforce numbers will no longer be able to purchase their government debt. Also, their strength in exporting is being diminished by rising costs, international competition, and a global economic slowdown.

Then there is China. The Chinese economy has been sputtering and is heading for a slowdown as its major trading partners are in an economic slump. The giant export powerhouse, seen by many as the economic engine for global growth in the coming years, is reeling from the global economic slowdown combined with its overuse of debt in building up their cities and industrial capabilities. Its developing middle class still only earns a fraction of the income of the western nations, and many years will elapse before it becomes an engine of global economic growth. Even as China rises, will the Chinese buy goods produced in America, Germany, or France? Or will the Chinese buy goods produced in China, dashing the hopes that China will be the source of growth for western economies?

The western world is now locked into a system that is unsustainable. Both at a consumer level and governmental level, budgets are maxed out, growth is driven by debt, and debt is no longer sustainable. Many have a goal to be financially independent and able to take care of themselves and their families. People want to think that they are in control of their financial situation and not be reliant on anyone for support now or in the future. However, this goal and dream for many may be a fast-fading illusion. Even if individuals are careful and responsible with their own finances, the financial system they have built their hopes upon may be crumbling beneath them.

In wrapping up his Sermon on the Mount, Christ told a parable of a man who built his house upon sand. Christ said:

> Every one that heareth these sayings of mine, and doeth them not, shall be likened unto a foolish man, which built his house upon the sand: And the rain descended, and the floods came, and the winds blew, and beat upon that house; and it fell: and great was the fall of it. (Matthew 7:27)

In his Sermon on the Mount, Jesus outlined the way we as Christ's followers should live. In the heart of His sermon, Jesus gave this advice on how to live.

> No man can serve two masters: for either he will hate the one, and love the other; or else he will hold to the one, and despise the other. Ye cannot serve God and mammon. Therefore I say unto you, Take no thought for your life, what ye shall eat, or what ye shall drink; nor yet for your body, what ye shall put on. Is not the life more than meat, and the body than raiment? Behold the fowls of the air: for they sow not, neither do they reap, nor gather into barns; yet your heavenly Father feedeth them. Are ye not much better than they? Which of you by taking thought can add one cubit unto his stature? And why take ye thought for raiment? Consider the lilies of the field, how they grow; they toil not, neither do they spin: And yet I say unto you, That even Solomon in all his glory was not arrayed like one of these. Wherefore, if God so clothe the grass of the field, which to day is, and to morrow is cast into the oven, shall he not much more clothe you, O ye of little faith? Therefore take no thought, saying, What shall we eat? or, What shall we drink?

or, Wherewithal shall we be clothed? (For after all these things do the Gentiles seek:) for your heavenly Father knoweth that ye have need of all these things. But seek ye first the kingdom of God, and his righteousness; and all these things shall be added unto you. Take therefore no thought for the morrow: for the morrow shall take thought for the things of itself. Sufficient unto the day is the evil thereof. (Matthew 6:24–34)

Our house is crumbling because the foundations that we have built upon are sand and cannot withstand the fury of the storms that are coming upon it. We have failed to heed the words of Christ and the Bible to build for ourselves and our families a house built on a solid rock foundation that can face any tempest.

Where did we go wrong as followers of Christ and His church? How did we get to the place where we are today and where will these events take us? This book explores the start of the financial crisis, the history behind it, and the direction that the crisis is heading. Most of all it seeks to explain the reasons why we are facing this crisis through a study of Bible prophecies and learn how we as Christians and the church can survive the systemic breakdown of our economic systems.

## Chapter 1

# 2008—The Awakening

Indeed, because he transgresses by wine, he is a proud man, and he does not stay at home. Because he enlarges his desire as hell, and he is like death, and cannot be satisfied, he gathers to himself all nations and heaps up for himself all peoples. "Will not all these take up a proverb against him, and a taunting riddle against him, and say, 'Woe to him who increases What is not his—how long? And to him who loads himself with many pledges'? Will not your creditors rise up suddenly? Will they not awaken who oppress you? And you will become their booty. (Habakkuk 2:5–7 NKJV)

**Liar Loans**

Another "For Sale" sign was planted in the neighborhood. This one read "Bank Owned." It was the fourth "For Sale" sign to go up in a month on the street. Nothing was moving. This was the fallout from the infamous "liar loans" and "NINJA loans." Liar loans were exactly what they sound like. Mortgage loans made on false pretenses with the full complicity of both borrower and lender. It was jokingly stated that the two basic requirements to get a liar loan were the ability to sign your name and a pulse. NINJA loans were short for "no income, no job application." As long as the borrower was buying real estate, that's all that mattered. Clearly, these borrowers could not afford to carry a mortgage, but they were offered one anyway. Buy it, flip it, and make lots of money was the craze of years of the real estate boom. Television shows promoted the idea of buying, renovating, and creating lavish houses with no thought about how to pay for it because someone else would buy it. How long? How long could the real estate market continue like this? How long could this kind of insanity go on? Some wondered. By the fall of 2008, the answer to that question had arrived.

The decline in the markets during the week of October 6, 2008, was relentless, dropping 10% by Wednesday, October 8. By late in the afternoon on Thursday, October 9, 2008, the stock market had fallen another 8% that day. The US stock market, represented by the S&P 500 index, had fallen 79 points down to 909 in its first close below the 1,000 level since 2003, with one more day to go until the weekend.

I kept myself busy trying to calculate the impact this week would have on client portfolios, trying not to worry about my own. I had been following the stock markets closely over previous few months as they fell more than 30%, or 400 points. The financial system was chaos in reaction to the meltdown in the housing market and mortgage investments in the summer of 2008.

Fannie Mae and Freddie Mac, the two giant mortgage companies in the United States, had announced that they were losing money that summer. They had a combined net loss of $25 billion for the third quarter and were projecting more losses in the coming quarters. Their stock prices had plummeted, further aggravating their capital problem. By September 2008, the government had to step in to nationalize these companies and injected $100 billion to keep these two companies solvent.[1] In September 2008, Lehman Brothers announced they were bankrupt too, having invested in subprime mortgages and even borrowing money to do so.

This giant housing bubble began in the year 2000 just after the stock market crash. With interest rates historically low, saving money in a bank account seemed pointless. The stock market was still recovering from the tech crash in 2001. The recession that year kept stock prices down. Then the fateful events of 9/11 happened, throwing the world into fear and turmoil. This even added more to the height of the proverbial "wall of worry," keeping the stock market depressed. So in 2002, housing just seemed to be the smart thing to invest in worldwide. The smart thing to do turned into a trend, which turned into rush, which turned into a craze. Prices become inflated due to the overwhelming demand, not only from people wanting a home in which to live but also from those wanting a quick profit. As buyers, homeowners, and speculators were all caught up in the tide of rising prices, it became like a feeding frenzy with everyone believing they had to get into the action. This housing bubble was not limited to the US. The housing bubble was being fully blown in almost every developed and developing nation in the world. Banks were all too happy to facilitate this mad rush to buy houses.

---

1  N. Eric Weiss, "Fannie Mae's and Freddie Mac's Financial Problems: Frequently Asked Questions," Congressional Research Service Report, September 12, 2008, (accessed March 2012).

Nothing typified this better than a television ad in Hungary. The ad for Raiffeisen Bank, an Austrian bank offering mortgages in Hungary, depicted a young couple sitting in front of a bank officer trying to get a mortgage. Every time the couple would try to tell the officer about their jobs, income, or financial situation, the banker, dressed so sharply and looking so professional, would cover her ears and sing "Pa pa pa pa pa pa," like a silly child who didn't want to hear her parents telling her to eat her broccoli. This went on for almost the full 30 seconds, the length of a typical commercial, until at the end the announcer said, "We don't care about your income, only your property value!" Perhaps this was clever, edgy marketing at the time, but one can only look back in amazement at the sheer folly of the times.

Bankers were guilty of greed and negligence as they lent their money as fast as they could for mortgages. When they lent all the money that they had, they took those mortgages and sold them to a mortgage company, such as Fannie Mae, who gave them cash in return so they could go lend some more. Local banks basically became sales agents for the big mortgage companies, earning lots of commissions with no worry about the borrowers ever repaying them. The borrowers then owed their money to the Fannie Maes and the Freddie Macs, the big mortgage lenders. The average homeowner had no idea that mortgages could be bought and sold by banks and that the ultimate owner of his or her house was essentially a revolving door.

Wall Street had been involved in the mortgage business by creating investments called mortgage-backed securities (MBSs). MBSs are basically investments like bonds that were secured or backed by the value of mortgages. Investors would buy these MBSs and in return would be paid the interest that these mortgages remitted. At the end of a specified period of time their principle would be returned in full. If the MBS held only good-quality mortgages, then the risk for the investors was very low because no homeowner would want to default on his or her mortgage and lose his or her home.

Then Wall Street brokers got "smarter" as they began to figure out more ways to package these mortgages. They wanted to package not only the good ones but also some with inferior quality. As the housing boom continued, more and more poor-quality mortgages, called subprime, were lent money to those with poor credit quality. If they could find a way to package some of the inferior-quality mortgages with the good, they could create more MBSs to sell and make money. Then banks could off-load these "subprime" mortgages in exchange for more cash so they could offer more mortgages to borrowers with even worse credit.

Wall Street created enhanced MBS products and then put them in a new package called a collateralized debt obligation (CDO). These were complex products where the actual holdings within these investments were difficult to determine, making it easier to hide these subprime mortgages in large quantities. Wall Street enabled the bad lending practices of banks as it figured out ways to package these subprime mortgages. Wall Street began to put any and all mortgages into these new types of investments—the good, the bad, and the ugly. The ugly were subprime mortgages, liar loans, NINJA loans, which we now just call toxic mortgages for the damage that they are still inflicting on the financial system today.

Wall Street sold these CDOs to sophisticated investors like pension funds and other institutions. The CDO investment structures became so complex that even the sophisticated investors didn't really understand the nature of them. Investors didn't understand what was in them or how they worked, but it would seem that no one wanted to admit he or she didn't understand. No one had the common sense to declare that the "king had no clothes!" Today, these sophisticated investors are suing the firms that sold them these investments for misrepresentation as they were characterized by the seller as having a AAA rating; they were anything but.

So then the circle was complete. Homebuyers borrowed the money from banks, who borrowed their money from mortgage companies, who borrowed their money from pension funds, who where holding money for the retirement of those very same homebuyers. The risks of a potential downturn in the housing market was transferred from the individual to banks, to the mortgage companies, and finally to institutions who were supposed to be safe-guarding the money for the average homeowners' retirement.

By investing in CDOs, pension funds had taken the danger from all of those toxic mortgages and placed them on right back on the backs of the individual homebuyers who had no idea that they were now exposed to that risk. Most people treated their house like their nest eggs and expected it to be a safe investment. They avoided risky investments like the stock market, only to find that they were fully exposed to the downturn in the stock market and in the housing market not only the value of their own homes but also of all the houses across the country. The stage was set for the meltdown.

Some analysts were warning about a real estate bubble even as early as 2005 and 2006. But most people were just riding the wave, too busy counting their commissions to notice that the wave was about to crash them into the rocks. Then in 2007, as the house-flipping started to slow and the markets started to cool off, the defaults started. Unable to sell their homes, which they just spent tens of thousands of dollars renovating and unable to pay their mortgages, the homeowners started to default on their mortgages and walk away from their investments. Banks started to receive "jingle mail"; envelopes that jingled with the keys of the house those owners were giving them back to the bank.

In March of 2008, a company named Bear Sterns, a venerable Wall Street financial firm, was in trouble. They had invested in CDOs and other toxic mortgage investments for their clients in two large "hedge" funds, which were sophisticated investments for knowledgeable investors. However, these investments were so complicated, so opaque, that even knowledgeable investors could not figure out exactly what these Bear Sterns funds had invested in and what the risks were of the fund.

By March of 2008, it was too late. Bear Sterns was insolvent. It had lost too much money and couldn't keep up the pace with redemptions from the funds. It was $28 billion dollars in the red. The failure of Bear Sterns would have a ripple effect on the whole financial community, so the government stepped in. Working with the US Federal Reserve, it bought up the assets of Bear Sterns and sold them at a discount to JP Morgan Chase & Co.[2] The government was hoping to stem the tide of the financial crisis that was coming. It were not successful.

By the summer of 2008, it was clear that the mortgage lenders Fannie Mae and Freddie Mac were also in trouble. They too had lost considerable sums of money as mortgagees defaulted on their loans. After suffering $15 billion in losses, the Federal Housing Finance Agency (FHFA) in September 2008 announced that Fannie and Freddie were to be put into a conservatorship in order to allow these agencies to keep funding mortgages.[3] These two agencies had more than $5 trillion in mortgages and debt as they funded much of the home buying in the United States. The US Treasury had to commit to fund more than $200 billion in capital for these

---

2   "JPMorgan Chase and Bear Stearns Announce Amended Merger Agreement and Agreement for JPMorgan Chase to Purchase 39.5% of Bear Stearns," JP Morgan Chase Press Release, March 24, 2008, http://www.sec.gov/Archives/edgar/data/19617/000089882208000320/pressrelease.htm (accessed March 2012).

3   "Statement of FHFA Director James B. Lockhart," Federal Housing Finance Agency Statement, September 7, 2008, http://www.fhfa.gov/webfiles/23/FHFAStatement9708final.pdf (accessed March 2012).

two agencies to keep them afloat since they lost their ability to raise capital from public sources. The mortgage crisis was in full bloom.

Wall Street had tried to make more money by spreading the risk to many investors, but the risk-spreading didn't end there. Fully expanding the risk to the entire taxpaying public, the federal government stepped in and bailed out the Fannie Mae, Freddie Mac, and all of the Wall Street firms that were in trouble due their investment in toxic mortgages. So a new saying was created: "socialization of losses and privatization of profits." This meant that losses by Wall Street were covered by the taxpaying public, but if they earned any profit, they kept the profits to pay their exorbitant bonuses.

**Habakkuk**

In the midst of all of these events, I was riding the train on my way to work, trying to focus on more important matters—spiritual matters. I was still in the process of awakening, coming from the darkness of a past life, but not nearly awakened to the marvelous light. God always seems to be careful not to blind us with the light, lest the shock to the senses makes us throw the covers back over our heads. I had slowly started to read the Bible again and to seek its truths in place of my own rationalizations. My plan was to read the Bible straight through from Genesis to Revelation to get the "big picture." The rays were penetrating and making its slow transformations. This morning I happened to be reading in the Minor Prophets and had come to Habakkuk. In the second chapter were these words:

> Indeed, because he transgresses by wine, He is a proud man, and he does not stay at home. Because he enlarges his desire as hell, and he is like death, and cannot be satisfied, he gathers to himself all nations and heaps up for himself all peoples. "Will not all these take up a proverb against him, and a taunting riddle against him, and say, 'Woe to him who increases what is not his—how long? And to him who loads himself with many pledges'? Will not your creditors rise up suddenly? Will they not awaken who oppress you? And you will become their booty.'" (Habakkuk 2:5–7 NKJV)

I did a classic double-take after reading this passage. I read it again. "Woe to him who increases what is not his. How long? And to him who loads himself with many pledges?" Could there be a more fitting description of our society today? Have we been increasing the things that really do not belong to us, because we are buying it with many pledges or in another word—"debt"? Our society, like none before it, has turned to borrowed money to fund lifestyles that would otherwise be unattainable to us. We wanted the lifestyles of the rich and famous, but we didn't have the cash for that life. However, we could borrow more easily than ever before—credit cards, loans, lines of credit, home equity loans. There were many ways to access cash, and with expectations of better jobs, higher incomes, and rising home values, there was no reason not to borrow.

It was the next part of the passage that got me worried. "Will not your creditors rise up suddenly? Will they not awaken who oppress you? And you will become their booty." Creditors rising up, oppressing us and then making us their booty—this did not sound very pleasant at all. Who was this text talking about? Who was this prophecy aimed at? Who was it trying to warn?

Looking at the context, Habakkuk seemed to be talking about some time in the future. In fact, he said it was the time of the end. Could he be talking about the mortgage situation and the debts that many of us had amassed? Little did most people realize the enormity of the debt situation at the time in 2008. The debt problem wasn't just mortgages or the housing market. It wasn't for about another year and a half that the full scale of the debt problem became so much more evident.

By 2010 it became clear that the debt crisis was created by not only the mortgages but also by nations and governments. The debt crises were created by US government and the US Federal Reserve that pumped trillions of dollars into the financial system, adding to the debt of the country. Japan continued trying to escape from a debt-death spiral by printing money. China built up cities with reckless abandon. European nations spent freely by borrowing money, then hid their massive debts behind a common currency.

"At the end it will speak," wrote Habakkuk, "It will not lie. Wait for it for it will surely come" (Habakkuk 2:3 NKJV). But how far in the future was he referring to? This started me on a journey in the Scriptures, looking for answers to not only this prophecy, but also into everything that the Bible had to say about a financial crisis in the end times of this world. So this is the story of the journey that has opened my eyes, changed my life (for the better), and has kept me walking humbly each day. It's a journey that has revealed so many truths, which has brought me squarely back to the fundamental beliefs as a Seventh-day Adventist Christian, preparing for the coming of the Lord. It's also a journey that tells of the dark days to come as well as trials and difficulties that will take nothing less than the faith of Jesus to overcome. It's a world of debt defaults, currency collapse, hyperinflation, and financial ruin—all prophesied as a warning to the church and to the world.

## Chapter 2

# Habakkuk 2—The Debt Default

"Woe to him who increases what is not his—how long? And to him who loads himself with many pledges"? Will not your creditors rise up suddenly? (Habakkuk 2:6, 7 NKJV)

Living in an upscale neighborhood in Toronto, Canada, housing was a valuable asset, growing in value each and every year we were told. That is, if you could forget about 1990 when prices dropped by nearly 50% or later that decade when again housing prices took a turn for the worse. In the 2000s, housing prices were thought to rise forever. By 2007, house prices had risen by 50% to 70% since the start of the decade. This made living easy; with home equity lines of credit so readily available, the house became an ATM. Debt was no longer to be feared. The value of the house was rising faster than the debt was being accumulated. Banks were happy to open their vaults for the homeowner.

Then in the fall of 2008, the financial markets froze and with it the housing market. House sales plummeted. Nothing was moving. Anyone trying to sell a house had to drop the price significantly. All of a sudden, the unstoppable real estate market came to a screeching halt. Borrowing against a house suddenly looked like a bad idea now with the uncertainty in the housing market. The debts already accumulated were weighing heavy against falling house prices. The liquidity crisis of the banks had exposed the serious debt problem for the world.

The second chapter of Habakkuk speaks of debt crises and creditors rising up. It speaks of a nation that has appetites that cannot be satisfied, like death a nation that tries to draw other nations to itself. Which nation is this, and when do these events take place? With not only my curiosity aroused but also with a sense of foreboding, I began a methodical and analytical study of the verses to try and understand this prophecy and other prophecies about a financial crisis.

There are very few references to Habakkuk 2 in the *Seventh-day Adventist Bible Commentary*, Spirit of Prophecy, or scholarly writings.

There are two references, however, to Habakkuk 2:2, 3, which says, "The Lord answered me, and said, Write the vision, and make it plain upon tables, that he may run that readeth it. For the vision is yet for an appointed time, but at the end it shall speak, and not lie: though it tarry, wait for it; because it will surely come, it will not tarry."[4] The commentary says that these texts likely a source of comfort for the Millerites when the Lord did not return in the spring of 1844.

In 1842 Charles Fitch prepared a prophetic chart to illustrate the visions of Daniel and Revelation, which was regarded as a fulfillment of the prophecy of Habakkuk 2:2.[5] William Miller, the great American reformer, used charts and tables to explain the various prophecies and prophetic timelines pointing to what he thought was the second coming of Jesus. Many joined him by believing in and preparing for this grand event.[6] Fitch's "1843" chart, still famous in circles, depicted beasts, dragons, times, and dates.[7] Never before had anyone laid out the prophecies in such a clear manner. This places the events of the prophecy of Habakkuk 2 in these last days, during the great antitypical Day of Atonement.

The verse that follows encourages the readers to wait for the fulfillment of the prophecies in spite of the apparent delay in its fulfillment. This is another reference to the end times through the Great Disappointment experienced by the Millerites when the second advent did not occur as they had hoped.

> Behold, his soul which is lifted up is not upright in him: but the just shall live by his faith. (Habakkuk 2:4)

The beginning of the prophecy marked the early years of the advent movement and the start of the "time of probation" for this world. Nevertheless, do the next verses follow in the same context? Indeed they do as they start with a solemn warning to a proud, apostate nation and with the most important theme for these end times—righteousness by faith. "The just shall live by his faith," said Habakkuk, contrasting them with

---

4   Nichol, F. D., ed., *The Seventh-day Adventist Bible Commentary*, Volume 4 (Washington, DC: Review and Herald Publishing Association, 1978, 2002), 1053.

5   E. G. White, *The Great Controversy*, 1888 ed., 392.

6   Ibid., 373.

7   White, A. L., *Ellen G. White: The Later Elmshaven Years, 1905-1915*, vol. 6 (Hagerstown, MD: Review and Herald Publishing Association, 1982, 2002), 247, 255.

those whose "soul which is lifted up" and "is not upright in him." While the text referred to "him" or "his" as an individual, the rest of the prophetic context indicated that this is about a nation and not just one man.

Habakkuk had originally written this prophecy as a warning to the king of Babylon who had been conquering nations and building his empire, but as the first few texts indicate, this is not confined to the ancient king of Babylon. It also applies equally to the Babylon of the end times. While it is dangerous and often erroneous to place prophecies where they should not be, either in the past or in the future, the context and remaining passages would give strong support to the view that this prophecy was meant for us living in these last days.

> Indeed, because he transgresses by wine, he is a proud man, and he does not stay at home. Because he enlarges his desire as hell, and he is like death, and cannot be satisfied, he gathers to himself all nations and heaps up for himself all peoples. (Habakkuk 2:5 NKJV)

Habakkuk described this nation as being proud and does not stay at home. Why? It is because he transgresses by wine. Wine is often used in prophecy to represent doctrines or ideology. What proud nation goes out to the world and tries to assert its doctrine to the world? What nation tries to gather all nations to himself? While there have been many nations that have tried to conquer the world, only one fits into the timeframe suggested by the opening verses. This would be none other than the United States of America. The past century has been about the rise to power of the United State in the world theater. Its appetite for power and resources has been insatiable.

What doctrine is it promoting? Democracy? Human rights? Individual freedoms? Perhaps on the surface, but below the surface it has been a doctrine of capitalism, profiteering, and materialism, covered in a veneer of a protestant Christian morality. While the people at the grassroots still hold to the values of the republic and Christian ethics, the country's politics has been commandeered by crony capitalism, corporate interests, and big government whose reach ever grows into the lives of its citizens. The past century has been a slow, but accelerating decline of the institutions of the United States. Occupy Wall Street is a faint shadow of the level of dissatisfaction of the masses with the failures of the government and corporation at every level, keeping the American dream alive for its people.

Will not all these take up a proverb against him, and a taunting riddle against him, and say, "Woe to him who increases what is not his—how long? And to him who loads himself with many pledges"? (Habakkuk 2:6)

Notice a phrase in the next verse; it is so telling as it is such a fitting description of the world that we live in—"Woe to him who increases that which is not his." That is exactly what we have done in the past three decades—increasing our material possessions, mostly at the cost of increased debt at the individual level, at the business/corporate level, and most importantly at the government level. Gone is the mindset of the parents of a generation or two ago who saved money in order to spend it. Everything is bought on credit now, and we borrow money, not just on the basis of what we can afford today, but on the expectation that we will have more money in the future to pay for the money we borrowed. Furthermore, borrowing has been encouraged and savings discouraged by extraordinarily low interest rates set by the central banks.

This is how the housing bubble was created. We spent more money by borrowing more money than we could afford with the expectation that we will have more money in the future to pay back our borrowings. The expectation was that the house purchased today could be sold for more in the future in order to not only pay off the mortgage but also make a handsome profit. The buying and selling of houses for profit become a national pastime, until the bubble burst.

**Sovereign Debt**

Again, is this prophecy just talking about individuals, or is it speaking about an entire nation of individuals and the governments that manage the economies? Is it a broader indictment of the nation and its leaders, who have the same mentality of borrow and spend, in order to promote their own agendas and goals? The mindset of the government would seem to be the same as that of its people—to borrow now and spend with the expectation that the growth of the economy in the future would allow for the repayment of those borrowed monies.

In fact, governments in North American and other developed nations have been engaged in this borrow, spend, and hope approach for the past 40 years. This has been the means for funding the growth of the economies over these four decades. Real organic growth has not been sustainable as our costs of living have increased. It is no longer possible to balance our personal income growth with corporate profitability and management of the government. As workers have demanded higher wages, companies have increased prices to cover these increased salaries, which have pushed consumers' need for more money to buy the same goods. In turn, this caused them to demand more raises, and the cycle continued. At the same time we have been demanding more from our governments—more services, more social security, and more health care. Governments have grown, requiring taxes and borrowing to fund the increased services.

Corporations have felt the pressure also because their margins were squeezed and productivity gains were not sufficient to maintain profits. They hit a wall where they can't raise prices and they can't decrease costs, at least not without making significant changes to their businesses. Some industries have hit this wall sooner than others. The automobile manufacturing industry hit that wall two decades ago as the industry found itself unable to compete with the Japanese and Korean manufacturers that were able to create better quality cars at lower costs. So the great doctrine of globalization began. Outsourcing became the key to profitability for corporations, and work began to find its way offshore and into countries with cheaper labor forces. This trend has been growing for the past thirty years. In 2011, the United States derived only 12% of its national income from manufacturing compared as to 29% in the 1990s.[8]

Thus, the great exodus of jobs began in the 1980s and with it much of the economic growth of the nation. The gross domestic product (GDP), the main measure of the economic output of a country, was stagnating, so something had to replace the lost production that had gone overseas. At this juncture the idea of a great consumer-driven economy was started. All of the lost production would be replaced by consumer and government spending. Enough new spending to keep the economy moving and provide for positive GDP growth was to be enacted, and this spending was to be fueled by debt.

To support this new level of spending by government and consumers, there was a tremendous growth in the financial services industry and financial innovations that would fund the borrowing needs of the both. Financial innovations like "interest rate swaps" would allow institutions to

---

[8] "The Facts about Manufacturing," The Manufacturer's Institute, National Association of Manufacturers, 1999, 2012 http://www.themanufacturinginstitute.org/~/media/4F04D20CAAED4F349132F5EF39C5C525/1999_Facts_About_Modern_Manufacturing.pdf (accessed March 20120), http://www.themanufacturinginstitute.org/Research/Facts-About-Manufacturing/~/media/A9EEE900EAF04B2892177207D9FF23C9.ashx (accessed December 2012).

lower their cost of borrowing, which could then be passed on to consumers. The real key to maintaining the higher level of borrowing would be to keep interest rates as low as possible.

To put the icing on this plan, the US dollar became the transactional standard for the world, creating great demand for the dollar and ensuring that there was strong demand so its value would not fall. As the dollar became the reserve currency for the world, and most major financial transactions were conducted in dollars, the currency didn't depreciate even though the amount of dollars in circulation continues to expand rapidly.

So it was that this Ponzi scheme was established, which is called the US economy. As long as more people borrowed and others were willing to lend more, growth would be sustained and all would be well.

Then came the Minsky moment; the point where the cycle of spending and borrowing came to a grinding halt. The Minsky moment, a term referring to the concept proposed by an economist named Hyman Minsky, is when indebtedness exceeds the threshold where debt is no longer sustainable. It is where borrowers can no longer afford the additional debt that they need to sustain the growth they need to keep paying for their borrowing. They are forced to sell assets to pay for debt, resulting in a sharp drop in the price of these assets because many others are doing the same thing, driving the price of the assets lower.

The Minsky moment arrived in 2008 when the whole world realized that the music had stopped, and there were not enough seats for everyone. The year when Bear Stearns and Lehman Brothers went bankrupt, and the entire financial system had to be bailed out by the government. When the housing bubble burst and individuals and institutions lost trillions of dollars as real estate prices cratered. This was the Minsky moment for many individuals and banks and the great financial crisis of our time was triggered. There was, however, one lender and borrower of last resort—the US federal government.

The US government lent and spent unprecedented amounts of money to bailout banks, to stimulate the economy and to try to avoid to complete collapse of the financial system. There was $700 billion in the Troubled Assets Relief Program (TARP) for the banks ($425 billion actually disbursed), $787 billion for the American Restoration and Reinvestment Act for stimulus funding; there was $200 billion for Term Asset-Backed Securities Loan Facility (TALF). Many others became known as the alphabet soup of government bailouts.[9] All together more than $1.5 trillion in government spending and loans were allocated to pull the economy and financial system out of its tailspin.

Corporations had also contributed to this expansion of debt and not just for their own operating capital. Many manufacturers with squeezed margins, unable to make a profit by producing goods, found a new way to make money—by lending money to allow customers to purchase their goods. Thus, leasing and factory financing became popular and easy ways for consumers to get the latest models of televisions, appliances, furniture, and cars. Things came to a point where automobile manufacturers were making most of their profits from their financing business while their production business was losing money.[10] General Motors Acceptance Corporation (GMAC), Ford Credit, and other finance companies became giant financial institutions, rivaling the size of any large multinational bank. However, many of these finance companies also failed under the weight of their own bad loans when the financial crisis hit.

Of course this debt based society was not restricted to the United States. Europe had been doing the same thing, building mountains of debt, while hiding behind the strength of the euro. Even weak economies like Greece could borrow money by issuing bonds denominated in euros, which gave the impression that the bonds were strong and stable. Each country in the eurozone was taking full advantage of its single currency, which allowed them to borrow money inexpensively and in large quantities. Greece and Portugal gave their citizens very generous social programs. Ireland turned itself into a major financial center. Spain, like America, enjoyed a housing boom. Meanwhile, the Germans made themselves busy producing high-quality goods to sell to their fellow eurozone members, making them an export powerhouse.

Governments borrowed money through major European banks to help fund the growth of their economies. There was little concern about countries defaulting on their loans. That is until the mortgage crisis in the US began to expose the weak links in Europe. Many banks had overextended themselves in lending money, particularly to the weaker countries in

---

9   "The Financial Crisis: A Timeline of Events and Policy Actions," St. Louis Federal Reserve Bank, http://timeline.stlouisfed.org/pdf/CrisisTimeline.pdf (accessed March 2012).

10  Danny Hakim, "G.M. Profit Beats Estimates, With Aid of Finance Unit," *New York Times*, October 16, 2003, http://www.nytimes.com/2003/10/16/business/gm-profit-beats-estimates-with-aid-of-finance-unit.html (accessed March 2012).

Europe. When the US housing crisis hit, banks found themselves exposed in many ways.

More recently the European Central Bank has been using debt to help maintain their solvency and liquidity. Not to be outdone by the Americans, they came up with their own alphabet soup; the European Financial Stabilization Facility (EFSF), the European Stabilization Mechanism (ESM), and the long-term refinancing operations (LTRO) to name a few. The EFSF was supposed to be a large fund to help to fix the European debt crisis with up to €780 billion in guarantee commitments from EU member nations, which could be leveraged to create €2.5 trillion in debt issuance support.[11] Each member nation and corporation was supposed to lend money to the EFSF to create a bailout fund, but several nations had to withdraw their support since they needed the bailout and were in no position to contribute to the fund. Commitments to fund the EFSF may further diminish as more nations find they need bailing out rather than contributing as conditions in Europe worsen.

The European Union (EU) then created the ESM, a permanent loan facility to rescue troubled countries to replace the EFSF. Well at least they created the concept of the ESM, which was yet to be ratified by the EU at the time of the writing of this book. LTRO was created by the European Central Bank to create liquidity for banks. As the banks had been buying up bond from peripheral eurozone countries, such as Greece, Ireland, and Portugal, they were stuck with unmarketable assets. LTRO would allow the banks to pledge these bonds to back to the European Central Bank in exchange for cash.

As a result, individuals, corporations, and governments were all complicit in the growth of debt and the inevitable debt crisis. Total debts have grown, particularly over the past three decades. Since the 1970s debt had continued grow rapidly to fuel economic growth, according to the Keynesian Model. The Keynesian Model said that growth in the money supply is required to have economic growth, and to grow the money supply, the government or central bank needs to make more money available continuously. By making more money available, individuals and businesses

---

11  European Financial Stability Facility, http://www.efsf.europa.eu/about/index.htm. http://www.efsf.europa.eu/attachments/faq_en.pdf (accessed March 2012, no longer available); Dirk Schumacher, et al, "Ten questions on the revamped EFSF," *European Weekly Analyst*, Issue No: 11/36, Goldman Sachs Global Economics, October 27, 2011, http://media.rtl.nl/media/financien/rtlz/2011/2810gs.pdf, (accessed December 2012).

will spend more which will provide for economic growth. This wasn't a difficult concept to sell to people who by nature love money and the things it can buy. The Keynesian Model was embraced by all and a consumer economy fully bloomed. Few worried whether this model was sustainable in the long run, so debts grew.

In fact, the growth of debt was on an exponential pace though this was not evident in the '80s or even the '90s. Given the size of the US economy, the growth in the debt was deemed to be manageable. National debt in 2000 was $5.6 trillion, but just ten years later it had ballooned to $11.8 trillion. As of this writing in 2012, the national debt stands at $15.6 trillion. According to a recent report by the McKinsey Global Institute, the total debt of the country, including private and public debt, is now more than 279% of GDP, or $43 trillion.[12] Debt has grown to a place where it can no longer be sustained because more debt is needed to pay for existing debt.

"How long?" the prophet asked. "Woe to him that increaseth that which is not his!" (Habakkuk 2:6). It would seem that the answer to that question is coming clear. "Until now" would seem to be the answer. In 2008, we hit a debt limit where the world power realized that their growth of debts were no longer sustainable. This resulted in the financial crisis, starting with a credit crisis in 2008. In September 2008, the financial markets nearly ground to a halt as financial institutions were no longer willing to conduct business with each other. Banks were hording cash for fear they would not have enough to operate, and they didn't trust anyone else to lend them any funds. Lehman Brothers, another venerable financial firm, collapsed.

The entire banking system had to be bailed out. Only one institution was willing to lend any money, and that was the US government through the US Federal Reserve. The Fed injected trillions of dollars into the financial system to keep it running and keep the banks afloat. By March of 2009 the liquidity injections and pledges of support by the Fed and the government had done its work of stabilizing the markets and the financial system. The stock market started its unprecedented rebound regaining nearly all of its losses. Still, another debt crisis was percolating.

Even as individuals, corporations, and banks were realizing that they needed to curb their borrowing and improve their balance sheets, governments around the world were spending feverishly to ensure that their

---

12  Charles Roxburgh, et all, "Debt and deleveraging: Uneven progress on the path to growth," *McKinsey Global Institute Report*, McKinsey & Company, http://www.mckinsey.com/insights/mgi/research/financial_markets/uneven_progress_on_the_path_to_growth, (accessed March 2012).

economies were growing. Governments were stepping in to fill the void that individuals and corporations made when they stopped borrowing and spending. Some governments had already seen their debt levels rise much faster than their economies. With the crisis in full effect, governments were hitting their own limits of borrowing. Nevertheless, they could not stop borrowing because borrowing was the way they were paying for their previous borrowing.

So it is now, that we see government debt still rising, with the US budget deficit of more than $1.5 trillion. Even though individuals and financial institutions had begun to deleverage, the overall debt of the nation continues to grow. The entire banking system, including what is called the shadow banking system of finance companies—hedge funds, structured investment vehicles, and government-sponsored enterprises—was also deleveraging.[13] The immense amount of liquidity created by the entire banking and shadow banking systems have been the main driver of loan growth and thus economic growth, but that has been turned off.

Governments and central banks are trying to replace this lost liquidity by increasing their borrowing and spending, but they have been unable to borrow enough to make up the difference. Credit provided by the banking system was the largest source of growth for the economy. When the Lehman event occurred as the result of debt defaults from the cooling of the housing boom, credit froze. In spite of everything, banks are not lending at the same pace they were in 2008. Even with the Fed providing an unlimited amount of credit, bank lending is still anemic.[14] With low interest rates, there is very little incentive to lend money. Also, with housing continuing to decline, banks are still facing losses from their real estate holdings, which take up the precious capital from their balance sheets.[15] Since the start of the crisis, the government has poured trillions of dollars into the banks only to see it vaporize as housing continues to fall.

---

13   Zoltan Pozar et al., "Shadow Banking," Federal Reserve Bank of New York Staff Report No. 458, July 2010, revised February 2012, Page 8, http://www.newyorkfed.org/research/staff_reports/sr458.pdf (accessed March 2012).

14   "Consumer Credit G.19," Economic Research & Date, Board of Governors of the Federal Reserve System, http://www.federalreserve.gov/releases/g19/Current/ (accessed March 2012),

15   "Home Prices Rise for the Sixth Straight Month According to the S&P/Case-Shiller Home Price Indices," S&P Dow Jones Indices Press Release, http://www.standardandpoors.com/indices/articles/en/us/?articleType=PDF&assetID=1245343891446 (accessed December 2012).

Currently, the US government has more than $15 trillion in debt. However, this is not the full extent of the debt. Other liabilities of the government include Medicare and Social Security, which are estimated at $60 trillion.[16] These obligations of the government are reliant on future tax income in order to cover these costs. These promises are made on the assumption of an ever-growing economy that would be able to fund these costs for generations to come and were made to keep up the illusion that all was well with the economy.

**The Bond Vigilantes**

"Will not your creditors rise up suddenly? Will they not awaken who oppress you? And you will become their booty" (Habakkuk 2:7 NKJV). This next part of the text is particularly worrisome, which suggests some type of debt default or event. "Creditors will rise up suddenly to awaken the oppressors." Who are these creditors? The text would suggest that they are the very nations that the US was trying to gather up unto themselves, the nations that lent money to America through US Treasury bonds. Of course, there are lots of domestic creditors too as much of the US debt is held by individuals and institutions who are residents. Both groups have been active of late, acting on their concern over the rapid rise in the amount of US debt.

The prophecy says that the creditors will rise up suddenly and that they will awaken the oppressors. Many nations holding US Treasury debt are now becoming alarmed at the rapid pace of the growth of debt in the country. Countries like China and Russia are ringing warning bells about the debt situation in the US, even though they have not taken a public and overt stand against the US and the US debt that they hold. When they do, the results will be sudden. One only has to look at the European debt crisis to see this effect.

When Greece initially began to reveal its budget and debt problems, the market was slow to react. In the fall of 2009, George Papandreou took office as the prime minister of Greece. After making promises about not raising taxes during his campaign as so many politicians do, he quickly realized that the budget situation was dire and quickly proceeded to blame the previous government. The result of this was not what he had hoped to accomplish, which was to gain a bit of leeway in dealing with Greece's

---

16  Dennis Cauchon, "US funding for future promises lags by trillions," *USA Today*, June 13, 2011, http://usatoday30.usatoday.com/news/washington/2011-06-06-us-owes-62-trillion-in-debt_n.htm (accessed March 2012).

budget problems. Instead, the market began to react to the news that the Greek budget was very unbalanced and that they were facing a serious deficit without much prospect for improvement. The bond market started to sell Greek bonds, driving the yields (interest rates) higher. This is the way that the bond market works, just like consumers must pay higher interest rates if they have poorer credit scores.

The term "bond vigilantes" was coined to describe the actions of active bond investors who demand market discipline to be placed on both bonds and bond issuers. Investors are willing to lend money at a given interest rate to governments in the form of bonds. However, as the investor/lender begins to see problems in the government of the country to which it is investing/lending, it will likely start to reduce the amount that it is investing. This is done by selling the bonds that it holds back for the brokers/dealers of the government bonds who will try to sell the bonds to someone else. However, if this country's bonds have become more risky in the eyes of other investors, these new investors may demand a discount on the bond in order to buy them. Therefore the dealers may not give the full amount that original investor lent in the first place. So new investors will demand a lower price for taking over existing debt or demand a higher interest rate in order to lend new money. In effect what both of these actions do is drive up the cost of borrowing for a country.

So in Greece the cost of borrowing money started to rise. At first somewhat slowly, but the selling picked up speed and momentum. As the Greek ten-year bond yields (interest rates) rose to from 4% in January of 2010 to 7% in April 2010,[17] the country was now effectively shut out of the market for raising money through issuing bonds. The market deemed 7% to be the breaking point as beyond this level; it became unsustainable, and a bailout or default was inevitable. The ten-year yield currently sits near 25%, making new bond issues impossible, quickly following in the steps of Greece was Ireland, then Portugal, Italy, and Spain.

This becomes a major problem for nations that rely on borrowing money to fund their budgets. If a country no longer has access to the international markets for borrowing, it will soon be unable to run its government and their country. Its only option was to go to the European Union to ask for funds, essentially a bailout, or to go to the International Monetary Fund (IMF) for loans.

---

17 "Greece Govt Bond 10 Year Acting as Benchmark," Bloomberg, five-year chart, http://www.bloomberg.com/quote/GGGB10YR:IND (accessed January 2013).

# Habakkuk 2—The Debt Default

Both of these actions come with consequences, which are more strict budgetary controls and austerity programs to try to reduce their budget deficits. Greece did get their bailout funds, which resulted in strict budget requirements and the accompanying austerity programs. Workers could no longer retire at the age of 61; instead, they would have to work three years longer.[18] Government workers would see their pay checks reduced as well as their benefits. Of course, government workers and pensioners didn't take this lying down. They rose up and began a series of protests, strikes, and government shutdowns. The creditors were rising up and began to oppress the Greek government. This is just a foretaste of what is to come; the ultimate debt crisis will be when the United States will not be able to honor their debt obligations. The prophecy will ultimately be fulfilled at that time.

The European debt crisis continues even as I write this, with Italy and Spain in the crosshairs of the bond vigilantes and the market. France is next in line; beyond the European borders, Japan will be targeted. Ireland and Portugal have already received their bailouts. So it will be with the debt crisis, which will move from country to country like a swarm of locusts devouring entire financial systems as they move and straining the remaining institutions and governments along the way.

Ultimately, this debt crisis will come to the shores of the United States. It is inevitable given the size of the US debt, the ongoing deficits, and the inability for the current government to function and take the necessary actions to right the listing ship. With $15 trillion in debt growing at a $1.5 trillion pace each year, the debt load has become unsustainable though the government continues to try to print their way out of debt. The talk is that the US will inflate their way out of debt, but the prophecy would seem to rule that out, at least initially. The text describes the creditors rising up and oppressing and that this nation will become their booty. How does one nation become the booty of another? The booty is typically tied to the spoils of war or battle. This will be a financial battle; the looser of which will become the spoils to the winner.

Will it be China, Russia, or Japan who will demand their pound of flesh for the debts that are owed them? In what form will these spoils take. Will the US be required to sell off key assets to satisfy debts? Selling assets is becoming a popular strategy for governments to raise badly needed cash.

---

18  "What makes Germans so very cross about Greece?" Charlemagne European Politics, *The Economist*, February 23, 2010, http://www.economist.com/blogs/charlemagne/2010/02/greeces_generous_pensions (accessed June 2012).

In Greece, as austerity is forced upon them, the Greek government is looking at asset sales as a key tactic.

**Violence in the Land**

Watching the events in Greece has been very instructive in how the situation might escalate in other nations that come under a debt crisis. Observing how the people reacted to the austerity measures imposed by the government was perhaps a preview of what we might expect in the US a short time in the future. The Greek people reacted with protests, strikes, and rioting to the financial measures the government proposed to bring their budget within the restrictions made by the European Union. It should be noted too that the riots and regime change in the Arab states which started in the winter of 2011 had a strong influence on the activism shown by the people in Europe and now in America with Occupy Wall Street.

Congressman Ron Paul in his 2010 address made this statement pointing to social unrest even before the Arab Spring, Greek riots or Occupy Wall Street. Congressman Paul, a long-time critic of the current central banking system, has been outspoken about what is now becoming obvious—the inevitable end of the borrow-and-spend approach to managing our economies.

> With no ability of the federal government to fund its commitments, international or domestic, major changes will occur in our system. The social unrest will elicit cries for government to exert unusual force to head off a complete breakdown of law and order. The ultimate trap will be set for a system of government claiming to protect a free society.
>
> If more power and police authority are not given to the federal government, it will be argued that only anarchy will result. If more government policing power is given, it will mean a lethal threat to civil liberties.[19]

Habakkuk also warned about the violence in the land.

---

19   Ron Paul, "State of the Republic Address," January 21, 2010, http://paul.house.gov/index.php?option=com_content&task=view&id=49&Itemid=60 (accessed January 2010, site no longer available).

# HABAKKUK 2—THE DEBT DEFAULT

> Because you have plundered many nations, all the remnant of the people shall plunder you, because of men's blood and the violence of the land and the city, and of all who dwell in it. Woe to him who covets evil gain for his house, that he may set his nest on high, that he may be delivered from the power of disaster! You give shameful counsel to your house, cutting off many peoples, and sin against your soul. For the stone will cry out from the wall, and the beam from the timbers will answer it. Woe to him who builds a town with bloodshed, who establishes a city by iniquity! (Habakkuk 2:8–12 NKJV)

As one reads this text, it can be taken in two ways; it can be understood from a personal or an individual level is that greed had been shown in society in trying to obtain more material wealth: "Woe to him who covets evil gain for his house." This again is so appropriate for our world today, a world where everyone wants to be a millionaire, a world where the difference between the haves and the have-nots is becoming greater, and the now infamous 1% versus the 99%. Those who have all the means to deliver themselves in times of disaster versus the masses are at the mercy of their circumstances. It can also be taken from a corporate or national level where the rich and powerful control industry and government make policies and decisions to benefit themselves.

"You give shameful counsel to your house, cutting off many peoples" (Habakkuk 2:10 NKJV). The government along with the too-big-to-fail banks have consulted together to pile on trillions of dollars of debt in order to maintain their status quo.[20]

So the prophecies of Habakkuk predict a coming debt crisis as a result of uncontrolled spending, violence in the land, and wickedness. However, in the midst of these dark prophecies there shines a ray of light.

> Behold, is it not of the Lord of hosts that the peoples labor to feed the fire, and nations weary themselves in vain? *For the earth shall be filled with the knowledge of the glory of the Lord, as the waters cover the sea.* (Habakkuk 2:13, 14, emphasis added)

Verse 13 says that that it is because of the Lord of hosts that the people labor in vain. The efforts of the people to build up their own "city" by

---

[20] You will find more on this topic in Chapter 5: "Too Big to Fail."

violence and fraud will fail as God's judgment will be upon them. In verse 14, Habakkuk saw the earth being filled with the knowledge of the glory of the Lord. The glory of the Lord is His character, which is revealed in His law. The earth is filled with the knowledge of God's glory, or His character, as the understanding of the God's law is made manifest to the world. This verse seems to be parallel with the closing of the three angels' messages in Revelation 14.

"After these things *I saw another angel come down from heaven, having great power; and the earth was lightened with his glory*" (Revelation 18:1, emphasis added). These prophecies foretell that God's glory will fill the earth through His remnant people. In these dark days, the "remnant" of God's people will rise up and show the world the glory of God through their Christ-like characters and their faithfulness and obedience to God's law. God's people are depicted as angels in this prophecy, acting as messengers from God.

In the very last verse of Habakkuk 2, the prophet declares that "the Lord is in His holy temple: let all the earth keep silence before him" (verse 20). In all of the turmoil that will come in the last days and people running to and fro, Habakkuk reminds us that the Lord is in His holy temple. The time of judgment has come, and we all stand in judgment before God. The great Day of Atonement has arrived where God is judging His people, where all things done in open and in secret will be brought to light. One key element of the judgment of His professed people will surely be how we have managed the resources that He has given us. Will He say to us, "Well done, thou good and faithful *servant*, enter thou into the joy of the Lord"? (Matthew 25:21, emphasis added). Or will the Judge say, "I never knew you: depart from me, ye that work iniquity"? (Matthew 7:23).

The backdrop of a financial crisis in this time of judgment will be appropriate for the evaluation of His people. The crisis will reveal their true priorities and who they really worship. As for the nations that are professedly Christian, their efforts to maintain their own wealth and status by piling on more debt will testify against them. While they try to establish their kingdoms on this earth, Jesus said, "My kingdom is not of this world" (John 18:36). Just like the Jewish nation at the time of Christ's first advent sought for a temporal kingdom, the people of today at His second advent will be doing the same.

Habakkuk tells of a debt crisis, defaults, and creditors rising up. Today, we see out-of-control government spending, signs of a currency crash, violence in the land, and financial losses. As suggested by Ron Paul, eventually, this all culminates in a broad effort by the US to print more money to meet their spending needs, particularly in the military. History tells us what happened to countries that overextended themselves and debased their currencies.

## Chapter 3

# A Measure of Wheat for a Penny: Hyperinflation

When he had opened the third seal, I heard the third beast say, Come and see. And I beheld, and lo a black horse; and he that sat on him had a pair of balances in his hand. And I heard a voice in the midst of the four beasts say, a measure of wheat for a penny, and three measures of barley for a penny; and see thou hurt not the oil and the wine. (Revelation 6:5, 6)

The fall of the Roman Empire has become a topic of great interest in these times as the parallels to the great American Empire are difficult to overlook. The great military conquests and the economic expansion of the Roman Empire would seem to be a type that is now seeing its great antitype in the United States. While Rome took much longer to build and to fall, the similarities are many and profound.

Among the many issues that finally brought Rome to its knees, one was its financial misfortunes or mismanagement. The cost of their military complex drove the empire to near bankruptcy, with the only resolution being that of debasing their currency in order to pay their bills. This same scenario is being played out today, with the US military budget taking more than $826 billion of the federal budget.[21] If the foreign military aid is added to that figure, it surpasses $1 trillion. The cost of the military and related spending is a full third of the US federal budget today, ballooning from $370 billion since the start of the "War on Terror" in 2001.[22]

**The Four Horsemen**

John the Revelator, in prophetic vision of the four horsemen of the apocalypse within the seven seals, wrote about the conditions in the world

---

21 "Spending Under CBO's March 2012 Baseline," Congressional Budget Office, http://www.cbo.gov/sites/default/files/cbofiles/attachments/Supplemental_byFunction.xls (accessed March 2012).

22 "Defense: US from FY 1997 to FY 2017," Government Spending Chart, usgovernmentspending.com, http://www.usgovernmentspending.com/spending_chart_1997_2017USr_13s1li111mcn_30t (accessed December 2012).

during the early days of the church even as the Roman Empire began to falter. First, he saw a white horse representing the purity of the apostolic church, which went forth to conquer the world with the gospel of Jesus Christ. Second, he viewed a red horse, representing the bloody days of persecution during the second and third centuries AD.

The third horse of the vision, found in the text in Revelation 6:5, as quoted above, was a black horse, reflecting the darkening character of the church, as compromise and apostasy entered its ranks, reaching to the very top of the organization. This was the time of Emperor Constantine who himself proclaimed to be converted to Christianity, then merging it with pagan practices in order to unify the people of the crumbling empire. This was the setting for the opening of the third seal, the third horseman of the apocalypse who was mounted on a black horse holding balances in his hand. These balances indicated that commerce was the main occupation of the church as the church traded in its sword of the gospel by which it had conquered earlier.

As this black rider emerged, a voice was heard in heaven from among the four living creatures that surround the throne of God. That voice could only be the voice of God, pronouncing a judgment upon the church and upon the earth. "A measure of wheat for a penny, and three measures of barley for a penny," said the voice (Revelation 6:6). "A measure of wheat" was a specific amount of wheat.[23] This was an amount equal to the portion given to a slave each day. Three measures of barley was an equivalent ration for a slave as barley is an inferior grain to wheat. This would be sufficient for a slave to prepare a small morsel of bread. This "measure of wheat" was then proclaimed to cost a penny, or a denarius, which was a day's wages for a common laborer at this time. The message being proclaimed was that of an economy in which the cost of living was extremely high. It proclaimed a financial crisis in which the cost of a small piece of bread would consume the entire wages of a day, a hyperinflationary state where the necessities of life were beyond the reach of the average worker.

Were these things so? Does history record such events taking place in the third century AD within the Roman Empire? Recent studies of

---

23 John Wesley's Explanatory Notes on the Bible, Revelation 6:6. States: "The word translated measure, was a Grecian measure, nearly equal to our quart. This was the daily allowance of a slave. The Roman penny, as much as a labourer then earned in a day, was about sevenpence halfpenny English," http://www.biblestudytools.com/commentaries/wesleys-explanatory-notes/revelation/revelation-6.html (accessed June 2011).

archeological records from ancient Egypt show remarkable findings that corroborate the occurrence of hyperinflation in the later Roman era. Egypt was a major source of wheat for the Roman Empire as the Nile valley was one of the most fertile lands of the day. Records of the sale of wheat from Egypt to Rome have been found,[24] indicating that Rome imported what was likely a third of their annual consumption from Egypt over the centuries of its existence. Shipped across the Mediterranean Sea, there was an efficient and cost-effective source of grain for the empire from the land of the Pharaohs. The cost of the wheat from Egypt appears to have been very stable for three centuries from the before the time of Christ to nearly 300 years after. Historians discovered a curious change in the price of wheat toward the end of the third century and into the fourth.

The price of wheat rapidly rose from about AD 290 to AD 300. In a very short period of time, the price of wheat skyrocketed a hundred times higher![25] It would seem that Rome endured a period of hyperinflation when the prices of goods were rising out of control. So what could cause such runaway inflation during those ancient times before central banks, stock markets, and electronic funds transfers were available? Isn't hyperinflation a modern phenomena arising from our modern financial systems?

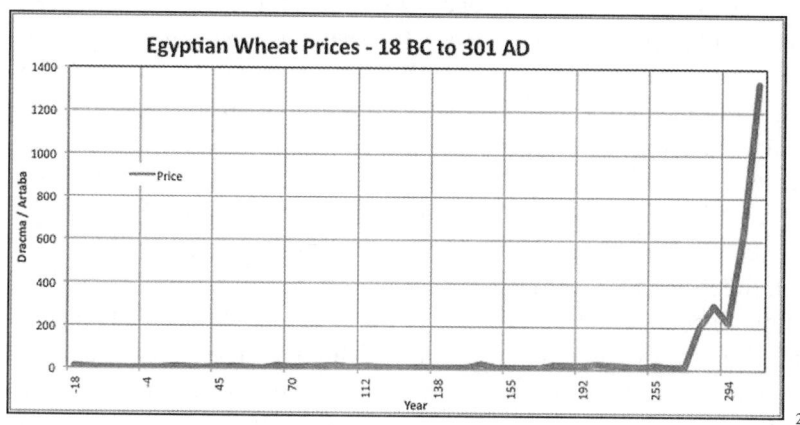

[26]

---

24  Pródromos-Ioánnis Prodromídis, "Another View on an Old Inflation: Environment and Policies in the Roman Empire up the Diocletian's Price Edict," Center of Economic Planning and Research, Athens, Greece, February 2006, http://www.kepe.gr/pdf/D.P/dp_85.pdf (accessed May 2011).

25  Richard Duncan-Jones, "The Economy of the Roman Empire Quantitative Studies," 2nd ed., (Cambridge: Cambridge University Press, 1982), 365.

26  Prodromídis, 26.

## Hyperinflation

Apparently, hyperinflation wasn't a modern-day creation but appears to have existed in the time of the Caesars, and the Caesars may have been the ones responsible for its creation. During the first century AD, the world was at relative peace due to the stabilizing influence of the powerful Roman government. The era was known as *Pax Romana* or "Roman peace," but this peace did not come easily or cheaply as Rome expended tremendous resources in order to maintain this state. The number of soldiers required to maintain order in the far reaches of the empire drained their economy deeply. In the third century as the Barbarian invasions began to take its toll on the empire, the cost of maintaining the military continued to increase. By the end of the third century, Rome had an estimated 68 legions, which represented about 500,000 soldiers[27] to defend the empire from invaders as well as protect the emperor from coups from within. Of course, all of these soldiers needed to be paid. As the military and its generals gained political clout, the soldiers demanded higher wages, further taxing the empire.[28]

The same scenario seemingly exists today in the US with the military budget ballooning to its current size of nearly $1 trillion over the years since 9/11. The military industrial complex is becoming an increasingly larger part of the US federal budget with little hope of reining it in. Even with the budget battles of late between the Democrats and the Republicans, where even social security is on the table for cuts, the military spending is barely considered as a source to cut spending. The mere mention of the military in any budget restraint dialogue is seen as unpatriotic and an affront to the men and women in uniform who give their lives to defend freedom. Challenging the military industrial complex may have serious consequences for anyone, even the president of the United States.

In the Roman era, things were likely not much different. The glory of the Roman conquests was the pride of the people, and they likely revered their soldiers as we do today, regardless of the costs and the corruption in high places. So the military budget held sway in the Senate and even over the emperor as the army needed to be maintained at all costs. So what was the solution to their budget crisis? Today, they would issue war bonds or get a special appropriations bill from Congress. Or perhaps the Federal Reserve would simply "print" more money. In the Roman era, however, the answer was simpler and more direct. Rather than pay their soldiers with

---

27   Ibid., 13.

28   Ibid., 14.

the usual denarius, a silver coin with the face of the emperor stamped on it, Rome started to mint a silver plated coin,[29] which of course contained less silver.

At first, it was only marginally less silver. How this was received by the populous is not known, but the effect on commerce could be seen. As mentioned earlier, the devaluation of the silver coins by Rome did not escape the notice of the Egyptian grain traders, and the result was that the cost of wheat started to rise. Year after year, Rome's budgets were stretched and the silver coins become less silver and more filler. Archeological findings show that the denarius minted in the early fourth century was only about a 0.5% silver.[30] A thin, silver covering over a brass or copper core was all that it had become, leading to a debasing of the value of the denarius. For those who used the denarius, some had the clout to demand more denarius for the same goods or service, such as the Egyptian grain traders or Roman soldiers, while others were unable to negotiate more, resulting in a real decline in their income and purchasing ability.

So it was that the exponential rise in the price of wheat occurred in the late third century AD. Merchants demanded more coinage for their goods as the value of each coin declined. The impact on the common people was then described by John in the opening of the third seal in his prophecy. "A measure of wheat for a penny, and three measures of barley for a penny," said the voice from the midst of the four living creatures in heaven (Revelation 6:6). "Hurt not the oil and the wine," the voice also said in the same verse. The oil and the wine being the symbols of the Holy Spirit and the blood of Christ, which represented that this economic crisis in the Roman Empire should by no means slow the work of the gospel as it continued to spread throughout the world.

The era in which this prophecy was fulfilled is very significant in the prophetic and historic understanding of the development of the Christian church. In this era Emperor Constantine announced his "conversion" to Christianity in an attempt to unite the people of Rome. Heretofore, the Romans persecuted the Christians, who were often blamed for any calamities faced by the empire since the time of Nero when he blamed the burning of Rome on the Christians. Constantine made being a Christian acceptable, so people could openly profess to be Christians without the fear of persecution.

---

29   Ibid., 16

30   Ibid.

This act came with compromises because the spirit of compromise and apostasy had already been at work in the church. The apostles all warned of this occurring, from Paul to Peter and James. "Certain men crept in unawares ... turning the grace of God into lasciviousness," wrote Jude. Luke also noted, "After my departing shall grievous wolves enter in among you not sparing the flock" (Acts 20:29). Indeed, these grievous wolves would enter into the church during the next 200 years, making merchandise of the gospel of Christ. These apostate leaders of the church used the gospel and the church to their own advantages adding power and prosperity to themselves.

The conversion of Constantine was a pivotal point in the history of the church. It became even more prosperous for the leadership of the church and even its members to use the church for their own means. Great errors began to enter into the doctrines of the church, and the pure gospel of Jesus became defiled to the point where the Revelator saw the rider on a black horse, signifying the extent of the church's fall. This was also the start of the third era of the church (Pergamos) in the prophecy of the seven churches given John in Revelation 2.

"I have a few things against thee, because thou hast there them that hold the doctrine of Balaam, who taught Balac to cast a stumblingblock before the children of Israel, to eat things sacrificed unto idols, and to commit fornication" (Revelation 2:14). It is instructive to note that Balaam is mentioned here. Balaam, the prophet who agreed to curse Israel for money, represents those in the church in the fourth century who were willing to compromise and change doctrines for their own personal advantage but in the guise of the "advancement" of the church.

This was the beginning of the era that would lead to the dramatic change in the church from a place of refuge for its members to an oppressive regime that preyed on the people. The church began to wield its power over people and even governments. In an environment where the population was suffering from wars, high taxes, and a crumbling economy, the church began to extract money from its members to support the bishops and other "leaders." By the early sixth century AD, with the fall of western Rome, the church became the dominant force, wielding both ecclesiastical and political power over most of Europe.

While this is a very short synopsis of what happened in the early church about the turn of the fourth century AD, having an understanding of what transpired and the condition of the world and the church at that time should help us to foresee what is to take place at the close of time. Looking forward to the economic environment today, we see all the symptoms of an ailing global economy, with the United States at the epicenter of the malaise. This consumer-based economy, which was fueled by debt, is now going through the early stages of withdrawal from its addiction to debt. Even still, the US federal government continues to pile on the debt, expanding their spending, particularly on the military, just like in the Roman era.

We are seeing other nations like Greece lose their ability to borrow money from the financial markets and turn to the European Central Bank and the International Monetary Fund, which is backed in a large part by the US to keep from defaulting on its debt. The US now seems to be the lender of last resort to the world in spite of their own struggles to manage their own budget.

The inability of the US Congress to achieve any meaningful progress toward balancing the US budget will continue to drive the country's debt levels ever higher. Eventually, the US will reach its debt limits—at the point when there will not be enough real buyers of US Treasury bills, notes, or bonds. Unlike Greece, Ireland or Portugal, however, there will be no one left to bailout the US. Rather, according the prophecies from Habakkuk, creditors may look for their money to be returned. What options will be left for the US when it reaches its credit limit and its creditors come calling? The US Federal Reserve will have to engage in some form of money printing or "quantitative easing."

Given the size of the deficit today, the Fed will have to take massive measures in order to fund the US federal budget. We know from the history of places like Weimar, Germany, and Zimbabwe, the impact of such massive money-printing efforts. Hyperinflation is the inevitable result of such actions. The US dollar will devalue, causing the cost of imported goods to rise dramatically. Since the US imports so much of what it consumes, this will have a dramatic impact on consumers and their ability to maintain their lifestyles. Imports, particularly oil and other energy products, in addition to electronics, raw materials, consumer goods, pharmaceuticals, and industrial goods, will see a rapid rise in prices.

One class of goods, of which the US is a significant producer, is food stuffs. Grains, meats, vegetables and fruits are produced in abundance; yet, these are the very things that Revelation 6:6 says that will become expensive or be in short supply. It is easy to reconcile these seeming incongruences when we look at how the commodities markets operate. Regardless of the producers and the natural cost advantages a country may have, goods will be sold at the prevailing market price. For example, in 2008 when oil prices rose to $140 per barrel, Canadians still paid the very high market prices for oil products and gasoline even though Canada had more than enough oil for its own use. The fact that Canada produced more oil than it needed didn't keep Canadians from paying very high prices for gasoline. Furthermore, other input costs such as fertilizer, fuel for machinery and transport, and processing will also add to the cost.

So when global food prices soar due to hyperinflation, natural disasters, and increased demand, even those in countries that produce an abundance of food, will have to pay exorbitant prices. Thus, the words in the book of James will be fulfilled.

> Go to now, ye rich men, weep and howl for your miseries that shall come upon you. Your riches are corrupted, and your garments are motheaten. Your gold and silver is cankered; and the rust of them shall be a witness against you, and shall eat your flesh as it were fire. Ye have heaped treasure together for the last days. Behold, the hire of the labourers who have reaped down your fields, which is of you kept back by fraud, crieth: and the cries of them which have reaped are entered into the ears of the Lord of sabaoth. Ye have lived in pleasure on the earth, and been wanton; ye have nourished your hearts, as in a day of slaughter. (James 5:1–5)

One critical factor is necessary for hyperinflation to take hold in the US, and that is when the dollar loses its status as the reserve currency for the world. Today, complete devaluation of the dollar would be unlikely because of its use in so many financial transactions, the natural checks and balances in the global system of currencies, as well as the destabilizing effect on the entire financial system. However, nations are currently moving to replace the dollar by using other currencies such as the euro or bilateral trade in their own currencies. China and Brazil[31] as well as Russia and Brazil[32] have made agreements to buy and sell oil in reals, renembi, and rubles rather than in dollars. Other such agreements are beginning to be

---

31  Jonathan Watts, "China and Brazil strike $30bn bilateral swap deal to reinforce economies," *The Guardian*, June 21, 2012, http://www.guardian.co.uk/world/2012/jun/22/china-brazil-bilateral-swap-deal, (accessed July 2012).

32  Michael Stott and Fernando Exman, "Brazil, Russia Plan to boost trade, investment," Reuters, May 14, 2010, http://www.reuters.com/article/2010/05/14/russia-brazil-idUSLDE64D0OG20100514 (accessed July 2012).

made globally as the fear increases that the US will devalue its currency to deal with debt problems and make its exports more competitive. In particular, those nations that hold a large amount of US Treasury bonds are becoming increasingly wary of the possibility of a decline in the value of the dollar and thus their investment.

When the US dollar ceases to be the reserve currency of the world, hyperinflation will become a possibility and a probability. It has been this reserve currency status that has allowed America to borrow and spend with abandon. It has been this reserve currency status that has created demand that has allowed the US to grow its economy as a financial hegemony, and it has grown despite losing most of its manufacturing jobs. Nevertheless, when the reserve status is gone and demand disappears, there will be little to support the dollar. Currency values are always relative to another currency, so a weakening of the dollar corresponds to the strengthening of other currencies. This will be painful for other nations as they see their exports become less competitive, but in the long run they will be in the position of strength.

Many symptoms and probable outcomes of a debt crisis and currency devaluation point toward a hyperinflation scenario, but the most important evidence is that of the historical experience of Rome. The biblical record of the events and the impacts on those living in those times should be an accurate prologue to the events in the near future. More importantly, the prophetic warnings in the Bible and the writings of E. G. White should be a clear warning to those living in the last days. The Bible makes clear references to a financial crisis in the end times and financial losses that will plague the world. In both the Old and the New Testaments, the Bible speaks of unprecedented financial troubles in the end times.

One of the most direct references and a clear link between the opening of the third seal of Revelation 6 the hyperinflationary environment during Roman era, the current economic condition, and the potential of future hyperinflation in our era is found in the following quote from E. G. White.

The same spirit is seen today that is represented in Revelation 6:6–8. History is to be repeated. That which has been will be again. (*Manuscript Releases*, vol. 9, 7)

"History is to be repeated," wrote Mrs. White. Verses 7 and 8 of Revelation 6 speak of the fourth rider, "Death" on the pale horse, representing the Dark Ages, the persecution and the spiritual darkness resulting from the apostasy and the withholding of God's Word during the papal reign, the beast power of Revelation 13. We recognize and often speak about the resurrection of the beast power, which is to parallel the fourth horsemen of the apocalypse. We also need to see that this reference also includes verse 6, which is specifically related to the financial conditions just prior to the final events. A measure of wheat will again cost a penny, and three measures of barley a penny. It will take a full day's wages just to buy a slave's portion of bread. The cost of survival will be high, and people will be preoccupied with their efforts to maintain their lifestyles. Those more used to luxury will likely be more inclined to try to keep up their way of life and more willing to compromise principle and belief to do so.

If there is to be a period of hyperinflation in the end times, why would this happen? Would God allow or even inflict the world with a massive financial crisis, including hyperinflation and have the US at the eye of the storm? Would God allow His people, those who call themselves Christians to suffer the same fate as the world? If this is to be the case, how should we as God's remnant people prepare and act in the face of this impending crisis. To see where our current crisis is headed, we go back to the start of the crisis—the housing bubble.

## Chapter 4

# The Gospel Bubble?

Beloved, when I gave all diligence to write unto you of the common salvation, it was needful for me to write unto you, and exhort you that ye should earnestly contend for the faith which was once delivered unto the saints. For there are certain men crept in unawares, who were before of old ordained to this condemnation, ungodly men, turning the grace of our God into lasciviousness, and denying the only Lord God, and our Lord Jesus Christ. (Jude 1:3, 4)

**A Tale of Two Crises**

Technology is a great asset for a busy commuter trying to keep up with reading and personal development. As an avid user of AudioVerse.org, a website with thousands of sermons and speeches on various religious topics, I enjoy hearing many wonderful speakers with spiritual insights. One speaker whom I respect and listen to often is Dennis Priebe, who speaks on the topic of righteousness by faith, its meaning, and it importance to us as Christians in the end times. He was at Pacific Union College in the '70s during the time of Desmond Ford and has a deep understanding of the issues around this very important topic.

In his sermons, Pastor Priebe warns about a new "gospel" that is prevalent today, even within Seventh-day Adventist churches, that focuses on justification by faith without accepting the imparted righteousness of Christ and the sanctifying power of His Spirit. In other words, many are preaching a gospel that says it's easy to be saved but without obedience to God. So "easy" that everyone can join in. As I sat on the subway on my way to work, listening to Priebe speak, I thought to myself, "Yeah, that sounds just like how the housing bubble grew and the financial crisis happened." Then it hit me like a two-by-four over my head: *Could we be headed for a gospel bubble?*

Just like the financial crisis' epicenter was the housing crisis, could we be heading for a spiritual crisis of epic proportions, the center of which is a gospel that teaches salvation without responsibility? As I made comparisons in my head, I began to worry. We saw the impact of giving homeownership and mortgages to people that should not have had them. Could the implications be translated to our church? Recall how the housing crisis started.

**The Housing Bubble**

As the US economy reeled from the crash of the technology stock market and the effects of 9/11, it fell into a recession in 2001. Then US Federal Reserve Chairman Alan Greenspan lowered the interest rates to the lowest they had ever been to help the economy recover. With interest rates below 1%, it was easy for business and consumers to borrow money, which in theory would help the economy to grow again. This had become the acceptable doctrine in economic cycles and monetary policy, Keynesian Model economics.

The concept was simply that the economic growth of a nation is driven by the creation of excess money supply, which is driven by an expansion of credit or increased government spending. In other words, for an economy to grow, a country must to make it easier to borrow money, which would encourage spending, or the government needs to increase spending on programs. Within this framework, credit expansion is driven by a central bank of a nation, through monetary policy, or by the federal government through fiscal policy. For a central bank like the US Federal Reserve, the main means of implementing this policy is through the control of the short-term money supply, and through interest rates. By lowering interest rates enough it would encourage businesses and consumers to borrow more money to invest or spend.

Moreover, the lower interest rates that are needed to encourage borrowing become a disincentive to save money. What would be the point of keeping money in a savings account if it earned little or no interest? With overnight rates at 1%, which is the rate at which banks can borrow money from the Federal Reserve, the rates for consumers was basically nil. Even corporate accounts with millions of dollars would earn less than 0.25% interest. This drove money into other short-term investments like treasury bills, certificates of deposits, commercial paper, and money market funds. These were all deemed to be safe liquid investments, in which funds could be moved in and out quickly.

Money market funds became a popular vehicle for investing short term money and large volumes of money moved into these instruments.

As always, when hot money is moving into certain types of investments, a proliferation of products occurs, and competition heats up among the fund companies to capture their share of this growing market. Competition always drives risk-taking behaviors, and the money market funds began to look at other types of investments to enhance the yield or return on their funds. By investing in new types of investments like asset-backed commercial paper, these funds could increase their yield by perhaps 0.25% or more.

In the grand scheme of things, 0.25% is not much difference, and perhaps not enough reward for taking more risk, but in the heat of a marketing battle, things are not always clear in the minds of fund managers and investors. So, money market funds were offering 0.75%—1.25% interest for investors to park their money in their vehicles. Investors were also still stinging from the crash the tech bubble in 2000.

The NASDAQ, a stock market that catered to many technology, internet, and computer companies, had been at an all time high in 2000 at 5048. Every company that had a business plan related to the internet saw its stock prices take off, even if it had yet to make a single penny in profits. It was the era of the dotcoms. New ideas were being introduced to the public. Web sites, search engines, online shopping, internet banking, online gaming, and web advertising were brand new concepts that would change the business world as we knew it. Investors, investment banks, private equity firms, and banks were all crazy for any investment idea related to this new thing called "the internet."

Hundreds of billions of dollars were being invested into this sector, and by 1999, the NASDAQ had risen 980% within 10 years.[33] Fortunes were made until reality reared its ugly head. It became clear that many of these new dotcom companies, whose stock prices had just tripled within a month of going public, were no more than pie-in-the-sky ideas that would never take flight, let alone become the next internet wonder company. Some were real winners, like Cisco, Amazon, and e-Bay, but there were many more failures than most investors would care to remember.

By the fall of 2000, the NASDAQ had crashed, falling 75% to 1720,[34] and investors lost billions of dollars. From those who spent their own money to start up a company, to relatives and friends who lent money, to banks

---

33  On NASDAQ's interactive stock charts, the index levels were at 414 (December 31, 1990) to 4,696 (January 31, 2000), http://www.nasdaq.com/symbol/ixic/interactive-chart (accessed March 2012).

34  Ibid.

that offered credit, to venture capitalists that committed their capital, to mutual funds that invested their unit-holders money, to investment banks that underwrote their initial public offerings, all experienced severe losses. Even the stocks that were eventual winners, like Apple, saw their stock prices plunge during the tech wreck. To make matters worse, over the next few years several stock scandals emerged. Three companies, (Enron, an energy marketing firm; WorldCom, a telecommunications company; Nortel, a communications equipment company) were all charged with irregularities in their accounting. When the all-out fraudulent behaviors of company leadership were exposed, these companies' stock prices crashed to the point that they were effectively worthless.

To top this off, on September 11, 2001, two commercial airliners were hijacked and flown into the World Trade Center in New York City, and a third plane was flown into the Pentagon in Washington D.C. Events no one will forget as it changed the complexion of the entire world. America was no longer safe from attacks. Flights were grounded, travel restricted, and trade halted, which added to the malaise of the times. This weighed heavy on the minds of everyone, including investors and savers. This was the environment in the first0s decade of the 21st century, which investors and retirees faced.

With the economy in full retreat under the weight of a recession, the tech crash, and a new element—a war on terror—prospects for safe investments seemed few. Yet, with the Federal Reserve turning on the credit taps and pouring money into the economy, a lot of "hot money" was looking for a place to be parked. Investors, still wary of the stock market, looked for something else to invest in, something safe. Although interest rates dropped so low, putting money in a savings account would pay very little if anything. So what else could they do?

The answer was right under the investors' noses or perhaps more precisely, right under their feet—their houses! Investing in one's house was the safest thing to do, or so people thought. As a result, people began to pour money into their houses. With low interest rates, refinancing a mortgage with much lower rates enabled homeowners to free up more cash flow each month. Banks were looking for ways to increase their revenues. Increased lending in the form of home equity loans seemed to be just the ticket. So the vault was opened and lending increased. Consumers/homeowners began to renovate their homes or sell and buy bigger homes. This was their opportunity to move up as low interest rates made bigger houses more affordable.

## The Gospel Bubble?

It was an opportunity for my growing family of five to move out of our three-bedroom townhouse to maybe a detached home with a two-car garage and a nice yard in a nice neighborhood. My wife and our agent were out "window shopping" when all of a sudden, there it was. The perfect home! They found it quite by accident. At the end of an afternoon of driving from one viewing to the next, and after exiting from another "not quite what we had in mind" property, Sharon saw a sign—no, not a bright light from above with an angelic choir singing kind of sign.

Two guys in a pickup truck were planting a new "For Sale" sign on the beautiful front lawn of a big house on a corner lot; it had a two-car garage and a perfect cedar hedge in the backyard. The two shoppers quickly walked over to the newly erected sign, and in their best nonchalant walk, they spied the house from their slow stroll around the sidewalk corner. As they neared the edge of the driveway, the front door of the house opened ,and an elderly lady poked her head out.

"Busted!" the two oglers thought.

"You don't have to stand out there, come on in if you're interested," the elderly madam called to the surprised women.

Accepting the invitation, though it wasn't quite the appropriate real estate agent protocol, they entered the house. The first view was a broad entrance way facing a spiral stair case. A large living room to the right with hardwood floors was connected to an elegant dining room. An eat-in kitchen had a walkout to the backyard. The appliances were old, maybe even the originals. In the family room was a fireplace, and the laundry room just off the kitchen was a perfect setup for a busy mom.

The lady of the house then said to her two guests: "Go on upstairs and have a look. I'm going to stay down here. It's too hard for me to get up and down the stairs with my hip. I don't go up unless I have to."

Upstairs were three spacious bedrooms and a grand master bedroom with walk-in closet and bathroom. From the bedroom window, the elementary school and park were in sight. Back downstairs, the three met up again.

"Would you like to see the flyer for the house?" the lady asked.

With a glass in her hand, the lady shuffled into the kitchen while her beverage sloshed in her glass and spilled out onto the floor. Quickly, without asking, my wife went to the kitchen counter and grabbed a paper towel and wiped up the floor after her. With a grateful wink, the lady thanked her and handed the flyers to the two ladies. The house was in a turnover neighborhood where older couples, whose children had long since moved way with their own families and who could no longer manage the house, were looking to sell in favor of a senior's condominium.

Shortly after this, my cell phone rang. While I was never told the timing of the call, I can't believe that it would have been more than about 20 seconds after my wife stepped out of the front door. Just about long enough to get to the sidewalk, I presumed.

"It's the perfect house, everything we want, and the price is about 15% below market value. The original owners are an older couple, and they're looking to downsize.

"You have to see it as soon as possible. It's not going to last long on the market!" I was told.

Events moved quickly that evening. From seeing the house, to signing the papers, to making an offer was about an eight-hour total time lapse. Confident that we'd beaten the rush, we went to bed that evening thinking that we may have found the place we had always wanted, and it was a bargain.

The next morning we got the news from our agent. Four other offers on the house came in last night. Our hearts sank. All of them were for about the same dollar amount, about 5% below the asking price. The vendors said they were firm on the price, and we'd have to up our offer if we wanted to be considered. They stipulated, however, that they didn't want more than the asking price. No bidding wars were needed. The old lady and her husband were going to decide who they wanted to live in their house. The house they had owned from the time it was built; the house where they had raised their children—a house dear to their heart. They wanted a young family in the house who would raise their children there, someone who would take great care of the house, someone who might go around wiping up spills that an old lady with her unsteady hands and shaky legs might make. Later that day toward the evening, we got the news. The house was ours.

Housing prices started to rise from the beginning of the decade as more people started to get in the "game." At first it was the families who were looking to move up as their families grew. Then it was opportunists who saw big upside in the real estate market. Next, renters worried that they might not ever get into the housing market if they didn't get in at that point. Every channel on TV seemed to have a show about renovating a house. It made sense to invest in a house since prices were going ever upward. After the renters the house flippers looked to make a quick buck. Borrowing money was so easy and cheap that it didn't make any sense not to. The housing market had worked itself into a frenzy. No one wanted to be left out.

Banks saw the opportunity to lend more money, so they invented more and more ways for people to borrow. They eased the terms of the mortgage. They extended the length of the mortgage to make the payments easier to carry. They offered cash back on mortgages for renovations, new appliances, or a vacation. They offered no–money-down mortgages. Then mortgages for 110% of the value of a house became available.[35] Banks were running out of money they had to lend, so they started to make more use of the special companies (such as the Federal National Mortgage Association, or "Fannie Mae" for short) that would buy the mortgages and take them off the banks' books, so banks could extend more loans. Banks realized they could write mortgages, sell them off, collect the commission, and have no responsibilities. So they did, and they began to find all sorts of ways to write more mortgages and bigger mortgages.

When banks and mortgage companies ran out of good homeowners to sell a mortgage to, they looked for anyone else who might want a mortgage—subprime borrowers, or people who shouldn't have bought a house. At the height of this mortgage craze, they had the now infamous NINJA loans.[36] NINJA loans stood for "No Income, No Job, (No) Assets." The loans didn't require applicants to have a job or income, or even a down payment. All they needed was some ID and a pulse. With liar loans[37] every possible fact that could be misrepresented was. People who were buying houses had no intention of living up to the requirements of homeownership; the most important requirement was that of living up to the contractual obligation of making payments on the mortgages. Buyers thought that they could just sell the house in a few months and make some easy money.

Thus, housing prices climbed as buyers tried to outbid each other. Homeowners extravagantly outfitted their homes in an effort to outdo their neighbors and to make it more attractive for sale. The housing bubble grew to astronomical proportions—an estimated $25 trillion, or about a quarter of the wealth of the entire world! The economic growth of the

---

35 Ryan Barns, "The Fuel That Fed the Subprime Meltdown," *Investopedia*, September 4, 2007, http://www.investopedia.com/articles/07/subprime-overview.asp#axzz2CDst9pBD, (accessed March 2012).

36 Alan Zibel, "Liar Loans' Threaten to Prolong Mortgage Crisis," Huff Post Business, August 18, 2008, http://www.huffingtonpost.com/2008/08/18/liar-loans-threaten-to-po_n_119650.html (accessed March 2012).

37 Ibid.

United States over the five-year period between 2001 and 2006 was driven by the housing sector. The bubble was being blown to massive proportions. All the while money continued to be lent based on these bubble values.

As with any bubble, it eventually bursts. The housing bubble, however, has yet to recover and may be still years in the future before it does. There continues to be an overhang of unsold houses, of bank-owned houses, and the shadow inventory, which is comprised of home mortgages currently in default or in foreclosure proceedings or simply sitting in limbo as the courts try to figure out who the legitimate owners are. These are not counted in the current inventory of houses for sale. In the height of the housing boom, there were so many mortgages written and so many that changed hands that it became difficult if not impossible to determine who had the legal title to a property. As mortgages were flipped from banks to finance companies and from one pool of mortgage-backed securities to another, the chain of ownership was clouded or even lost.

The electronic registry system called MERS (Mortgage Electronic Registry Systems) had been the central depository for mortgages across the country. Transactions on MERS came under question as the proper documentation that needed to accompany a mortgage transfer or ownership transfer was missing or improperly executed. When the bubble burst and banks began to foreclose, they found that it was difficult in many cases to establish who had a clear title to a house in order to implement foreclosure proceedings.

Many foreclosures proceeded anyway. Mortgage holders who called their banks to try to arrange for refinancing or mortgage alterations found the banks unwilling or unable to make changes as they didn't have clear titles to the properties. Many mortgagees couldn't find out who actually owned their mortgage, so they could try to renegotiate to save their house. With a tremendous amount of mortgages in foreclosure, MERS allegedly began authorizing foreclosures without the proper documentation and clarity on ownership required for such action.

The offices of attorneys general in every state filed lawsuits against the major banks in order to resolve these issues, putting the foreclosure process on hold. Many homeowners then sat in limbo, not knowing who held the mortgage, owned the house, whether they would face foreclosure proceedings, and whether they would lose their house. All the while these people in limbo were not paying their mortgages, which ironically has been a boost the economy as they have had more disposable cash to spend on other items.

The impacts and consequences go well beyond just the US housing market. The crisis is global and the fallout is still in progress in other parts of the world. China is having their own housing crisis as they built too many houses for their fledgling consumer economy. The impacts may be with us for years to come.

Looking ahead, the real estate market in the US may take another hit, with prices falling yet again as banks step up their foreclosure process. With the "settlement" of the alleged foreclosure fraud issues by the states' attorney generals and the banks, the banks will have a green light to move ahead with more foreclosures, putting even more houses on the market. The bottom of the housing market may be a lot further off than many are hoping.

## Two Gospels

So how does this relate to the gospel of Jesus Christ and our salvation? What do I mean by a "gospel bubble"? Could a gospel bubble mean growth in church membership but without the increase in true followers? Any nominal growth without real underlying growth is by definition a bubble.

Two versions of gospel are being taught: one with conditions and one without. Some churches teach a gospel that is easy-to-get and costs nothing to maintain. They espouse justification by faith without obedience to God's Word. They preach that Christ died for our sins, so there in nothing more for us to do. The gospel without submission makes it easy to accept, but what of the consequences? The Bible addresses this in Titus 3:5–7.

> Not by works of righteousness which we have done, but according to his *mercy he saved us*, by the *washing of regeneration*, and *renewing of the Holy Ghost*; which he shed on us abundantly through Jesus Christ our Saviour; that being justified by his grace, we should he made heirs according to the hope of eternal life. (emphasis added)

The three-part process for justification and sanctification cannot be separated. We cannot separate God's mercy from rebirth and the renewing of the Spirit.

Still, many Christians would try to offer justification (forgiveness) only without the admonition of Christ to "go, and sin no more" (John 8:11). So what must be the result? Just like NINJA loans, will we get applicants who want the benefits of salvation but without any intention of surrendering to Christ and following Him? Members want the assurance of salvation without the sacrifice of self. "For the time will come when they will not endure sound doctrine; but after their own lusts shall they heap to themselves teachers, having itching ears; and they shall turn away their ears from the truth, and shall be turned unto fables" (2 Timothy 4:3, 4). We see this happening as churches experience a growth in the number of people attending church, without a real increase in the number of true seekers and followers. The result must be a gospel bubble.

This is not to suggest that we shouldn't cast our net widely and reach out to as many as possible. Rather, we need to preach the full gospel: forgiveness + renewal + surrender. If the gospel we preach does not come with the requirements for renewal and surrender, we will fill our pews with those who have no intention of discipleship. Nicolaitans, those who "say they are Jews, and are not" (Revelation 3:9), turn the grace of God into lasciviousness. We are not to be judges, nor are we to decide who should attend church and who should not. If we rightly teach the Word of God, the power of His Word will draw the true seekers and the repentant.

The early Christian church thrived and grew when it had member-disciples who were dedicated to following Christ, obeying His commands and doing His work. When nominal Christians joined the church, it began to falter and ultimately fell into apostasy.

While it is dangerous to push an analogy too far, a couple more points can be made in comparing the housing bubble and crisis to the gospel work. The housing bubble didn't really turn into a massive problem until the lending practices became very lax and mortgages were given to those who should not have had them. The bubble did not really expand while true homeowners were spending lots of money on their houses but still borrowing within the normal limits. Only when the standards of practice in lending were loosened, and those who had no intention of homeownership were added, did the bubble take off.

As the bubble expanded, it began to affect the behaviors of those who were not subprime borrowers. The environment for everyone in the housing market changed. It created a perilous condition for all, even those who didn't have a mortgage. Now bursting, the bubble's wreckage is affecting everyone in the world. The impact of this new "gospel" on the church is happening now. It's not just about the nominal members, but about how it is impacting the entire church, changing the very foundations of our beliefs and the focus of our church's mission. This bubble will not burst until we near the close of probation, but the damage is currently accumulating. We need to stand for the truth today because it is affecting our brothers and sisters even now.

It is no small thing to be a disciple of Christ as it is neither cheap nor easy. It will cost us everything we have. God is an all-consuming fire. The true follower, however, would have it no other way. Being half a Christian is a most miserable life. Being only a part Christian would mean that we didn't know the full grace of God in our lives, which is not only forgiveness of sins, but also freedom from the grasp of sin in our lives through the transforming power of Christ.

If we only had forgiveness and not victory, we would be bound to repeat our mistakes over and over. We, with the apostle Paul, would exclaim, "O wretched man that I am! who shall deliver me from this body of this death?" (Romans 7:24). There is only one way to receive complete salvation, and that is a full surrender to Jesus. There is only one gospel because any other gospel than that which gives us victory over sin is no gospel at all. Paul didn't end crying, "O wretched man that I am"; he went on to proclaim, "I thank God through Jesus Christ my Lord" (Romans 7:25). "That the righteousness of the law might be fulfilled in us, who walk not after the flesh, but after the Spirit" (Romans 8:4).

The fallout from the "housing bubble" has damaged our financial institutions and shaken them to the core of their business. The fall of the "gospel bubble" will cause a shaking of the church to its core. Financial institutions appealed to a higher power to rescue them, the US Federal Reserve. They argued that they were "too big to fail," or in other words that they were too important to the world economic system and to allow them to fail would cause worldwide economic destruction. This new doctrine of "too big to fail" has become the mantra for the Fed and the US government, which in turn has now created a new risk—a new moral hazard. The church will also need to look to a higher power to survive the bursting of the gospel bubble, a gospel that has become a new moral hazard for the church.

## Chapter 5

## Too Big to Fail

What shall we say then? Shall we continue in sin, that grace may abound? God forbid. How shall we, that are dead to sin, live any longer therein? (Romans 6:1, 2)

A dozen people called about asset-backed commercial paper (ABCP) and the safety of money market funds by ten o'clock in the morning. Coventree, a company that created these some of these ABCP investments, had fallen victim to the mortgage crisis.[38] These instruments that were deemed to be very safe were in trouble. Nobody wanted to touch them. If a money market fund was holding these investments, and they needed to sell them to raise cash for investors who were redeeming their money, they were out of luck. These investments could not be sold because there were no buyers. That morning was spent reassuring people that there were no ABCPs in our products. This episode was only a prelude to a much bigger event to come.

Cash is the lifeblood of the financial system. Without it, the system cannot survive. It would die as quickly as we would die if we lost all our blood. Cash is found in many forms: in actual currency like notes and coins, as deposits in bank and brokerage accounts, and as electronic funds found in the computers of global financial systems. The most prevalent form of money is in the form of ones and zeros, a binary computer language that records the assets and liabilities of companies and financial institutions. The world has much more electronic money than actual currency. Moving a million or a billion dollars can be done in a split second, as long as it takes to punch the "enter" key on a computer. Taking billions of dollars out of the financial system can be done quickly and with little effort. What would happen then if money was being taken out of the system at the speed of

---

38  Jacquie McNish and Jeff Gray, "OSC says Coventree withheld looming ABCP crash from investors," *The Globe and Mail*, September 28, 2011, http://m.theglobeandmail.com/report-on-business/osc-says-coventree-withheld-looming-abcp-crash-from-investors/article2183316/?service=mobile (accessed March 2012).

electricity? Well, what would happen to a human body if a knife was stuck in a main artery?

In the days after the failure of Lehman Brothers, the global financial markets nearly ground to a halt. It was a year later when the details became public. The chairman of the Congressional Banking Committee's Capital Markets Subcommittee, Paul Kanjorski (D), discussed the events after the failure of Lehman. He revealed that the banking system was literally minutes from a total shutdown on September 11, 2008. In his statement on C-Span, Rep. Kanjorski said that by 11:00 AM of the morning of September 11, 2008, more than $500 billion in cash had been taken out from the money markets in the matter of an hour and a half.[39] This was an electronic run on the banks.

The Federal Reserve estimated that $5.5 trillion in cash would have been withdrawn from the system by the afternoon, and the US and the world financial systems would have collapsed. The US Treasury quickly announced that they would guarantee up to $250,000 per account for any depositors, which seemed to calm the markets. When the decision was made to allow Lehman to go under, the impact on the short-term money markets was not well understood. The size of Lehman Brothers, while substantial, was not so great that its failure would have a catastrophic impact on the financial system. What wasn't well understood was the impact that a Lehman Brothers failure would have on the money markets, in particular, the commercial paper market.

Commercial paper is a short-term debt instrument issued by companies to fund their short-term borrowing needs. These issuers are usually high-quality companies that have a strong risk rating by the rating agencies. Also, the fact that these instruments are short-term, meaning that the principle is usually repaid within in 90 to 120 days, the risk is deemed to be low. Investors, typically large companies or money market funds that have cash to invest, buy commercial paper to earn interest at higher rates than can be earned in a bank account. The issuers usually rolled these instruments, meaning that after 90 or 120 days when the borrowed money had to be repaid, they simply issued more paper to pay off the last set of investors and maintain the cash funding for their company. Companies used these borrowings as a part of their permanent capital structure, helping to pay for things like operating costs, inventory, and the all important payrolls.

---

39  Paul Kanjorski, "Rep Paul Kanjorski Reviews the Bailout Situation," C-Span *Washington Journal*, February 9, 2009, http://youtu.be/pD8viQ_DhS4 (accessed February 2009).

Lehman Brothers facilitated large amounts of commercial paper issuance by guaranteeing the amounts issued. Lehman Brothers also borrowed $785 million from a money market fund called the Reserve Primary Fund to help fund many of Lehman's real estate investments.[40] Money market funds were supposed to be one the safest investments possible after bank deposits and government securities.

Lehman Brothers' investments in real estate were losing value. No one wanted to buy them anymore. When there are only sellers in the market, prices tumble. The asking price was falling lower and lower, which meant that losses for Lehman Brothers were mounting. By September 12, 2008, it was clear that the losses incurred by Lehman Brothers were greater than their capital base and the company was insolvent. On the weekend of September 12, the US Treasury Secretary Hank Paulson gathered the heads of all of the major banks at the New York Federal Reserve offices for an emergency meeting. While the purpose of the meeting was to find a means to rescue Lehman Brothers, the bankers spent most of their time ensuring that their own banks would survive a Lehman Brothers bankruptcy.[41] The CEO of Merrill Lynch, John Thain, found a buyer for his own company during that weekend meeting. Merrill was sold to Bank of America for $50 billion.[42] Bankers were busily working to try to minimize losses from any transactions outstanding with Lehman Brothers. Still, the group had not understood the impact of a Lehman Brothers bankruptcy on the markets.

When the morning of Monday, September 15, came around, the markets were quiet; no phones were ringing; no voices emanated from the squawk box. All was silent, not from relief or calm, but out of sheer terror of what was about to happen. Lehman Brothers had warned the US Treasury and the Federal Reserve that allowing them to go bankrupt would have catastrophic consequences, but their warnings fell on deaf

---

40   Christopher Condon, "Reserve Primary Money Fund Falls Below $1 a Share," *Bloomberg*, September 16, 2008, http://www.bloomberg.com/apps/news?pid=newsarchive&sid=a5O2y1go1GRU (accessed March 2012).

41   Joe Nocera and Edmund L. Andrews, "Struggling to Keep Up as the Crisis Raced On," *New York Times*, October 23, 2008, http://www.nytimes.com/2008/10/23/business/economy/23paulson.html?pagewanted=all&_r=0 (accessed March 2012).

42   Charles Gasparino, "Bank of America to Buy Merrill Lynch for $50 Billion," *CNBC.com*, September 14, 2008, http://www.cnbc.com/id/26708319/Bank_of_America_to_Buy_Merrill_Lynch_for_50_Billion (accessed March 2012).

ears.[43] The government didn't want the public relations disaster stemming from another bailout of a financial institution. Hank Paulson kept repeating, "No more bailouts."

The markets opened that morning, but the short-term money markets were completely frozen. Banks were not doing any transactions with each other, offers found no bids, sellers found no buyers.

As the news of the Lehman Brothers bankruptcy was released and the size of losses at Lehman Brothers became known, the fallout started. First, the markets learned that the Reserve Primary Fund had $785 million in commercial paper issued by Lehman Brothers, which meant gigantic losses for the fund. Investors started pulling their money from the fund. There were $40 billion in redemption requests in the first day.[44] Many other money market funds were also seeing huge redemptions.

In the panic selling, the Reserve Primary Fund "broke the buck," which means that its value fell below $1. The value of each unit of a money market fund was pegged at $1 at all times. This was to reflect the fact that the value of the fund was stable and the investment safe. Nevertheless, as the panic-driven redemptions continued, the fund had to sell assets even at losses in order to fund their redemptions.

Furthermore, the fund had to recognize that the value of the commercial paper from Lehman Brothers might be worthless. This resulted in the fund "breaking the buck," something that had happened only once before in the history of money market funds. By the end of the week investors had pulled more than $172 billion from money market funds. At this point the US Treasury Department and US Federal Reserve stepped in to calm the markets. They guaranteed the value of money market funds from losses a next year and extended loans to banks to buy high–quality, asset-backed commercial paper.[45] These actions of the US Treasury and US Federal Reserve acted to calm the markets, and the redemptions stopped.

---

43 · Lauren Ezell, "From Bear to Lehman: Documents Reveal and Alternate History" *PBS Frontline*, May 1, 2012, http://www.pbs.org/wgbh/pages/frontline/business-economy-financial-crisis/money-power-wall-street/from-bear-to-lehman-documents-reveal-an-alternate-history/ (accessed March 2012).

44 Chairman Mary L. Schapiro, "Testimony on 'Perspectives on Money Market Mutual Fund Reforms," *U.S. Security and Exchange Commission*, June 21, 2012, http://www.sec.gov/news/testimony/2012/ts062112mls.htm (accessed September 2012).

45 Henry M. Paulson, "Treasury Announces Temporary Guarantee Program for Money Market Funds," US Department of the Treasury Press Release, September 29, 2008, http://www.treasury.gov/press-center/press-releases/Pages/hp1161.aspx (accessed October 2008).

Hank Paulson, realizing the gravity of the moment, also announced on September 19 the intent of the US Treasury to create a troubled assets relief program, which would help financial institutions. In his statement he said:

> The federal government must implement a program to remove these illiquid assets that are weighing down our financial institutions and threatening our economy. This troubled asset relief program must be properly designed and sufficiently large to have maximum impact, while including features that protect the taxpayer to the maximum extent possible. The ultimate taxpayer protection will be the stability this troubled asset relief program provides to our financial system, even as it will involve a significant investment of taxpayer dollars. ...
>
> Right now, our focus is restoring the strength of our financial system so it can again finance economic growth. The financial security of all Americans – their retirement savings, their home values, their ability to borrow for college, and the opportunities for more and higher-paying jobs – depends on our ability to restore our financial institutions to a sound footing.[46]

Paulson realized that these subprime mortgages that many of the banks had been investing in, were worth far less than they were sold for. In fact, their values were both plummeting and clogging up the financial system. On October 3, 2008, President George W. Bush signed into law the Emergency Economic Stabilization Act of 2008, which established the $700 billion Troubled Assets Relief Program (TARP). The belief was that by taking a bold move to throw $700 billion at the problem would solve the issue and stabilize the market; however, they were wrong. The $700 billion was far too small in comparison with a $25 trillion mortgage market that was melting down. If the housing market declined just 10% that would be a $2.5 trillion impact, but unfortunately, the declines were much greater. The stock markets were not convinced that the measures taken were sufficient to stem the tide of the mortgage crisis.

---

46 "Statement by Secretary Henry M. Paulson, Jr. on Comprehensive Approach to Market Developments," US Department of the Treasury Press Release, September 19, 2008, http://www.treasury.gov/press-center/press-releases/Pages/hp1149.aspx (accessed March 2012).

Bank stocks continued to fall throughout the month of October 2008. Citigroup, the giant megabank, saw its stocks fall to $3.50 in October, down from about $48 a year earlier. In fact, Citi's stock had been falling since the fall of 2007 from a high of $55 per share when a little-known analyst named Meredith Whitney published a report identifying the problems that the banks had from their exposure to the mortgage market. This report shook the financial world in a similar fashion to the boy who exclaimed that the king was wearing no clothes. The king was indeed naked as it became clear that the big Wall Street banks did not have enough capital to cover themselves. Whitney emerged as the superstar analyst who brought down the big banks.

Of course, by mid 2008, half of Wall Street was now exclaiming that it too saw the problems with the banks and predicted the financial crisis, while the other half continued to proclaim that all was well and that these banks were still sound and that the Treasury and the Fed had acted to avert disaster.

Led lower by the banking stocks, the entire market began its record descent down. Slowly, but surely the markets were beginning to understand the severity of this downturn as they began to understand the root causes thereof. Yes, mortgages were not being paid anymore as the subprime borrowers were defaulting on the loans that they couldn't afford in the first place. The values of the investments that packaged these mortgages to sell to investors were falling rapidly. The banks that invested in these mortgages were being punished by the stock market for their bad investments. The banks would have to recognize large losses on their books as they reduced the holding value on the balance sheets of these deteriorating assets. These investments become known as "toxic assets" as their characteristics where like acid or rotting flesh eating away at the rest of the body.

To compound the problem, the share price of the banks fell; their capital position was eroded further, hampering their abilities to lend more money. Without lending, the economy would sputter and stop growing as companies no longer had access to the financing they needed to grow their businesses. Small and midsized businesses, in particular were being strangled from the lack of credit. These mid-market companies, which have always been the heart of job growth, were now forced to lay off thousands of workers as their businesses struggled.

Then it became painfully obvious that the economic growth of the previous seven years had been driven by the boom in the housing market. Construction spending had been the main driver of GDP growth between

2002 and 2006.[47] The housing bubble fueled the credit bubble as it seemed absolutely everyone took advantage of their easy access to credit backed by housing prices, which they were told would be going up forever. The easy credit fostered more spending on everything from iPods to renovations to vacations, but without the benefit of this housing boom and credit expansion, the economy was in a free-fall. Credit was no longer easy to get; consumer spending was no longer a driving force for growth; instead it was a ball and chain. With business and consumer spending at a standstill, the economy, the stock markets, and confidence were all down the drain.

The banks were in trouble. Their stock prices were at decade lows. Their balance sheets were full of toxic investments. The economy had ground to a halt, and no one was borrowing—at least no one they were willing to lend to. They weren't making any money, and worst of all, there would be no bonuses. Investment banks feared that they would face the same fate as Lehman Brothers. Many investors threatened with lawsuits because they lost millions of dollars, having been sold investments that were supposed to be AAA safe, only to find that they were worthless. The US Treasury had already announced that $700 billion would be spent to help the banks survive, but with the financial markets headed lower, the Treasury and Fed stepped up their efforts to save the system.

They followed up their TARP announcement with these measures:[48]

- October 7, 2008: The Federal Reserve announced the creation of the Commercial Paper Funding Facility.

- October 7, 2008: The FDIC announced an increase in deposit insurance coverage to $250,000 per depositor.

- October 8, 2008: The Federal Reserve Bank of New York was authorized to borrow up to $37.8 billion in securities from American International Group (AIG) ("borrow" means they took toxic assets from AIG in exchange for cash).

- October 14, 2008: The FDIC announced the Temporary Liquidity Guarantee Program to guarantee the senior debt of FDIC member banks.

---

47  Gross Domestic Product Data, US Bureau of Economic Analysis, http://www.bea.gov/newsreleases/national/gdp/2012/xls/gdp3q12_2nd.xls (accessed March 2012).

48  "The Financial Crisis: A Timeline of Events and Policy Actions," The Federal Reserve Bank of St. Louis, http://timeline.stlouisfed.org/pdf/CrisisTimeline.pdf (accessed March 2012).

- October 21, 2008: The Federal Reserve announced the creation of the Money Market Investor Funding Facility (MMIFF).
- October 13, 14, 2008: The Federal Reserve increased its swap lines with the Bank of Japan, Bank of England, European Central Bank and the Swiss National Bank.
- November 10, 2008: The Federal Reserve approved the application for the American Express company to become a bank-holding company, allowing it to have access to the various government financial support programs.
- November 11, 2008: The US Treasury and the Federal Housing Finance Agency announced a streamlined process for loan modifications.
- November 18, 2008: General Motors, Ford, and Chrysler requested access to the TARP program.
- November 23, 2008: The Treasury, Federal Reserve, and FDIC jointly announced a program to guarantee $306 billion in mortgages held by Citigroup in exchange for preferred shares. (Any gains in the mortgages would be kept by Citigroup; any losses would be paid for by the guarantee Privatization of profits and socialization of losses! "Heads, I win; tails, you lose.")
- November 25, 2008: The Federal Reserve announced the creation of the Term Asset-Backed Securities Lending Facility (TALF) for lending up to $200 billion to holders of AAA securities.
- November 25, 2008: The Federal Reserve agreed to purchase $600 billion of debt from Fannie Mae and Freddie Mac through auctions conducted by "primary dealers"[49] and other asset managers.
- December 2, 2008: The Federal Reserve announced the extension of three liquidity facilities, the Primary Dealer Credit Facility, the Asset-Backed Commercial Paper Money Market Fund Liquidity Facility and the Term Securities Lending Facility, to the end of April 2009.

---

49  Primary dealers are financial institutions that deal directly with the US Federal Reserve system to purchase and market government securities. Primary dealers are required to make bids when the Federal Reserve conducts its open market operations to sell Treasury Securities.

- December 19, 2008: The Treasury authorized loans to GM and Chrysler of $13.4 billion and $4 billion respectively from TARP funds.
- December 22, 2008: The Federal Reserve approved the application for the CIT Group Inc. (a finance company that provides loans to many small and medium-sized businesses) to become a bank holding company.
- December 24, 2008: The Federal Reserve approved the application for GMAC to become a bank holding company. (GMAC or General Motors Acceptance Corp is the financing arm of General Motors Corporation)
- January 16, 2009: The Treasury, Federal Reserve and FDIC jointly announced a program to guarantee $118 billion in mortgages held by Bank of America in exchange for preferred shares. (Heads, I win; tails, you lose, again.)
- February 10, 2009: US Treasury Secretary Timothy Geithner announced a Financial Stability Plan and the creation of a Public-Private Investment Fund (PPIF) to purchase troubled assets (did not work very well, gained little traction).
- February 10, 2009: The Federal Reserve announced that they would expand TALF up to $1 trillion and expand the securities eligible for the program.
- February 17, 2009: President Obama signed the American Recovery and Reinvestment Act of 2009 into law, providing $787 billion in stimulus spending for "shovel ready" projects.
- February 18, 2009: President Obama announced the Homeowner Affordability and Stability Plan, a $75 billion fund to help refinance mortgages held by Fannie Mae and Freddie Mac. The US Treasury also announced the increase of preferred stock purchase agreements with Fannie Mae and Freddie Mac to $200 billion.
- March 2, 2009: The Treasury announced an increase of $30 billion in aid to AIG under a new restructuring agreement. AIG announces a fourth quarter loss of $61.7 billion.
- March 18, 2009: The Federal Reserve announced the purchase of an additional $750 billion in mortgage-backed securities, which raised its total purchases for the year to $1.25 trillion. The Fed also

- planned to purchase an additional $100 billion of federal agency debt and $300 billion of longer-term Treasury debt.
- April 2, 2009: The Financial Accounting Standards Board provided a new set of guidelines for accounting for troubled assets. (Banks no longer have to mark to market assets which have no market value or no active market and recognize losses!)

It became clear that the US federal government and the Federal Reserve would do anything within their power to ensure that the banking system would maintain the status quo, regardless of the long-term economic and societal impacts. In spite of these measures, the stock markets continued to decline through the winter of 2009. The S&P500 stock index had fallen to 666, from a peak of 1590 in the fall of 2007, losing 60% of its value along the way.[50] The retirement savings of many Americans had been nearly wiped out. Stock markets around the world had fallen off a cliff, and it seemed like financial Armageddon was here.

On March 15, 2009, Ben Bernanke, the chairman of the US Federal Reserve Board, in an interview on the CBS program *60 Minutes* predicted that the US would come out of its worst recession in recent history by the following year, and that he already saw "green shoots" of economic recovery.[51] A few days after this interview, the Fed announced its program of massive purchases of US Treasury securities, mortgage-backed securities, and agency debt, which would eventually become known as the first program of "quantitative easing" or QE1. This measure would see the Federal Reserve buy more than $1.25 trillion in debt from financial institutions, more than doubling the size of their balance sheet. This was on top of the trillions of dollars already pledged in earlier announcements. These were very expensive green shoots.

The stock market understood the announcement and the measures that the Fed was undertaking. The Fed was not going to let the banks fail at any cost. With that realization the stock markets began to rally hard and over the next year, hardly looking back. The markets nearly doubled their lows and regained about half of what they had lost. Banks that looked to be on the precipice of collapse were able to claw their way back from the edge.

---

50  "S&P500," S&P Dow Jones Indices, http://www.standardandpoors.com/indices/sp-500/en/us/?indexId=spusa-500-usduf--p-us-l-- (accessed March 2012).

51  Scott Pelley, correspondent, "Ben Bernanke's Greatest Challenge," *60 Minutes*, March 15, 2009, http://www.cbsnews.com/8301-18560_162-4862191.html (March 2009).

Since the beginning of the financial crisis, the large US financial institutions had adopted an attitude of we're "too big to fail." These commercial banks and investment banks were and still are critical to the function of the economy. They pressed their case to the government that they could not fail, or it would be a mutually assured destruction. Until the financial crisis hit, the government and regulators had been largely turning a blind eye to the excesses in the lending practices by the financial institutions. Since the Clinton administration, banks had been lobbying successfully that there should be less regulation and that they could better police themselves. Now that disaster had struck, the banks lobbied for aid and for the government and regulators to rescue them. They were too big to fail. Financial institutions spent a significant $41 million lobbying in Washington in 2008. In 2011, the figure rose to $61 million.[52] The National Association of Realtors also spent $17 million lobbying in 2008.[53] Apparently, money well-spent based on the amount of financial support the industry received.

Furthermore, these banks, particularly the Wall Street investment banks, have had close ties to the government under every administration. During the first few years of the Obama Administration, many were taking note, particularly from the right, that there were many former Goldman Sachs executives and directors in the White House.[54] Though the fact is that there were many former Goldmanites in the previous administration as well, these facts played well in the media for the Republicans. There was Stephen Friedman, chairman of the President's Foreign Intelligence Advisory Board who was a former co-chairman at Goldman; Gary Gensler, commissioner of the Commodities and Futures Trading Commission who was a former partner at Goldman; Robert Hormats, undersecretary of Economic, Energy and Agricultural Affairs, was former vice chairman at Goldman; Mark Patterson, chief of staff to the treasury secretary, was a former vice president at Goldman; Dianna Farrell, deputy director at the

---

52  "Annual Lobbying on Commercial Banks," Commercial Banks Industry Profile, 2008, OpenSecrets.org Center for Responsible Politics, http://www.opensecrets.org/lobby/indusclient.php?id=F03&year=2008 (accessed March 2012).

53  "Annual Lobbying on Real Estate," Commercial Banks Industry Profile, 2008, OpenSecrets.org Center for Responsible Politics, http://www.opensecrets.org/lobby/indusclient.php?id=F10&year=2008 (accessed March 2012).

54  Michael Abramowitz, "Goldman Alumni Now Call the Shots in Washington," Washington Post, September 19, 2008, http://www.washingtonpost.com/wp-dyn/content/article/2008/09/18/AR2008091803843.html (accessed March 2012)/"Goldman Sachs Alumni: Currently Servicing," http://www.trendsresearch.com/reports/goldman-inter.pdf (accessed March 2012).

National Economic Council, was a former analyst at Goldman; Phillip Murphy, ambassador to Germany was once head of Goldman Sachs in Frankfurt. To be fair, it should be noted that Hank Paulson, treasury secretary under George W. Bush was the former chairman and CEO of Goldman; Jeffery Rueben, a former managing partner at Goldman preceded Robert Hormats; Robert Steel was undersecretary for domestic finance and a former vice chairman at Goldman; Robert Zoellick was deputy secretary of state. Unfortunately, it must be said that the above names were just a few of the former Goldman and Wall Street executives. With these close ties between Washington and Wall Street, the cry of "too big to fail" was heard loud and clear.

It can't be overlooked, either, that the US Federal Reserve system is owned by its member banks and, to a large extent, operates for the benefit of its members. The Federal Reserve does, in fact, implement the nation's monetary policy, and yet they are independent of direct control by the federal government. While this independence is by design to ensure that monetary policy is free from political influence, the fact that the Federal Reserve can take actions that effectively spend taxpayers' money has become a concern for both citizens and politicians.

Over the course of the financial crisis, the Fed has continued to expand its balance sheet by buying up more debt from its primary dealers and other financial institutions, leading to a devaluation of the dollar and a potential liability to the taxpayers of America. More simply put, who will bailout the Federal Reserve when its balance sheet is full of toxic assets and becomes insolvent? Still, the Fed implemented round two of the quantitative easing program in 2010, buying up $600 billion[55] in US Treasury securities from its primary dealers and then "Operation Twist"[56] in 2011, which saw the Fed selling short-term securities and buying long term to keep interest rates lower. Both of these actions resulted in additional cash for financial institutions and came at times when the stock markets were floundering.

The banks argued that they were too big to fail, that they were too important to the financial system and the economic well being of the country.

---

55  Ben S. Bernanke, "The Economic Outlook and Monetary Policy," Board of Governors of the Federal Reserve System, August 27, 2010 http://www.federalreserve.gov/newsevents/speech/bernanke20100827a.htm (accessed August 2010).

56  Press Release, Board of Governors of the Federal Reserve System, September 21, 2011 http://www.federalreserve.gov/newsevents/press/monetary/20110921a.htm (accessed September 2011).

The government agreed that the banks were too big to fail and determined that the financial system status quo must be maintained at all costs. The Federal Reserve made sure that the banks did not fail and provided them with unprecedented amounts of monetary support to keep them afloat. In the spring of 2009, banking stocks were recovering and the markets were rallying along with them.

Unfortunately, the real economy continued to remain depressed. Unemployment continued to remain high with weekly unemployment claims remaining at nearly half a million people.[57] New jobs were not being created. Large layoffs continued at a high pace. Where were the green shoots? Where was the economic recovery that Chairman Bernanke predicted? What did the banking system do with the all of bailout money and the access to funds and guarantees?

Looking at the Federal Reserve's Consumer Credit data, it is clear that the banks did not increase its lending to consumers. Over the three years since the financial crisis started, total consumer credit declined 4.4% in 2009, and 1.7% in 2010, but it did manage to increase 3.6% in 2011,[58] but that was due to a $109 billion increase in non-revolving loans by the federal government, mostly in the form of student loans. So what happened to the trillions of dollars that was injected into the banking system? Businesses were not expanding and hiring, so there was not much lending to corporate America, and consumers didn't get any credit. Where did the money go?

Clearly, the banks were still in dire need of cash and capital to shore up their balance sheets against the losses they incurred from their mortgage-related investments. The trillions they received were still not enough to cover the losses in order to put the banks in a position to extend credit.

Banks must meet capital adequacy ratios, or in other words, they must have sufficient equity in their business in order to be able to lend. They were not in a position to do so with the amount of toxic mortgages still on their books. With the economy still sputtering and the potential for further housing price declines still looming on the horizon, the banks may have been keeping more cash on hand in the event of another crisis.

---

57 Unemployment Insurance Weekly Claims Data," Employment and Training Administration, US Department of Labor, http://www.ows.doleta.gov/unemploy/wkclaims/report.asp (accessed March 2012, data no longer available).

58 "Consumer Credit G.19," Economic Research & Data, Board of Governors of the Federal Reserve System, http://www.federalreserve.gov/releases/g19/Current/ (accessed December 2011).

Primary dealers were able to take the money from the Federal Reserve at 0.25% interest and purchase longer term US Treasury securities with a yield of 3% and get a risk-free return of 2.75%. Many of the banks also went right back to investing in mortgage-backed securities from government agencies and other asset-backed securities. With the Federal Reserve now purchasing these securities, the values continued to rise. Banks also increased their revenues from trading activities benefiting from the rising markets. While they had little motivation to take risks from lending, they had much more incentive to take the excess funding they received and put it into the markets.

So here was the moral hazard; if there is no worry about failing, what risks can be taken to make money? If a bank is deemed to be too big to fail, what incentive is there to limit risk-taking to earn higher profits?

Starting in the fall of 2011, the European debt crisis took center stage in the financial news. The debt situation in Greece continued to worsen, requiring the country to ask for further support. Though the Greek debt is relatively small, how their debt problems are solved would set a precedent for other eurozone nations, particularly Italy and Spain. Whatever course of action is taken to resolve the Greek debt crisis would likely be taken by other nations. A Greek debt default could not be allowed since this would set the tone for Portugal, Spain, Italy and any other nation that could not pay back its debts.

The European Union and the eurozone finance ministers, specifically of Germany and France, could not allow a direct default of the debts by these peripheral eurozone countries because most of their debts were held by the large European banks.[59] The European Union basically declared that their key banks are too big to fail. The European Central Bank (ECB) also embarked on a program they called long-term refinancing operations[60] (LTRO), which would see the ECB accept almost any bond as collateral in exchange for a three-year cash loan. The ECB would become the repository for these toxic bonds while the banks would be safe from any defaults. The ECB conducted two LTRO programs, one in the fall of 2011

---

59  Stephen Castle, "With Details Settled, a 2nd Greek Bailout Is Formally Approved," *New York Times*, March 14, 2012, http://www.nytimes.com/2012/03/15/business/global/greece-gets-formal-approval-for-second-bailout.html (accessed March 2012).

60  "ECB announces measures to support bank lending and money market activity," Press Release, European Central Bank, December 8, 2011, http://www.ecb.int/press/pr/date/2011/html/pr111208_1.en.html (accessed March 2012).

and the next in the winter of 2012 for amounts of €500 billion and €489 billion respectively.

These LTRO programs have provided liquidity to more than 500 European banks to help shore up their capital positions. Also, the LTRO programs and the direct purchases of European sovereign bonds have worked to bring down the bond yields for key countries like Italy and Spain to try to avert a Greek-like disaster. The two-fold effect of LTRO has helped to calm the markets and stabilize the financial system, but it is still yet another form of a bailout of the financial institutions. It is another example that governments will do whatever they feel they need to do to keep the status quo.

Recently, a new term has been coined to replace the "too big to fail" moniker, which would no doubt be unpopular with the executives. Twenty-nine global banks have been named systemically important financial institution (SIFI) by the Financial Stability Board.[61] For those banks designated as SIFI, there is an implicit guarantee that the respective government of each of these institutions, along with the global financial community, will not allow these banks to fail. Regulators are seeking ways to ensure the stability of these institutions without overly restricting their business activities; however, this may be proving to be difficult.

The way in which financial institutions can take risks or increase the amount of risk can be very subtle. A slight change in their credit-granting procedures, looking at new or different investment opportunities or expanding into new areas of business, can all add risks and profits and still remain within accepted guidelines. Recall that the banks were investing in what was believed to be AAA rated securities, which led to the mortgage bubble, and it was only a slight variation from the types of securities previously purchased. Clearly, this did not work out well.

"Too big to fail" has created an environment of moral hazard in which banks will take undue risk for the sake of profits and give their executives bonuses with the belief that the government will bail them out. This risk-taking behavior continues to put the world economy at risk due to mal-investments trying to perpetuate the failed economic systems, which will eventually implode. The most recent revelation by JP Morgan Chase that they have again lost billions of dollars due to their investing activities

---

61 "Policy Measures to Address Systemically Important Financial Institutions," Financial Stability Board, November 4, 2011, http://www.financialstabilityboard.org/publications/r_111104bb.pdf (accessed March 2012).

is a case in point regarding this problem.[62] Likely, they are not alone in this type of risk-taking behavior.

**Too Big To Fail**

We see the folly of this attitude and the moral hazard it created. If you believe you'll be bailed out, what risks wouldn't you be willing to take? This is a question for you to think about for a moment. Of course, you are not a bank, and there is no one providing you with an unlimited supply of cash, but I believe we do have a moral hazard in our spiritual lives. Many of us have grown up in the church and in our faith. We believe in the Grace of God and the fullness of His salvation for us. Christ paid the price, so we don't have to. What more can we do to add to our salvation? Jesus has bailed us out! God is too big to fail us. No matter what we do, He will forgive us. While that is true, the moral hazard is immense. We were debtors, but we are now free! But free to do what? This is the question.

"What wrong with…?" We have struggled with this question since our youth.

"What's wrong with jewelry?"

"What is wrong with an occasional drink?"

"What is wrong with …" well the list can be endless. I've asked those same questions from the time when I was little.

"Why can't I do that?"

"I don't see anything wrong with it."

"God won't care if I do that!"

This led to an attitude of "what can I get away with doing and still be a Christian?"

Ultimately, I believed that God is "too big to fail." I believed that I could take lots of risks with my relationship with God because He is too big to fail. I knew that God would always take me back. I can be like the world, but God's grace is sufficient for me. He will save me.

We can go down this road for some time taking more and more risks with our relationship, with our faith, and with our love. Yet, somewhere down the road something will change in us. The risk we run is that eventually we will not want the things that God offers. Of course God is too big to fail, but the question is this: will we want the salvation that He offers.

---

62   Dawn Kopecki and Michael J. Moore, "JP Morgan's $4.4 Billion CIO Loss Drives Profit Down 9%," Bloomberg, July 13, 2012, http://www.bloomberg.com/news/2012-07-13/jpmorgan-s-4-4-billion-cio-loss-drives-profit-down-9-percent.html (accessed July 2012).

Something will change in our appetites, in our motivations and in our desires. Taking risks with God's grace is not sustainable for us. Bit by bit it will move us away from God, all the while making us think that we are still saved. "The time will come when they will not endure sound doctrine; but after their own lusts shall they heap to themselves teachers, having itching ears; and they shall turn away their ears from the truth, and shall be turned unto fables" (2 Timothy 4:3, 4).

When we appreciate God's grace and understand the price He paid to bail us out, our response should be to see how close we can get to Him, rather than how far can we stray and still be saved? Our every desire should be to see how much like Christ we can become and serve Him? We still are perhaps asking, "What's wrong with that?" If so, we may need to reexamine our relationship with Him. In these times God is looking for people who want to be closer to Him than to anything in this world; people who will take risks *for* Him, not with Him; people who will be too close to Him to fail; people who won't fail Him when the time comes to take a stand. Paul wrote:

> What shall we say then? Shall we continue in sin, that grace may abound? God forbid. How shall we, that are dead to sin, live any longer therein? Know ye not, that so many of us as were baptized into Jesus Christ were baptized into his death? Therefore we are buried with him by baptism into death: that like as Christ was raised up from the dead by the glory of the Father, even so we also should walk in newness of life. (Romans 6:1–4)

The problem in my life, was that not only was I taking risks with my relationship with God and not recognizing my true condition, but I also had a serious misunderstanding about how and, most importantly, when I needed to get ready for end-time events. God through His Word and His messengers started to open my heart and mind to see more clearly not only what I was lacking, but also how urgent my need was for change. When I began to understand that I had been "planning" for the wrong event my whole life, my life changed.

## Chapter 6

# The Salvation Option

After this I looked, and, behold, a door was opened in heaven: and the first voice which I heard was as it were of a trumpet talking with me; which said, Come up hither, and I will shew thee things which must be hereafter. (Revelation 4:1)

In September 2009, Robert Toll, the 68-year-old CEO of Toll Brothers, the largest home builder in the US sold 1.7 million shares of stock in his own company, taking in about $31 million.[63] Robert Toll founded this company with his brother in 1967 and has grown the company over the past 40 years. The day after a Wall Street brokerage equity research department issued a recommendation to its clients to buy Toll Brothers stock, the forecast for the stock price rose to $29 from $23.

So we must conclude one of two things: 1) either Robert Toll had made a bad decision in selling his stock and didn't know what his company was worth, or 2) that there was something wrong with the research. It would be my guess that Toll knows his business, the market, the economy, and what his stock is worth. In fact, he and his brother have exercised their stock options and then cashed in more than $100 million worth of shares in the company in 2011 since the stock has recovered from its lows in March of 2009.

A stock option allows the holder to buy a stock at a predetermined (usually low) price; however, you do have to exercise it by a certain date (called the exercise date). Stock options are often included as a component of executive compensation, and options often have greater value than the salary component of the total compensation package. Options provide a way to defer the taxable benefit until after a vesting period, over which the executive is incented to raise the value of the company's stock.

Upon exercising the options, the executives would receive the specified shares of the company after which the executive may choose to hold

---

63  James R. Hagerty, "Toll's CEO Tallies Gains in Stock Sale," *Wall Street Journal*, September 14, 2009, http://online.wsj.com/article/SB125288064880607045.html (accessed September 2009).

or sell them. It should be noted that it is certainly within Mr. Toll's rights to sell stock of his company, and any CEO may have many reasons to sell company shares, particularly given his age. Mr. Toll still holds a large number of shares in his company, and the amount sold is only a small fraction of his holdings. This is a matter of public record as are all transactions by executives of publicly traded companies, and this is all above board and transparent.

With hindsight being 20/20, we can see that he made a good decision as the Toll Brothers, Inc. stock price never rose past $23, but rather fell over the two years following 2009. As of the spring of 2012, it has just regained the $23 to $24 level. It would seem that the brokerage reports were too optimistic, and Mr. Toll made a good decision in exercising his options.

Still, back in 2009 few CEOs bought their own stock. Stock purchases by company insiders were few and far between. Very few companies were initiating any share buyback programs. The insider transactions were currently running about at about a 30:1 ratio of sells vs. buys.[64] In other words, 30 times more stocks of their own company are sold by executives than are bought. During 2010 and 2011, insider selling was many times higher than insider buying. Insider buying and selling is at times a good indicator of where stocks are headed.

Corporate executives do know their business and industries, timing their own investment decisions based on this knowledge. Analysts from brokerages may try to entice investors with favorable stock reports, which often turn out to be too optimistic. Being knowledgeable about what is going on can be very profitable, allowing the holder of the knowledge to take actions that others cannot. Insiders, who know the time and seasons, are like those holding options and who have the ability to take advantage of their knowledge using their options to their benefit. This is not about Wall Street or corporate CEOs; rather, it's about our brothers and sisters in the Seventh-day Adventist Church—you and me—insiders to God's plan for the end of this earth. But exactly what are we doing with this knowledge and hope?

Many of us who have grown up in the church, or who have been members for some time, know about the signs of the times and the events leading up to the second coming of Jesus. We are the insiders to God's magnificent plan of salvation and the coming apocalypse. How fortunate for us that we know this. This is valuable. We can know what events to look for so

---

64  Izabella Kaminska, "Trimtabs: Insider buying is non-existant," FTAlphaville, September 1, 2009, http://ftalphaville.ft.com/2009/09/01/69351/trimtabs-insider-buying-is-non-existent/? (September 2009).

we can get ready. It's like we have a "salvation option" in our hands, which we can exercise when the appropriate time comes. Do we hold the knowledge of the end-time events like a protective hedge that we can use when the time is right so we aren't on the wrong side of the judgment? In the meantime are we enjoying the world and its luxuries until it comes time to give it up and exercise the salvation option? It seems that many Adventists treat God's wonderful gift of salvation, His righteousness that He gives to us by faith and the incredible prophecies of the end times, like an "option" that we can exercise as the end comes nearer and we see the signs.

We just have to exercise this "option" before the close of probation to be saved. We know the signs; we see wars and rumors of wars; we see that natural disasters are increasing in frequency, that nations are angry. When we start to hear rumbles about a Sunday law, then we know it's time to get really serious about our spirituality. As long as we are ready before the close of probation, all will be well, and if we study the prophecies enough, we will be able to see the warning signs of its close. Besides, we believe we are maintaining our daily Christian walk sufficiently, and where we lack, God will change us in a twinkling of an eye from corruption to incorruption when He pronounces that those who are righteous will be righteous still and those who are filthy will be filthy still ... right?

What would happen if we didn't have this timing right? What if the exercise date that we are working toward, the close of probation, was the wrong date? What would be the consequence of misunderstanding the meaning of probation, this tarrying time, the time since 1844? What if we are focused on the wrong event? Also, if the close of probation is the wrong event, what might be the right event?

For the answer, we need to go back to the sanctuary and the service of the Day of Atonement. Revelation tells us that when Christ entered the most holy place, the door was opened (Revelation 4:1), revealed the throne room of God, and the judgment was started. Though many would like to close this door, it cannot be closed. God's law is shown in its full light; its requirements are made known and judgment has commenced, first, with the dead and then onto the living. God's is judging His people now, not sometime down the road.

Just think about the word "probation" in its judicial sense. Probation is an alternative sentence for someone who has been found guilty of a crime. Rather than going to jail, the judge can give a sentence of probation, which allows one to live among the free, law-abiding citizens as long as he or she obeys certain condition. So what is God's probation for the world? Could it be that all are found guilty under the law, but God has given an alternative sentence to live by His grace in His Spirit and live under certain conditions?

He gives a probationary sentence to provide the opportunity for all to show that they can live in accordance with His will, through His spirit. Only as one continuously lives in accordance to the conditions of the probation, can his sins be blotted out from the books in heaven. Only when the Holy Spirit lives inside, guides and purifies, can the conditions of probation be fulfilled, the sinner be justified, and his or her sins be blotted out.

Many of us think that the close of probation is an event where we will be cleansed of our sinful nature. Others believe that we need to fully overcome our sins by God's Spirit by the time probation comes to an end. We look toward the close of probation as an important milestone in our journey as Seventh-day Adventist Christians—the time when final decisions are made, and the seal of God is placed upon our forehead. There are a number of problems with this view, however. First, the concept of what is to happen at the close of probation is incorrect. Second, if we are working toward that date to "be ready" we will be too late to receive the seal of God. Third, we are not recognizing the important role that God has given us in His last-day plans.

Let's deal with the first issue of what happens at the close of probation. Many Adventists believe that we are sealed at the close of probation, which means that we can no longer commit sin. The word "seal" can be used in two ways. In one definition, a seal is a mark or stamp that establishes a mark of ownership. The other use of the word "seal" indicates a secure closure that keeps things in or keeps things out. Many of us believe that the sealing of God makes it impossible for us to sin. That this seal will keep sin out and keep God's goodness in. Unfortunately, this is not the correct meaning of the word seal in as used in Revelation 14.

The seal of God in Revelation 14 is simply a mark that God places on His people, indicating who has made their final decision and have prepared themselves for the end times. It identifies those that God says will follow Him under any circumstances. When the sealed people pass the final test in the time of trouble, it demonstrates to the universe that God can identify true faith and love in the heart. The seal does not remove the ability to make choices or to sin from those bearing God's seal. Even after the close of probation God's elect could sin, which is why Satan unleashes all of his fury at them to try to get them to sin and disprove God. These saints will not sin, however, because God's Spirit lives in them and has trained them to obey and not sin. Only as we allow the Holy Spirit to cleanse us of our sins now will we be prepared for the close of probation—the great time of Jacob's trouble.

Ever wonder why, God doesn't just wipe out the sinful tendencies in our lives. Luke 11 tells us that if an unclean spirit is driven from us and returns to find the space he vacated swept and cleaned (but still empty), he will return with seven others more wicked than him, and the condition of the person will be many times worse. For every bad habit or tendency that we get rid of, we need to replace it with good ones through the help of the Holy Spirit. It takes time for us to develop good habits, to learn to trust in Him, to pray, and to fully yield to Him. It doesn't happen overnight and God won't make it happen by the force of a miracle. By our daily choices we enable the Spirit to live inside us and work to change us. It takes time, and we must start now.

So what does happen to us at the close of probation? Nothing! At least nothing on the inside. The close of probation simply happens whether all have made their choice for God or not, and He decides when He has given everyone enough time. God's preparatory work is done well in advance. Nothing miraculous occurs at that point time. Probation just closes because no more time is needed.

If the close of probation is not the time by which we must be ready, what is the time? By the time Sunday laws are passed? Before persecution begins? Unfortunately, this will be too late as well. We need to be ready to be sealed, to have overcome our sins and have a pure heart before the latter rain is poured out. We cannot partake of the outpouring of the Holy Spirit unless our hearts are cleansed and we have won our victory over every sin. Just as the disciples needed to have a true conversion of the heart before Pentecost, we too must have the same experience like Peter or Thomas. Christ breathed on the disciples the Holy Spirit in the upper room, before He ascended to heaven, to help prepare them for the larger outpouring of the Spirit. We need the same experience of receiving the Spirit in a smaller measure to cleanse us from sin, so that God can pour out the Spirit in greater measure in latter rain power. Ellen White wrote:

> I saw that many were neglecting the preparation so needful and were looking to the time of "refreshing" and the "latter rain" to fit them to stand in the day of the Lord and to live in His sight. Oh, how many I saw in the time of trouble without a shelter! They had neglected the needful preparation; therefore they could not receive the refreshing that all must have to fit them to live in the sight of a holy God. ... *I saw that none could share the "refreshing" unless they obtain the victory over every besetment, over pride, selfishness, love of the world, and over every wrong word and action.* We

should, therefore, be drawing nearer and nearer to the Lord and be earnestly seeking that preparation necessary to enable us to stand in the battle in the day of the Lord. Let all remember that God is holy and that none but holy beings can ever dwell in His presence. (*Early Writings*, 71, emphasis added)

The third angel's message is swelling into a loud cry, and you must not feel at liberty to neglect the present duty, and still entertain the idea that at some future time you will be the recipients of great blessing, when without any effort on your part a wonderful revival will take place. Today you are to give yourselves to God, that he may make of you vessels unto honor, and meet for his service. Today you are to give yourself to God, that you may be emptied of self, emptied of envy, jealousy, evil-surmising, strife, everything that shall be dishonoring to God. *Today you are to have your vessel purified that it may be ready for the heavenly dew, ready for the showers of the latter rain; for the latter rain will come, and the blessing of God will fill every soul that is purified from every defilement.* It is our work today to yield our souls to Christ, that we may be fitted for the time of refreshing from the presence of the Lord—fitted for the baptism of the Holy Spirit. (*The Review and Herald*, March 22, 1892, emphasis added)

We need to be prepared to receive the latter rain from God. The Spirit is already being given in parts of the world where great work is being done. If we neglect our duty to prepare, we will miss our opportunity, and we will be left to our own delusions.

Oh, that the people might know the time of their visitation! There are many who have not yet heard the testing truth for this time. There are many with whom the Spirit of God is striving. The time of God's destructive judgments is the time of mercy for those who have had no opportunity to learn what is truth. Tenderly will the Lord look upon them. His heart of mercy is touched; *His hand is still stretched out to save, while the door is closed to those who would not enter.* (*Testimonies to the Church*, vol. 9, 97, emphasis added)

It is important for us to recognize that probation closes at different times for different people, for it closes at the moment one dies and is laid to rest. The close of probation for those of us who know the truth is sooner than for those who have not had the opportunity. The close of probation for Seventh-day Adventists will be as the latter rain is being poured out. If we have not been prepared by having given our all to Christ, if we do not enter while the door is open now, we will find that our time of probation will have been effectively closed. With greater light comes greater responsibility. We have been given a tremendous amount of light, so we have greater accountability during these end times.

God needs His special messengers to prepare for the outpouring of the Holy Spirit, so when it comes, they will go to the whole world with power. Great numbers will hear the message and be convinced of the truth. They will join the ranks of God's remnant people; yet, they have much work to do in order to prepare themselves for the close of probation. They will need to accomplish in a short time what Adventists have had many years to do. They too will need to learn to overcome their sins and learn to fully trust in God before the final trials come.

This is the critical difference for Seventh-day Adventists. We have a unique message that has been entrusted to us to give to the world. It is simply not enough for us to gain salvation for ourselves. We are called to be a witness to the world of God's love, His law, and His righteousness. If we do not fulfill this function, then we will have failed in our mission. If we reject this calling, we reject Him who has called us. Those who knowingly reject the present truth message will be left to a strong delusion, indeed, long before the close of probation. This happened in Ellen White's time; it will happen, and is happening, again.

In order to fulfill our mission of preaching the three angels' messages, we need to be prepared by the Holy Spirit now, so we can be empowered by Him when He is poured out upon us. The Spirit cannot live inside an unsanctified vessel. God cannot pour out His Spirit upon us while we are harboring sin in our lives.[65] Getting ready by the close of probation is too

---

[65] The Lord has shown me some who profess the present truth, whose lives do not correspond with their profession. They have the standard of piety altogether too low, and they come far short of Bible holiness. Some engage in vain and unbecoming conversation, and others give way to the risings of self. We must not expect to please ourselves, live and act like the world, have its pleasures, and enjoy the company of those who are of the world, and reign with Christ in glory.

We must be partakers of Christ's sufferings here if we would share in His glory hereafter. If we seek our own interest, how we can best please ourselves, instead of seeking to please God and advance His precious, suffering cause, we shall dishonor God and the holy cause we profess to love. We have but a little space of time left in which to work for God. Nothing should be too dear to sacrifice for the salvation of the scattered and torn flock of Jesus. Those who make a covenant with God by

late for those whom God has called to be His voice. Those individuals will not be able to withstand the shaking. That is why "*now is the time*, while the four angels are holding the four winds, to make our calling and election sure." (*Early Writings*, 58, emphasis added).

> *Now is the time* when we are to confess and forsake our sins, that they may go beforehand to judgment and be blotted out. Now is the time to "cleanse ourselves from all filthiness of the flesh and spirit, perfecting holiness in the fear of God. (*The Review and Herald*, November 19, 1908, emphasis added)

> *Now is the time* to receive grace and strength and power to combine with our human efforts that we can form characters for everlasting life. When we do this we will find that the angels of God will minister unto us, and we shall be heirs of God and joint heirs with Jesus Christ. (*Maranatha*, 334, emphasis added)

> *Now is the time* to lay up treasure in heaven, and to set our hearts in order, ready for the time of trouble. Only those who have clean hands and a pure heart will withstand that trying time.

> *Now is the time* for the law of God to be in our minds (foreheads), and written in our hearts. The Lord has shown me the danger of letting our minds be filled with worldly thoughts and cares. I saw that some minds were led away from present truth and a love of the holy Bible, by reading other exciting books; and others were filled with perplexity and care for what they shall eat, drink and wear. I saw some, looking too far off for the coming of the Lord. Time has continued on a few years longer than they expected, therefore they think it may continue a few years more, and in this way their minds are being led from present truth, out after the world. In these things I saw great danger; for if the mind is filled with other things, present truth is shut out, and there is no place in our foreheads for the seal of the living God. This seal is the Sabbath. I saw that the time for Jesus to be in the most holy place was nearly finished, and that time can last but a very little longer; and what leisure time we have should be spent in searching the Bible, which

---

sacrifice now will soon be gathered home to share a rich reward and possess the new kingdom forever and ever. (*Early Writings*, 47)

is to judge us in the last day. (*Broadside2—To Those who are receiving the seal of the living God*, January 31, 1849, emphasis added)

The thoughts must be centered upon God. *Now is the time* to put forth earnest effort to overcome the natural tendencies of the carnal heart. (*Testimonies for the Church*, vol. 8, 315, emphasis added)

Many are uncomfortable with the idea that we must put forth "earnest effort." We prefer to think that salvation a free gift and there's nothing for us to do. But, on the contrary, there is much for us to do to accept that gift—study, pray, repent, serve, and prepare. Not that these can add one iota to what Christ has already done, but these make us more open to receive the Spirit of the True Witness so we will be a more useful vessel for God's Spirit to use. These activities help us to grow in our relationships with Christ, and I would submit that there is only one kind of true Christian, a growing Christian, one whose relationship with Christ is a daily focus, seeking ever to grow, seek to serve Him, and seek to prepare for the end of time. We need to make "now" the time to prepare.

Spiritual growth often comes when we realize that the premise we were operating under was wrong. I began to realize that I don't hold a "salvation option" that lets me have the world and Jesus. I needed to throw out the "option" and buy the real asset—an active, abiding life in Christ where God can reap the real dividends that come from a life given to Him. I knew that God is too big to fail, but I began to realize that that would not make me free to take risks with my relationship with Him.

We need to avoid that moral hazard. Understanding that the door[66] is opened to the most holy place and no one can shut that door, I could not ignore the light that is shining from it.

---

66   Thank God today that there is an open door which Satan and his agents may seek in vain to close. The arm of Almighty Power has opened this door, and no other power can close it. John in holy vision saw a door opened in heaven. "And the temple of God was opened in heaven, and there was seen in his temple the ark of his testament." Looking down the stream of time, the prophet sees a people whose attention is directed to that open door, and then to the ark within, which contains the commandments of God. The third angel of Rev. 14 is represented as flying through the midst of heaven, saying with a loud voice, "Here are they that keep the commandments of God, and the faith of Jesus." This angel presents a message that is to be proclaimed to the world just before Christ comes in the clouds of heaven to take his elect to himself. Just prior to this event, then, the attention of the people is to be called to the trampled-down law of God. (*The Present Truth*, November 3, 1885)

> After this I looked, and, behold, a door was opened in heaven: and the first voice which I heard was as it were of a trumpet talking with me; which said, Come up hither, and I will shew thee things which must be hereafter. And immediately I was in the spirit: and, behold, a throne was set in heaven, and one sat on the throne. And he that sat was to look upon like a jasper and a sardine stone: and there was a rainbow round about the throne, in sight like unto an emerald. ... Out of the throne proceeded lightnings and thunderings and voices: and there were seven lamps of fire burning before the throne, which are the seven Spirits of God. ... the four beasts had each of them six wings about him; and they were full of eyes within: and they rest not day and night, saying, Holy, holy, holy, Lord God Almighty, which was, and is, and is to come. (Revelation 4:1–3, 5, 8)

I saw that probation isn't a future event for which I needed to prepare, but a daily evaluation of my life. Most importantly, as a Seventh-day Adventist Christian who has been given much light, I realized I have a greater responsibility to be prepared for the latter rain, which I could not receive until I have overcome every sin through the power of Christ.

So our test will come much sooner than any of us expected, sooner than death decrees, Sunday laws, or any persecution. No great prophetic landmarks exist for this event, the outpouring of the Holy Spirit, just the collection of a large group of consecrated young men and women, seniors, parents, teens, and children who make "now" the time to be prepared.

This was an eye opener for me, to realize that I had a wrong understanding of the time of my probation. It was a difficult lesson to learn, but there were still many more. Furthermore, I could see the beginning of the financial crisis around me and its impacts. I could also see the mounting problems and the trajectory of the crisis. I saw the parallels with the issues in the church, a reflection of our decaying human nature. The question "why?" remained in my mind. How far will these financial problems go? What else does the Bible say about the crisis? Did God have a purpose for allowing this situation to happen?

## Chapter 7

# The Bride, the Builders, and the Crisis

They ... shall build the old waste places: thou shalt raise up the foundations of many generations; and thou shalt be called, The repairer of the breach, The restorer of paths to dwell in. (Isaiah 58:12)

In the 19th chapter of the book of Revelation we are given a view of the second coming of Christ. John the Revelator heard a large number of beings saying, "Let us be glad and rejoice, and give honour to him: for the marriage of the Lamb is come, and His wife has made herself ready" (Revelation 19:7). Later in chapter 21, as the vision progresses, an angel showed John the bride, the Lamb's wife. It was that great city, the holy Jerusalem descending out of heaven from God (Revelation 21:9–11).

No doubt most of you have read or heard this before, and perhaps you've thought to yourself, "Why is the bride of Christ the new Jerusalem?" Why a city? Why not a woman? After all, a woman is the symbol of the church. Why is the bride of Christ a city?"

The explanation is an important lesson for us, not just of theological significance, but one that impacts us in our day-to-day lives both today and in the near future. The explanation will reveal the challenge before us, the financial crisis, and why it's happening. The symbol of the city will be the key to understanding some of the experiences that we will be going through as we approach the end times.

**The Bride**

First, a little more about the city—in Revelation 19:7 John is told that the marriage of the Lamb is come. In the next verse, in Revelation 19:8, it tells us that the she is adorned as a bride in fine linen, clean and white. You would expect that linen to be the righteousness of Christ. In Revelation 3:18, Jesus said, "Buy of white raiment ... that the shame of thy nakedness [does] not appear." Surprisingly, it says that the bride's gown is the righteousness of the saints (Revelation 19:8)! Or in some versions, like the New King

James Version, the righteous acts of the saints. Apparently, the saints have something to do with getting the bride ready. The saints here on earth have a part in preparing the heavenly Jerusalem in their righteousness or their righteous acts. The Father doesn't just create New Jerusalem and give it to Christ; the saints are active in its preparation. Revelation 19:7 says, "His wife has made herself ready."

In the book of Isaiah, the prophet wrote about this work. "They shall build the old wastes, they shall raise up the former desolations and they shall repair the waste cities, the desolations of many generations" (Isaiah 61:4). In chapter 58 he noted, "They ... shall build the old waste places: thou shalt raise up the foundations of many generations; and thou shalt be called, The repairer of the breach, The restorer of paths to dwell in" (Isaiah 58:12). So the work of God's people in preparing the bride of Christ is to restore the city, to rebuild the broken down walls, and to repair the breach. Furthermore, in Isaiah 60 it is said, "All they that despised thee shall bow themselves down at the soles of thy feet; and they shall call thee; the city of the Lord" (verse 14). Therefore, it is the people of God that is the city, which is why the bride of Christ is represented as the city. The last several chapters of Isaiah are full of this imagery of the building of the city.

Isaiah described the results of the work: "The abundance of the sea shall be converted unto thee, the forces of the Gentiles shall come unto thee" (Isaiah 60:5). In prophecy, remember that the sea stands for peoples and multitudes in prophecy (see Revelation 17:15). "Therefore, thy gates shall be open continually; they shall not be shut day nor night; that men may bring unto thee the forces of the Gentiles, and that their kings may be brought" (Isaiah 60:11).

Finally in Isaiah 66:20 we read, "They shall bring all your brethren for an offering unto the Lord out of all nations upon horses, and in chariots and in litters and upon mules, and upon swift beasts to my holy mountain Jerusalem." What an amazing picture of a church that will powerfully convert many and give them as an offering to the Lord before His second advent. We, as a church, still have some work to do in order to get there.

**The Builders**

These prophesies of Isaiah have a dual application, one for the return of the Israelites from exile in Babylon to rebuild the second temple in Jerusalem, and one for the return of spiritual Israel, living in the last days, returning from the exile in spiritual Babylon, and preparing the church for the second coming of Jesus. In the story of the return of the exiles from

## The Bride, the Builders, and the Crisis

Babylon there are important lessons for us to learn that are vital today. The story of the restoration of the temple of Jerusalem and the walls of the city have a powerful parallel for the restoration of the temple and the preparation of the bride, the New Jerusalem.

In the year 538 BC, King Cyrus of Persia, gave the decree that the Israelites could go back home to rebuild the temple of Jerusalem. Only a small group of about 50,000 people returned to Judea to take on this work (see Ezra 2:64, 65). The Israelites had been in captivity for 70 years, and in the meantime the land of the Hebrews had become populated by other peoples. Some of these were remnants of the ten tribes of Israel who remained after the nation had been captured by Nebuchadnezzar. Others from Assyria settled in the region, and they intermarried with the Jews who had remained (see *Prophets and Kings,* 567). These people were known as the Samaritans. While they professed to worship God, they had created idols to represent Him and were, therefore, idolaters.

The Samaritans went to Ezra and Zerubbabel and offered to help rebuild the temple, but Ezra refused the help of these apostate worshippers. God had instructed the remnant from Judah who had left Babylon to rebuild the temple and to accept the help of the Samaritans would go against God's Word. Zerubbabel also understood the injunction from God that they should not associate or make covenants with the heathen, for accepting their help, their idolatrous practices would have seeped into the temple worship. He declined their offer saying "Ye have nothing to do with us to build an house unto our God; but we ourselves together will build unto the LORD God of Israel, as king Cyrus the king of Persia hath commanded us" (Ezra 4:3).

This didn't sit well the Samaritans so the Samaritans tried to disrupt the work. They "weakened the hands" (Ezra 4:1) of the workers by using every means at their disposal. They hired counselors against the Jews. They ridiculed and scorned the Jews to discourage them. They threatened them with violence. They covertly tried to sabotage the building efforts. They were fraught with legal challenges as well. They even went to the new king to cast false accusations about the intent of the Israelites.

The rebuilding of the second temple was not an easy task, and it took many years to accomplish. In the book of John the people exclaimed, "Forty and six years was this temple in building" (John 2:20) when Jesus remarked, "Destroy this temple, and in three days I will raise it up." The record of the building of the temple and the city can be found in the books of Ezra, Nehemiah, and Haggai. Only a small group of people who returned from Babylon undertook the work. There were many obstacles, not the least of which was the opposition and harassment by the Samaritans. The workers became discouraged and soon left the work of rebuilding the temple to build their own houses and pursue their own gain. The work of rebuilding the temple, thus, came to a halt.

**The Crisis**

At this point God intervened. God wanted the temple to be built and needed to arouse His people to continue the work. In order to awaken them from their complacency, He allowed a famine and an economic crisis into the land to teach the people to rely on Him and go back to the work of rebuilding the temple. He sent His prophet Haggai to tell the people the reason for their impoverished condition and to reprove them. The events are told in the book of Haggai.

> Thus speaketh the Lord of hosts, saying, This people say, the time is not come, the time that the Lord's house should be built. Then came the word of the Lord by Haggai the prophet, saying, Is it time for you, O ye, to dwell in your cieled houses, and this house lie waste? Now therefore thus saith the Lord of hosts; Consider your ways. Ye have sown much, and bring in little; ye eat, but ye have not enough; ye drink, but ye are not filled with drink; ye clothe you, but there is none warm; and he that earneth wages earneth wages to put it into a bag with holes. … Consider your ways. Go up to the mountain, and bring wood, and build the house; and I will take pleasure in it, and I will be glorified, saith the Lord. (Haggai 1:2–8)

Haggai further wrote:

> Ye looked for much, and, lo it came to little; and when ye brought it home, I did blow upon it. Why? saith the Lord of hosts. Because of mine house that is waste, and ye run every man unto his own house. Therefore the heaven over you is stayed from dew, and the earth is stayed from her fruit. And I called for a drought upon the land, and upon the mountains, and upon the corn, and upon the new wine, and upon the oil, and upon that which the ground bringeth forth, and upon men, and upon cattle, and upon all the labour of the hands. (Haggai 1:9–11)

# The Bride, the Builders, and the Crisis

So God used an economic crisis to get the attention of His people. He sent his prophet Haggai to tell them of their error and why the famine had come to them. Haggai explained to the people that their current condition was the result of their neglect in doing the work of God in building the temple. The people repented of their ways and once again began the work of rebuilding the temple. Four years later the temple was finished. But the work was not done as the walls of the city were not yet completed.

It took another decree by King Artaxerxes in 457 BC (see *Prophets and Kings*, 699), allowing the city of Jerusalem to be rebuilt. Within a few years the walls of the city were finally finished. Ezra then taught the people the law of God and taught them to obey it. The people harkened unto God and followed his statutes and reestablished the nation of Judah, of which Jerusalem was the center. This was an important accomplishment because ultimately, Jesus the Son of God went to Jerusalem and entered the temple.

Thus was fulfilled Haggai's prophecy, that the glory of the second temple will be greater than the first. Even though this second temple was nowhere near the grandeur of the temple built by Solomon, Haggai said that the glory of the second will be greater (see Haggai 2:9). The old men of Israel cried when they saw the new temple as it was only a shadow of the former (see Ezra 3:12; *Prophets and Kings*, 563). They didn't understand the words of Haggai when he noted that "I [God] will shake all nations, and the desire of nations shall come: and I will fill this house with glory" (Haggai 2:7). This temple would be a witness to the beginning of the mystery of God, "God was manifest in the flesh, justified in the Spirit, seen of angels, preached unto the Gentiles, believed on in the world, received up into glory" (1 Timothy 3:16). The mystery will cause the glory of God to be revealed to the whole world, the mystery that God was manifested in the flesh.

Jesus, as a baby, was dedicated at the temple. Then as a child of twelve years old, Jesus learned of His mission on earth as He saw the sacrifices at the temple. Entering His ministry, Jesus cleansed the temple from the moneychangers that defiled God's house. He taught and healed many, blessed the children, and revealed the glory of God to the entire nation. Jesus the Son of man and Jesus the Son of God went into the temple and filled it with His glory.

Very closely connected with the building of Jerusalem was another event. The final decree by King Artaxerxes in 457 BC to rebuild the city was the start of another prophecy, the prophecy of the 2,300 days in Daniel, chapter eight. This prophecy foretold of another temple that was to be cleansed: "Unto two thousand three hundred days; then shall the sanctuary be cleansed," said the prophet in Daniel 8:14.

Moving forward to 1844, when the 2,300 days prophecy of Daniel was completed, a new group of "Israelites" were called out of Babylon to begin the work of restoring the "temple" and to complete the city so that the bride of Christ will be ready. Temple? Yes, we are the temple of God! "What don't you know that your body is the temple of the Holy Ghost, which is in you, which you have of God, and you are not your own?" (1 Corinthians 6:19). We are the temple that needs to be restored.

Beginning in 1844 when the investigative judgment began, the law of God was made plain. God's plan was, and still is, to restore man to a proper connection with Him, so that the soul temple could be cleansed and then He could cleanse the heavenly temple. Just as the Hebrew nation had to confess all of their sins before the Day of Atonement began, we as spiritual Israel need to confess all of our sins. Moreover, due to the finality of this atonement, not only will we need to confess our sins, but we will also need to overcome them. For this purpose, God leads a new group of people for this end-time work.

God inspired William Miller to lead a small group out of the many churches to dedicate themselves to God and to prepare for the second advent of Christ. Though Miller misunderstood the sequence of God's plans, He nevertheless used Miller and established a group who would be dedicated to restoring man in the image of God.

Restoration comes through a complete understanding of the requirements of God for not only the spiritual being, but also the mental and physical states. This restoration of the soul temple was in order that God's people would be prepared to receive the latter rain and have the Spirit of Christ live within us. When they had reconstructed the temple, they rebuilt the city of God, the waste places, and the broken down walls. They reestablished the city so that many people from all walks of life, including Gentiles, could enter into the gates, and they would be called the city of God. Today as spiritual Israel, rebuild by perfecting our characters by faith in the power of Christ so that the bride will be adorned with the "righteousness of saints" (Revelation 19:8). This was God's purpose for this new remnant of His people heading into the end times.

The work of the Great Awakening started in earnest in the early 1800s, but once again, discouragement set in. Difficulties surrounded them, and harassments assailed them. At first the work progressed with the earnest work of many of our pioneers. God sent His special messenger for the end times, Ellen White. God sent them a special health message in 1863 to strengthen them and maintain their energy. Picking up where Miller had left off, this group of people continued to preach that the second coming of Christ was near, but Christ did not come. Many sincerely believed that Jesus would return within their lifetime, but they passed away without seeing that glorious day.

As the years wore on and generations came and went, the workers began to be disheartened. They lost their zeal for the work of restoration. They lost their interest in the work of building the temple. They began to say that it was not yet time for the second coming of Christ. They began to build their homes and settle into the daily routine of maintaining their lives, largely forgetting about the work of building the temple and the city. The people became more interested in their earthly homes than in a heavenly home.

One hundred and sixty-six years would pass, and the work seems to be at a standstill, but God is intervening once again. Just like the time of Nehemiah, Ezra, and Haggai, God is trying to awaken His people, and in the same way as at the time of Ezra, God is using a famine on the land—an economic crisis as His means of accomplishing the awakening. A financial crisis, which continues to progress and will be more calamitous that any crisis ever before, will get the attention of His people. His message is the same: stop working to earn money to put into bags with holes. He says I will blow on your wealth and it will become little. "Consider your ways," He said (Haggai 1:7). He then invited us to go up to the mountain and to bring wood for the temple (see Haggai 1:8, 9), to buy of Him "gold tried in the fire," to buy of Him "white raiment" to cover our nakedness (Revelation 3:18), white raiment to adorn the bride of Christ.

Just like in the time of Haggai, God will rouse His people from their lethargy to begin again the work of rebuilding the temple. Once the temple is rebuilt, then the city can be completed. What is the city of God? It is His people and His church. The forces of the Gentiles will flock to the church when they see examples of true Christianity lived in the lives of God's remnant people. When they see Christ in each and every member and the church is filled with love and unity, it will become an irresistible force.

Nevertheless, before the city can be built, the temple must be completed. So God must rouse His people, purify and prepare them. Said Ellen White:

God has shown me that He gave His people a bitter cup to drink, to purify and cleanse them. It is a bitter draught, and they can make it still more bitter by murmuring, complaining, and repining. But those who receive it thus must have another draught, for the first does not have its designed effect upon the heart. And if the second does not effect the work, then they must have another, and another, until it does have its designed effect, or they will be left filthy, impure in heart. I saw that this bitter cup can be sweetened by patience, endurance, and prayer, and that it will have its designed effect upon the hearts of those who thus receive it, and God will be honored and glorified. It is no small thing to be a Christian and to be owned and approved of God.

The Lord has shown me some who profess the present truth, whose lives do not correspond with their profession. They have the standard of piety altogether too low, and they come far short of Bible holiness. Some engage in vain and unbecoming conversation, and others give way to the risings of self. We must not expect to please ourselves, live and act like the world, have its pleasures, and enjoy the company of those who are of the world, and reign with Christ in glory. (*Early Writings*, 47)

This economic crisis will be sore on all peoples. Many will feel the heavy hand of reproof of God through the weight of financial stress upon them and their households. It will indeed be a bitter cup for many as our dreams of luxury and ease will be dashed. Our hopes for a comfortable retirement will fade. Our confidence in our own self sufficiency will be shaken, and we will learn to rely on God. We will repent and return to the work of building the temple and the city.

The building of the temple will become a priority in our lives. We will become faithful stewards of the resources that God has placed in our hands to complete the work. Nothing will be too valuable to sacrifice for this purpose, and when we focus on building the temple and rebuilding the city God will look after His workers. Just like His providence was upon Ezra and the exiles, He has promised to look after us as well. Even in the midst of the economic crisis, we will never lack what we need to sustain our lives and carry out His purposes. We go back to Isaiah for words of encouragement.

> Ho, every one that thirsteth, come ye to the waters, and he that hath no money; come ye, buy, and eat; yea, come, buy wine and milk without money and without price. Wherefore do ye spend money for that which is not bread? and your labour for that which satisfieth not? hearken diligently unto me, and eat ye that which is good, and let your soul delight itself in fatness. Incline your ear, and come unto me: hear, and your soul shall live; and I will make an everlasting covenant with you, even the sure mercies of David. (Isaiah 55:1–3)

God offers us all of the necessities of life. He invites us to come and buy of Him wine, milk, and bread, with no money and with no price. He says if we eagerly listen to Him, we will flourish spiritually. God makes an everlasting covenant even the "sure mercies of David." So what are the "sure mercies of David"? Looking at Psalm 89, we can see that God made an everlasting covenant with David that God would not forsake him.

> My mercy will I keep for him for evermore, and my covenant shall stand fast with him. His seed also will I make to endure for ever, and his throne as the days of heaven. If his children forsake my law, and walk not in my judgments; *if they break my statutes, and keep not my commandments; then will I visit their transgression with the rod, and their iniquity with stripes.* Nevertheless my lovingkindness will I not utterly take from him, nor suffer my faithfulness to fail. (Psalm 89:28–33, emphasis added)

God promised that the kingdom will always be in the hand of the descendents of David, which was ultimately fulfilled in the death and resurrection of Christ when He reclaimed the kingship of this world, taking it back from the usurper. Christ, the Son of David, became the everlasting King of this world and the promise of God was fulfilled.

God made provisions in case David did not listen to His voice as he should have. God promised that the kingship would always be with David's lineage, but if he should stray, God reserved the right to reprove David and his descendents in order to bring them back to Himself. These were the "sure mercies of David"—God would not reject his people; instead, He would work to ensure that they always followed Him.

So are these the physical descendents of David, the nation of Israel? Jesus said, "My kingdom is not of this world" (John 18:36). The kingdom that Christ ushered in with His death and resurrection was not an earthly kingdom but a spiritual and heavenly kingdom, and all people could be part of the kingdom by believing in Him. We are to be heirs of God and joint heirs with Christ by faith, and we are to be a nation of kings and priests unto God because we are joint heirs with Christ. Thus, we become the kings of the kingdom that God promised to keep in David's line; therefore, God fulfills His promise to David. Unfortunately, we are in no condition to be able to fulfill the position of being an heir of God and joint heirs with Christ. So God will invoke the "sure mercies of David" contingency to ensure that His people are prepared to take on the role that has been appointed to them. God will reprove His people for the errors in their lives so that they can finish rebuilding the temple and then finish rebuilding the city.

This is the reason why God will allow an economic crisis to touch His people. In so doing, He awakens His people from the slumber of materialism. In order to fulfill the covenant, He will permit this financial calamity to occur in the world. We don't need to be worried or afraid of the events to come as long as we are actively working to join with God to finish the work of laboring for souls. God always looks after those to whom He gives a special mission. Be it the children of Israel and manna, Elijah fed by ravens, or Jesus feeding His disciples. We should be confident that God will look after the needs of His remnant (see Isaiah 33:16), to which He has assigned the task of building the temple and the city. It is His work, and He will never let it fail or see His workers ashamed because of want. However, most of us are not actively serving Him in our lives and we should be prepared to accept the "sure mercies of David" by which God will reprove us of our worldliness and bring us back to Himself.

My wife has always had a great eye for style and color as well as how to use space. Each room was furnished beautifully with pictures and decorations that pulled together the finishing touches. The kids got to arrange their own rooms. One girl's was a light blue to match her curtains and bed covers, and the other daughter's was a bright green to match her hockey team colors. My son's room was an "I don't care ... whatever" shade of off-white suited for a soon-to-be teenager.

The house was now a home, a wonderful place to raise the family with all of the amenities we wanted. It was certainly not an extravagant house, not like some of the monster homes we continue to see being built, I thought to myself. It was plenty big for our family of five, even as the kids were soon to grow up to be teenagers. Backyard barbeques were my favorite thing, with just the family or with friends. So life was good, and all was well, which made it easy to forget that we are just pilgrims here, just sojourners on this earth and a heavenly mansion awaits. I was content in my life and not really lacking anything, except that the building of the temple languished.

## Chapter 8

# Laodicea and the Root of All Evil

Unto the angel of the church of the Laodiceans write; These things saith the Amen, the faithful and true witness, the beginning of the creation of God; I know thy works, that thou art neither cold nor hot: I would thou wert cold or hot. So then because thou art lukewarm, and neither cold nor hot, I will spue thee out of my mouth. Because thou sayest, I am rich, and increased with goods, and have need of nothing; and knowest not that thou art wretched, and miserable, and poor, and blind, and naked. (Revelation 3:14–17)

The Bible tells us that "the love of money is the root of all evil" (1 Timothy 6:10). Human nature desires all of the things that money affords. While we may not explicitly profess to love money, a true examination of our wants and needs, our goals, and plans would reveal that what we desire requires money. We in the developed world are captive to a system that requires the possession of money as the chief resource in order to function. Even the most altruistic person will find that without money even his or her most benevolent purposes are futile. Money really does make the world go around. It is inescapable. Trapped in such an environment it is nearly impossible for us to be completely immune to the effects of money. It's a relentless force that pulls us in like a powerful gravitational force into a black hole of dependency.

In the Lord's Prayer, Jesus taught us how to pray:

Our Father which art in heaven, Hallowed be thy name. Thy kingdom come, Thy will be done in earth, as it is in heaven. Give us this day our daily bread. And forgive us our debts, as we forgive our debtors. And lead us not into temptation, but deliver us from evil. (Matthew 6:9–13)

Stop here for a moment. Consider what we are asking for in this prayer: "deliver us from evil." This is not only a prayer that we have repeated often, but it is also a template for how we should pray. We should ask God for deliverance from evil. If we take the two thoughts together—the love of money is the root of all evil and to pray "deliver us evil"—it makes a rather profound thought.

If we pray for God to deliver us from evil, and the love of money is the root of all evil, then does it not follow that God, in fulfilling our prayer request, will deliver us from the root cause of our sin problem—the love of money? If so, just how would God deliver us from the love of money?

There are numerous references to money and riches in Scripture. Also, many of these verses give warning to the dangers of it. Take a look.

- Lo, this is the man that made not God his strength; but trusted in the abundance of his riches, and strengthened himself in his wickedness (Psalm 52:7).

- He that hasteth to be rich hath an evil eye, and considereth not that poverty shall come upon him (Proverbs 28:22).

- No man can serve two masters: for either he will hate the one, and love the other; or else he will hold to the one, and despise the other. Ye cannot serve God and mammon (Matthew 6:24).

- Woe unto you that are rich! for ye have received your consolation (Luke 6:24).

- How hardly shall they that have riches enter into the kingdom of God! For it is easier for a camel to go through a needle's eye, than for a rich man to enter into the kingdom of God (Luke 18:24, 25).

- They that will be rich fall into temptation and a snare, and into many foolish and hurtful lusts, which drown men in destruction and perdition (1 Timothy 6:9).

- Charge them that are rich in this world, that they be not highminded, nor trust in uncertain riches, but in the living God, who giveth us richly all things to enjoy; that they do good, that they be rich in good works, ready to distribute, willing to communicate (1 Timothy 6:17, 18).

God has made a few individuals rich in possessions, like Abraham and Job, but both of them trusted in God more than their wealth. Abraham was faithful in offering up his most prized possession, his son. Job trusted God even when his riches were taken. For the vast majority of us, riches are a snare, and money is a temptation; yet, so many still seek to be rich in this world's goods.

Money matters are a very touchy subject, which is infrequently addressed from the pulpit or in publications other than a fairly cursory treatment, usually as an offering appeal. Given its very personal nature, which people generally don't want to discuss publically, to have a broad discourse on the subject is difficult. Also, like many other issues, very few could neither claim strict adherence to biblical principles on money matters nor claim absolute faithful stewardship of all that have been entrusted.

One of the few who has spoken very boldly about the issue of money, and our relationship to it, would be Pastor David Gates. He speaks boldly not only in words but also in action in his life and work with Gospel Ministries International. His life exemplifies a life totally dedicated and reliant on God for every material need.

**David Gates**

Pastor David Gates, for those who are not familiar with him or his work, is an extraordinary minister for God, completely funding and operating a global mission organization on faith alone. His story is both an inspiration and a challenge to the majority of us who live comfortably in our homes relying on our jobs to earn a paycheck to maintain the necessities of our daily lives. Pastor Gates totally relies on God for all of his daily needs. This includes food, shelter, living expenses for him and his family, as well as his entire mission organization infrastructure, which includes many mission airplanes, TV stations, radio networks, medical facilities, and staff. These are all funded essentially by unsolicited donations provided by the generosity of donors who are moved by the Spirit of God.

Pastor Gates' operating premise is that God will look after the funding as long as the workers are doing His work. He and his staff take no salary or wages. Yet all of their needs are consistently met. He operates his vast mission enterprise on the same principles as George Mueller, the famous missionary minister who ran orphanages in nineteenth-century England, completely relying on God's providence.

Pastor Gates has extraordinary stories of faith, purchasing airplanes and television networks even before he had a nickel to spend. When a need or opportunity was presented to him and he was moved by the Spirit, he stepped out in faith and made the purchases even before he knew where the money might come from. Some call this incredible faith. Some charge him with being foolhardy or presumptuous. Nevertheless, "the proof is in the pudding" as the saying goes. The fruits of his work testify to the Spirit that is leading him.

His saga began when he and his family decided to go to the mission field in South America to minister to people in a remote area. Since there were no funds to support such a mission, he decided to test God's providence and move out in faith, trusting that God will look after his needs. As a registered nurse, Pastor Gates was able to provide medical missionary services to the people of this remote village. The people responded positively to his care for them. Pastor Gates and his family were richly blessed and well supported by the people of the village. People came from villages further in the jungle to see Pastor Gates, and he soon saw the need for a medical missionary plane to fly into remote areas where it would be impossible to get to by foot. Pastor Gates was moved to purchase a plane for this purpose, though he had no money. He arranged to purchase a plane without any money in hand, and on the day payment was due, he received a check to cover the cost. He has continued to operate in this fashion to grow his ministry work around the world.

While we may not all be called to live like David Gates and follow his model today, the time will surely come when we will have to rely on God's sustaining grace for every morsel of food and drop of water. Pastor Gates just has a head start on the rest of us in preparing for that time. He has greatly increased his chances of survival throughout those trials to come. Not because he developed some extraordinary personal power, but because he has learned to explicitly trust in God's providence.

Pastor Gates is operating under the same mode as Jesus did while He ministered here on earth. Jesus said, "Foxes have holes and the birds of the air have nests but the Son of Man has nowhere to lay His head" (Matthew 8:20 NKJV). He also sent out His disciples saying, "That they should take nothing for their journey, save a staff only; no scrip, no bread, no money in their purse" (Mark 6:8). Christ and His disciples went from town to town, preaching the gospel, healing the sick, and receiving food and shelter from those who gladly accepted the tidings that they bore. This was the means for Christ and the early evangelists.

The early Christian church operated on a similar model. Members gladly sacrificed their property and possessions to give to the work of spreading the gospel. It was through their great personal sacrifices that the work progressed so quickly, and Paul could exclaim that the gospel had been preached to every creature. Even poor congregations like the Philippians gave freely to support the work of Paul, to whom he wrote, "My God shall supply all your need according to his riches in glory by Christ Jesus" (Philippians 4:19).

Another model for the support and maintenance of the work of the church is the Levitical model, established in the time of Moses. The Levites did not receive a portion of the land that each of the other tribes was given when they moved into the Promised Land . The Levites, as the priesthood of the nation of Israel, were to receive their support from the other tribes. The tithes and offerings for the temple were to be used by the Levitical priesthood for their maintenance. Even the offerings taken to the temple—the burnt offering, the meat offering, the drink offerings, the yearly temple dues—all were to be used for the support of the priesthood. This is more like the model currently employed by the church to look after the needs of the church organization.

So are these two models in opposition to the other? The answer should be no. God has richly blessed us, particularly in the developed countries, such that we should not only be able to support the organized church but also support independent initiatives in ministry. These two approaches are not in opposition to each other, but they, in fact, complement each other.

The church organization in general should be a conservatively managed institution, carefully using the resources it has been given by its members. The governance of the church should reflect its established policies and the will of the majority of its members while being sensitive to those to the left and to the right of the middle. Fiscally, it ought to be conservative, never overextending itself to put at undue risk the assets for which it has been made a steward. This is never an easy task as there are many competing needs within the church. The church as steward should act in faith, but it also needs to weigh concrete evidences of business plans, budgets, audits, and reports. This is not to say that the church organization should not step out in faith to enter into projects and endeavors that require new funding. Rather, the leaders need to find an appropriate balance between faith and faithfulness.

Individuals, small groups, and local church organizations may find it appropriate, however, to enter into ventures that the broader church cannot or should not do. Individuals, as convicted by the Spirit of God, could undertake projects that the church organization cannot endorse due to a lack of identified resources. Individuals can pledge their greatest resources—their time and energy—to their projects, to which the church could never commit. These individuals, as they are led by the Spirit, could take on ventures with greater risk than the greater church body ought to take as an organization. Individuals can have strong convictions about actions that they must take, but they may not be able to share or articulate that conviction sufficiently to move the entire church body. This should not invalidate their conviction, but at the same time, the church organization should not make it a practice to move without clearly defined plans properly supported by evidence and analysis. Individuals are free to carry out their convictions in their own terms and with their own or local resources.

It should go without saying, however, that as individuals and small local groups seek to engage in their own ministries, these activities should be complementary to their local, regional and national church initiatives. Furthermore, these activities should be funded outside of the regular tithes and offerings. God has blessed us with more than enough resources to provide for the greater church body and to carry on our local ministries. The more we give the more God will provide, according to the promise given in Luke 6:38: "Give, and it shall be given unto you; good measure, pressed down, and shaken together, and running over, shall men give into your bosom. For with the same measure that ye mete withal it shall be measured to you again."

The Bible shows two different financial models for ministry, and they can be complementary, each adding to the strength and effectiveness of the other. A local church participating in its conference and divisional programs and taking local initiatives through the efforts of its dedicated members can be powerful tools for the accomplishment of much good. Perhaps there is a greater distinction, however, between the ministry model that Christ used compared to the Levitical model. That difference would be the timing. The Levitical model has been, and continues to be, effective in a time where the large church body needs to be maintained indefinitely over a long period of time. This model provides for a consistent approach to funding and operating a "church," allowing for sustenance and gradual growth in its congregation. The model that Christ, His disciples, and the early church used was "take nothing for your journey" (Luke 9:3), was more suited to allow for an intense personal ministry and to provide for the rapid growth.

This intensive ministry was made possible largely by the impartation of the Holy Spirit, during the ministry of Christ and after the time of Pentecost. The Spirit of God, given to the disciples, enabled them to go out and accomplish great feats of evangelism. The early church was able to mobilize quickly because of the work of evangelists like Paul, who were mostly self-supporting. While there were churches that supported the gospel work of the evangelists, Paul, for example, worked as a tent maker in order to support himself and his ministry. Paul did go on his missionary journeys with the blessing of the brethren in Jerusalem, but Paul's example was that of a self-supporting minister of God. Working and living frugally, Paul dedicated himself and his resources to the work.

This model of a self-supporting ministry, working in cooperation with the organized church, is an important example for today. With the expectation that we are nearing the very end of time, when the Spirit of God will be poured out soon, our operating model may benefit from reflecting these two modes. Both are acts of faith and dedication on the part of the members, but now requiring greater sacrifices and commitment than either on its own. Yet there is another aspect that must be considered in the context of a financial crisis. Joel wrote:

> *Lament like a virgin girded with sackcloth for the husband of her youth.* The meat offering and the drink offering is cut off from the house of the Lord; the priests, the Lord's ministers, mourn. (Joel 1:8, 9, emphasis added)

> Gird yourselves, and lament, ye priests: howl, ye ministers of the altar: come, lie all night in sackcloth, ye ministers of my God: for the meat offering and the drink offering is withholden from the house of your God. (Joel 1:13)

Joel was prophesying about a time when the meat offering and the drink offering is cut off from the house of the Lord. The meat offering and the drink offering were those parts of the daily sacrifices that were made in the sanctuary. The meat offering was, in fact, not the lamb, goat or bull, but rather bread or flour. In Leviticus the meat offering is explained.

> When any will offer a meat offering unto the Lord, his offering shall be of fine flour; and he shall pour oil upon it, and put frankincense thereon: and he shall bring it to Aaron's sons the priests: and he shall take thereout his handful of the flour thereof, and of the oil thereof, with all the frankincense thereof; and the priest shall burn the memorial of it upon the altar, to be an offering made by fire, of a sweet savour unto the Lord: And the remnant of the

meat offering shall be Aaron's and his sons': it is a thing most holy of the offerings of the Lord made by fire. (Leviticus 2:1–3)

The meat offering was given to the Lord, but only a portion of it was to be offered on the altar. The remainder of the meat offering was to be for Aaron and his sons, the priests. This was given in order to sustain the Levitical priesthood with their needs. These meat offerings and tithes were given to support the tribe of Levi.

In days of Moses there was no currency used, but rather commodities were given as tithes. Deuteronomy tells that the tithes were "of thy corn, or of thy wine, or of thy oil, or the firstlings of thy herds or of thy flock" (Deuteronomy 12:17). So what would it mean when Joel prophesied that the meal offering will be cut off? Looking at whom this passage is directed may give the answer. Joel said to the priests and the Lord's ministers that they should grieve for the condition of the church for which they were responsible and prepare themselves for the time when their support will be cut off. The cutting off of the meat offering would indicate a loss of financial support for the church, a cutting off of the tithes and offerings that support the church organization today. Perhaps not by all members, but in sufficient measure that it would cause great perplexity in the church.

Christ spoke of perplexity in the end times. "There shall be signs in the sun, and in the moon, and in the stars; and upon the earth distress of nations, with perplexity; the sea and the waves roaring" (Luke 21:25). The Greek root word for "perplexity," *aporio*,[67] means "to be without resources, to be wanting, to be embarrassed, to be left not knowing which way to turn." A cutting off of resources in the end times and a cutting off of meat offerings will cause the church and the ministers of the Lord to grieve as the church seems about to fall.

Ellen White also spoke about this time: "The church may appear as about to fall, but it does not fall. It remains, while the sinners in Zion will be sifted out—the chaff separated from the precious wheat. This is a terrible ordeal, but nevertheless it must take place" (*Selected Messages*, Book 2, 380). Speaking about the end times just before the close of probation and the time of trouble, Mrs. White foretold of the time when the church may

---

[67] The word "perplexity" in Luke 21:25 is *aporia* in Greek, which means to be "the state of one who is in perplexity." The root word of the word *aporia* is *aporeo*, which means "to be without resources, to be in straits, to be left wanting, to be embarrassed" (http://www.blueletterbible.org/lang/lexicon/lexicon.cfm?Strongs=G640&t=KJV). See also 2 Corinthians 4:8, "we are troubled on every side, yet not distressed, we are perplexed [*aporeo*] but not in despair."

appear as about to fall. The combined impact of a financial crisis, "natural" disasters, persecution and satanic deceptions will cause a condition in the church that will appear as though it is about to fall, but it does not.

When the chaff is separated from the wheat, many members leave the church, but they are quickly replaced by others who will accept the truth and take a stand for God. Final decisions will be made by all. Throughout this time, the financial support for the church is likely to dwindle due to the loss of members, the loss of jobs by those who stand for the truths, and due to an overall decline in the state of the global economy.

Under these conditions, the church will have to continue its work for its own members and for evangelism. Members will have to make extreme sacrifices to ensure that the work carries on, both financial sacrifices and of their own personal time. Mrs. White recounted her vision.

> I also saw that God had not required all of His people to dispose of their property at the same time; but if they desired to be taught, He would teach them, in a time of need, when to sell and how much to sell. Some have been required to dispose of their property in times past to sustain the Advent cause, while others have been permitted to keep theirs until a time of need. Then, as the cause needs it, their duty is to sell. (*Early Writings*, 57)

Without jobs, properties, or any earthly support, the members will have to carry on the gospel work; still, this will be the most successful time for the work as many are brought into the church. It will be Christ's model of evangelism that will remain in the end as the Holy Spirit is poured out on the people.

This example set by Christ's ministry, one that is wholly reliant on God, isn't the only example in the Bible, however. Israelites during the exodus from Egypt were fully reliant on God for their food, water, and protection. Even their clothes did not wear out due to the sustaining power of God. Elijah was also sustained by God throughout the drought and famine. All of these characters are types of the remnant and the experience they will have to go through. All were called to leave their homes and minister, relying totally on God for their support. Most of us are far from this model of stewardship and service.

Not all are called to leave everything and trust fully on God for every detail of their daily sustenance, at least not yet. We have been allowed to have some possession here on earth, not so much for our physical benefit, but more as a test to see how faithful we can be in our stewardship. This is seen in the example of Nicodemus and the rich young ruler. Both of these rulers came to Jesus seeking the way to eternal life. To the rich young ruler, Jesus said, "Sell all that you have and distribute to the poor ... and come, follow me (Luke 18:22). Yet to Nicodemus, Jesus explained that he needed to be born again (see John 3:1–17. In the end, Nicodemus did forsake everything and became a follower of Christ, and he used his wealth to sustain the early church and helped it to grow.

> He employed his wealth in sustaining the infant church that the Jews had expected to be blotted out at the death of Christ. In the time of peril he who had been so cautious and questioning was firm as a rock, encouraging the faith of the disciples, and furnishing means to carry forward the work of the gospel. ... He became poor in this world's goods; yet he faltered not in the faith which had its beginning in that night conference with Jesus. (*The Desire of Ages*, 177)

We have to a large extent, however, been unfaithful in our role as stewards of God's goods and have squandered much on riotous living. While many will protest that they have been faithful in their tithes and offerings and have done what the Lord has required of them, this would not stand up to close scrutiny in comparison to the life of Christ, of His prophets, nor to the counsel we have been given through the Spirit of Prophecy of how to live in these probationary times. We are captives in this world, which is made functional by money.

So how will God deliver us from evil, which is the love of money? How can He extricate us from this system of money that has us locked into mortgages, payment plans, bills, and retirement savings? Does He even intend to deliver His church from the grips of mammon?

Perhaps God will deal with this case by case, but given the breadth of the problem to the extent that the church in North America, in particular, has been lax in the prosecution of her duties as stewards of God's wealth, God may have to take broader measures. The medicine He must administer and we must take, may be quite severe—severe in its strength, its duration, and in the depths and breadth of its application. A global financial crisis and a prolonged economic depression may be the fire that is used to purge the dross in which we are encased. The solution for the Laodicean condition is given to us.

> I counsel thee to buy of me gold tried in the fire, that thou mayest be rich; and white raiment, that thou mayest be clothed, and that the shame of thy nakedness do not appear; and anoint thine eyes with eyesalve, that thou mayest see. (Revelation 3:17)

This begs the question, just how does one buy gold tried in the fire? There are two ways for us to make this purchase. Peter wrote:

> That the trial of your faith, being much more precious than of gold that perisheth, though it be tried with fire, might be found unto praise and honour and glory at the appearing of Jesus Christ ... wherefore gird up the loins of your mind, be sober, and hope to the end for the grace that is to be brought unto you at the revelation of Jesus Christ; as obedient children, not fashioning yourselves according to the former lusts in your ignorance: but as he which hath called you is holy, so be ye holy in all manner of conversation; because it is written, be ye holy; for I am holy. (1 Peter 1:7, 13–16)

Furthermore, Mrs. White wrote:

> We are nearing the end of this earth's history, and the different lines of God's work are to be carried forward with much more self-sacrifice than is at present manifest. The work for these last days is in a special sense a missionary work. The presentation of present truth, from the first letter of its alphabet to the last, means missionary effort. The work to be done calls for sacrifice at every advance step. From this unselfish service the workers will come forth purified and refined as gold tried in the fire. (*Counsels on Health*, 216)

The two great commandments we were given are revealed in these two statements: love God with all your heart and love your neighbor as yourself (see Mark 12:30, 31). We love and honor God by revealing in ourselves His character and holiness, and we love our neighbor by working for their salvation. These two commands, holiness unto God and reaching the lost, will let us procure the gold tried in the fire that Jesus invites us to buy. In this work will be trials and struggles that will grow our faith, that will stretch the bounds of our trust in Jesus, and that will put the resources that God has entrusted us with to its proper use.

What if we fail the make that wise purchase that Jesus recommended? Will He simply stand at the door and knock passively until our probationary time is up and walk away? If we don't hear His voice calling, will He turn away silent and sadly remand us to the choices we have made? Rather, will He escalate His appeals to us to leave no stone unturned to endeavor to reach us? Will he cut off our cable TV and our cell phones, spoil our food, and ruin our fashions. Would He go as far as to take away our homes and possessions until, finally, we turn to Him or demand that He leave us alone? Will He take our half-hearted prayers for deliverance from sin and put it to the test? If we have ever prayed the Lord's Prayer and said the words: "Deliver us from evil," will He not see if we really meant what we said and deliver us from the root of our evil, our love of money?

Remembering the patience and the perseverance of the Jehovah of the Old Testament suggests that God will do what He deems necessary to give us every opportunity and warning to ensure our redemption and to work for the preparation of His harvest. Beginning with the exodus from Egypt, through the wanderings in the wilderness, the oppression by many heathen nations, by famine and pestilence, God worked to draw His people back to Himself. Why would He not use the same tenacity, particularly in these end times, to arouse His people from slumber when so much is riding on the preparation of the remnant? Will God not invoke the "sure mercies of David" clause in His covenant to turn us back to Him?

## Eliminating Lukewarm

So if our love of money is the impediment to spiritual growth out of our Laodicean condition, then would not God use every means at His disposal to change our hearts. The economic storm that is gathering looks to be of "biblical" proportions, well suited for the job of turning hearts back to God, or at least to eliminate lukewarm as an optional state for His people. It will be a perfect storm of collapsing global output and consumption, unsustainable government debt, insolvent financial institutions, demographic time-bombs, unprecedented financial frauds, social-political upheaval, and natural disasters, all occurring at an accelerated pace.

Personally, I found that eliminating the lukewarm can be a painful process, not just financially but also spiritually and emotionally. I recognized that I had been trying to lead a double life, trying to have Christ and the world. I finally realized my true state rather than trying to rationalize all of my actions. The panic set in, like I'd missed the alarm clock having just awakened at 8:00 AM when I had to be at work by 9:00, still needing to get the kids up and ready for school.

I had a sense of remorse of looking back at all of the missed opportunities to follow God's leading and understood that I had turned my back on them. I felt real sorrow for having taken for granted all the blessings given to me by my loving Father. I began to think about how to change all the things in my life that I've built around me for many years, realizing that nothing short of divine intervention is going to make it happen.

Then I began to see doors beginning to open, allowing changes to start. I wondered what my family and friends would think when they saw the changes in my attitudes and behaviors. A total transformation had begun on the inside, but I knew that it would take time to change all the things on the outside. Financially, it could have been much worse for me, but God in His mercy spared me of any real disasters. Challenges remained, however.

In my own situation, He hit me just hard enough to awaken me. He showed His love toward me in how He eliminated lukewarm. After all, Jesus said, "As many as I love, I rebuke and chasten: be zealous therefore, and repent" (Revelation 3:19). He will not leave us to face the consequences or our Laodicean condition without supernatural intervention that is irresistible, at least not without a real concerted effort on our part to deny Him. God will make the options binary, trust in Him or trust in mammon. If we choose the latter, we will have no one to blame but ourselves for the result.

God has given us repeated warnings, ample time to consider, and countless blessings to persuade us of His faithfulness He extends to us His merciful invitation to repent, to humble our hearts, and to pray, to seek His face, and turn from our wicked ways, then He will hear from heaven and will forgive our sins and heal our land (see 2 Chronicles 7:14). Does this mean that we will not feel the effects of the financial crisis? Perhaps not, but we can certainly have a peace that passes all understanding and stand in the midst of the storm, confident that our God will supply all of our need (see Philippians 4:19). Furthermore, God has given us so many examples in the Bible and history to help us understand the things that are about to happen, so we need not bear the brunt of the impact unprepared. Even the current financial crisis may have had a prior dry run so we can see the events to come if we have been paying attention. In 1873, a great depression gripped the world, which would bring about end-time events and the second advent.

## Chapter 9

# The Panic of 1873—A Prelude to a Sunday Law

As God's people thus review the past, they should see that the Lord is ever repeating His dealings. They should understand the warnings given, and should beware not to repeat their mistakes. (*Testimonies to the Church*, vol. 7, 210)

Most people would think that the longest depression in the United States was the Great Depression of the 1930s; however, they would be mistaken. In 1873, a depression occurred that lasted 65 months, which was considerably longer than the Great Depression of 1930 and lasted 42 months.[68] This depression was appropriately called the "Long Depression," lasting from 1873 to 1879. Even after the depression ended, the US economy slipped in and out of recession for another two decades.

The Long Depression was an American depression, but had global consequences, which included many countries in Europe, the heart of the global economic system at the time. The Unites States was still a developing industrial economy and the slowdown in Europe had a significant impact across the Atlantic. Many factors led to and triggered the Long Depression:

1. The American Civil War, which began in 1861 and lasted until 1865, was the bloodiest war in US history and resulted in the loss of more American soldiers than all other wars combined. During the war, federal spending rose dramatically due to the war efforts, but following the war, economic growth fell for six years. After two years of growth, the US slipped into a long depression. The war cost an estimated $6.1 billion,[69] which is a massive cost, when compared to annual GDP of $7.6 billion for the entire country in 1865. With their infrastructure destroyed and their population

---

[68] "US Business Cycle Expansions and Contractions," The National Bureau of Economic Research, http://www.nber.org/cycles/cyclesmain.html (accessed March 2012).

[69] Patricia L. Faust, ed., *Historical Times Illustrated Encyclopedia of the Civil War* (New York: HarperPerenniel, 1991), 187.

ravaged, the war devastated the economy of the South, causing its average annual income to drop by 40% as compared to the North.[70] This income disparity lasted until the 1920s. The economic damage from the war was severe in its depth and length.

2. In 1870, the Franco-Prussian war erupted, embroiling these two countries that were the main economic powers in Europe at the time. The Prussians quickly gained support from their neighbors, the Northern German Confederation and the southern states of Baden, Wurttemberg, and Bavaria. These states all unified under Prussian King Wilhelm I. Using railroads for effective mobilization of the army and their new steel breach loading cannons, the Prussian army proved much more efficient and effective than their French counterparts. The Prussian army eventually laid siege on Paris and captured the city. The war left France in ruins. Wilhelm I demanded reparations of 20 billion francs from France.[71]

3. In the late 1860s, after the Civil War, part of the reconstruction efforts included the rebuilding of infrastructure, railroads in particular as they were the means of mass transportation. The building of the railroads become a speculative bubble as many looked to profit from their construction after the Civil War. The rampant speculation in railroad companies caused an over building of rail lines, which eventually ended with the bursting of the bubble. This resulted in a major bank failure in the Philadelphia-based Jay Cooke & Company, the major financiers of the railroad boom.[72] The crisis quickly spread, and the New York Stock Exchange was closed for 10 days.

4. Following the Franco-Prussian War, the European economies were trying to rebuild. There was a significant focus on the infrastructure, and similar to the US, there was over-investment and speculation in railroads and shipping. Particularly with the war reparations from France, there was an excess of liquidity

---

70   Stanley Libergott, "Wage Trends, 1800–1900," Bureau of the Budget, National Bureau of Economic Research, http://www.nber.org/chapters/c2486.pdf (accessed August 2012).

71   *Encyclopedia Britannica Online*, s.v. "Franco-German War" (accessed January 2013).

72   "1873: Off the Rails," Historical Collections, Harvard Business School, http://www.library.hbs.edu/hc/crises/1873.html (accessed September 2008).

looking for a place to be invested. An asset bubble was formed and resulted in a stock market crash at the Vienna stock exchange.[73]

5. There was a movement by both Germany and the US to go to a gold standard in currency, and demonetize silver.[74] This meant taking out silver coins from circulation as legal tender. This action resulted in a tightening of monetary policy due to the fall in value of silver. (While there is tremendous amount of interest in gold again, monetary policy is certainly very loose. However, while policy is loose, actual credit creation is not taking place, which is creating a de-facto tight monetary policy today.)

6. An outbreak of equine influenza (horse flu) caused almost 100% of unvaccinated horses in North America became ill.[75] While there were no effects to humans from the horse flu, it was a massive problem for the economy in North America since horses supplied much of the transportation power for the economy at the time. The outbreak was traced back to the area around Toronto, Canada. The Great Boston Fire of 1872 was the result of a lack of fire trucks, which were horse-drawn at the time. Even the US Cavalry was fighting on foot against the Apaches, who were also on foot.[76]

---

73 "History of the Exchange Operating Company Wiener Börse AG," weinerbörse. at (Vienna stock market), http://www.vienna-stock-exchange.com/ (accessed September 2008).

74 Milton Friedman, "The Crime of 1873," The Hoover Institution, Stanford University, March 1989, https://www.google.com/search?q=The+Crime+of+1873&ie=utf-8&oe=utf-8&aq=t&rls=org.mozilla:en-US:official&client=firefox-a#hl=en&safe=active&client=firefox-a&hs=4io&tbo=d&rls=org.mozilla:en-US%3Aofficial&sclient=psy-ab&q=the+crime+of+1873+milton+friedman&oq=The+Crime+of+1873+mil&gs_l=serp.3.0.0.62168.65119.0.67366.4.2.0.2.2.0.114.201.1j1.2.0.les%3B..0.0...1c.1.gpxcFZwWgtg&pbx=1&bav=on.2,or.r_gc.r_pw.r_qf.&bvm=bv.1354675689,d.aWc&fp=e959f31022a630cb&bpcl=39650382&biw=1440&bih=683 (accessed March 2012).

75 Adoniram B. Judson, MD, "History and Course of the Epizoötic among Horses upon the North American Continent in 1872–73," Public Health Reports and Papers, American Public Health Association, 1873, http://www.lrgaf.org/medical/james-law-epizootic.pdf (accessed September 2008).

76 "How equine flu brought the US to a standstill," horsetalk.co.nz. http://www.horsetalk.co.nz/features/equineflu-131.shtml (September 2008).

The Long Depression led to many financial hardships, poverty, crime, and a decline in the morality of the people as does any long-lasting severe economic crises. What should interest us as Seventh-day Adventists is what happened as a result of the depression.

> In many towns in Ohio and New York in the fall of 1873 women concerned about the destructive power of alcohol met in churches to pray and then marched to the saloons to ask the owners to close their establishments. They met with success but it was only temporary so by the next summer the women concluded that they must become organized nationally. This led to the founding of the National Woman's Christian Temperance Union - the oldest continuing non-sectarian woman's organization in the world.[77]

This was the formation of the Woman's Christian Temperance Union (WCTU). The fall in morality gave rise to the temperance movement led by groups like the Women's Christian Temperance Union. They worked to stem the spread of alcoholism and other vices, spoke for workers' rights and women's rights, and campaigned for environmental issues and for a general improvement in the morality of the people. In 1875, the WCTU sought to pass legislation prohibiting the liquor traffic and collected petitions to send to Congress. In 1876, newly elected Senator Henry W. Blair introduced a bill in the Senate for the prohibition amendment to the Constitution of the United States.[78]

Along with the temperance movement was a call to return to Christian principles as they were closely supported by many churches. One of the ideas promoted was the observance of a "the Lord's Day," a common day of rest for everyone, during which everyone could attend church and improve their spiritual condition. Many states enacted laws that forbade any work on Sunday and promoted Sunday as a day of rest. Many Seventh-day Adventists refused to obey those laws and were subsequently fined or imprisoned. "Four Seventh-day Adventists ... were tried on May 27, 1892, at Paris Tennessee, on charges ranging from chopping wood and hauling firewood to plowing a strawberry field. After being fined $25 apiece, three

---

[77] "The History of the WCTU," Christian Woman's Temperance Union, History, http://wctu.org/history.html (accessed March 2012).

[78] Elizabeth Pu Gordon, *Women Torch-Bearers: The Story of the Women's Christian Temperance Union* (Whitefish, MT: Kessinger Publishing, 2005), 102.

of the defendants were marched through the street of Paris in the chain gang and forced to perform street labor," according to Warren L. Johns.[79]

The Seventh-day Adventist Church opposed the enactment of "Sunday laws" as being not only unconstitutional but also against its values. Other protestant churches accused the brethren of being against the temperance and morality that they were trying to promote. Adventists were painted as being anti-Christian, immoral, and unpatriotic. In the journal *The American Sentinel* in 1888, the editors, E. J. Waggoner and Alonzo T. Jones, defended their views.

> The Sentinel has had occasion frequently to criticise some of the workings of the Women's Christian Temperance Union. Upon the part of those who favor the establishment of a *religious* instead of a *civil* government here, this fact has been made the means of an attempt to create prejudice at the expense of the SENTINEL. They try to make it appear that the AMERICAN SENTINEL is opposed to temperance.[80]

Of course the Seventh-day Adventist Church is a strong proponent of temperance and healthy living, and these accusations were not aimed at the issue of temperance, but rather the issue of establishing a religious government in place of a civil one and merging church and state.

These events culminated in 1888 with a bill sent before the US Senate for a national Sunday law, which was introduced by Henry W. Blair, the same senator who introduced the prohibition bill in 1876 in support of the WCTU's efforts to curb liquor traffic.[81] At this point the WCTU came in support of Blair, amassing one million signatures on a petition supporting

---

79   Warren L. Johns, *Dateline Sunday: The Story of Three and a Half Centuries of Sunday-law Battles in America* (Mountain View, CA: Pacific Press Publishing Association, 1967), 54.

80   E. J. Waggoner, A. T. Jones, eds., *The American Sentinel*, October 1888, Volume 3, Number 10, page 76, http://docs.adventistarchives.org/docs/AmSn/AmSn18881015-V03-10a__B.pdf?q=docs/AmSn/AmSn18881015-V03-10a__B.pdf (accessed March 2012).

81   E. J. Waggoner and A.T. Jones, eds., "Our Position Again Stated," *The American Sentinel* 4, no. 1 (January 1889): 6, http://www.adventistarchives.org/docs/AmSn/AmSn18890101-V04-01__B.pdf#view=fit (accessed March 2012).

this bill. Blair managed 15 million signatures in total for his petition or about 30% of the population of the United States at that time.[82]

This bill was strongly opposed by the Seventh-day Adventist Church, which sent one if its church leaders, Alonzo T. Jones, to testify before a Senate committee to lobby against the bill. Jones successfully argued that the bill was unconstitutional and was also against Christ's teaching, using His words "Render therefore unto Caesar the things which are Caesar's, and unto God the things that are God's."[83]

In spite of the popular tide favoring a national day of worship, the Senate voted against the bill based on the concept that the will of the majority cannot determine morality. A small group of about 30,000 Seventh-day Adventists and 10,000 Seventh-day Baptists had a significant impact on the political and constitutional landscape of America through these events. However, the fact that the country came close to adopting a law requiring national Sunday worship should not be lost or forgotten. Blair resubmitted an amended bill the following year, which was also struck down.[84] However, Blair and those who supported a national day of worship, continued to introduce smaller amendments and by-laws regulating activities on Sunday.[85]

The establishment of a national law to require religious observance is a key milestone on the prophetic road to the end of times, according to the prophecies in Revelation, Daniel, and Isaiah. The fact that the nation came close to this event would indicate the nearness of the second advent at the time of this occurrence. We know through the writings of Ellen White that it was God's desire to return at that time; however, as His people were not ready, the advent was delayed.

> Had Adventists, after the great disappointment in 1844, held fast their faith and followed on unitedly in the opening providence of God, receiving the message of the third angel and in the power of the Holy Spirit proclaiming it to the world, they would have seen the salvation of God, the Lord would have wrought mightily with their

---

82  Seneca Vaught, "The Blair Bill 1888: Religious Reform or Social Engineering?" http://www.oakwood.edu/historyportal/ejah/2011/blair.htm (accessed March 2012).

83  E. J. Waggoner and A.T. Jones, eds., *The American Sentinel* 4, no. 1 (January 1889): 7.

84  Ibid.

85  Gordon B. McKinney, *Henry W Blair's Campaign to Reform America: From the Civil War to the U.S. Senate* (Lexington, KY: University of Kentucky Press, 2013), 142, 143.

efforts, the work would have been completed, and Christ would have come ere this to receive His people to their reward. But in the period of doubt and uncertainty that followed the disappointment, many of the advent believers yielded their faith. ... Thus the work was hindered, and the world was left in darkness. Had the whole Adventist body united upon the commandments of God and the faith of Jesus, how widely different would have been our history!

It was not the will of God that the coming of Christ should be thus delayed. God did not design that His people, Israel, should wander forty years in the wilderness. He promised to lead them directly to the land of Canaan, and establish them there a holy, healthy, happy people. But those to whom it was first preached, went not in "because of unbelief." Their hearts were filled with murmuring, rebellion, and hatred, and He could not fulfill His covenant with them.

For forty years did unbelief, murmuring, and rebellion shut out ancient Israel from the land of Canaan. The same sins have delayed the entrance of modern Israel into the heavenly Canaan. In neither case were the promises of God at fault. It is the unbelief, the worldliness, unconsecration, and strife among the Lord's professed people that have kept us in this world of sin and sorrow so many years. (*Evangelism*, 695, 696)

Events and circumstances were in place to bring about the final conflicts, but the church was unprepared and the members bickered among themselves and were concerned about worldly positions in preparing to be ready for the outpouring of the Holy Spirit. So the opportunity passed and the harvest remained ungathered, the cycle had to be reset to run its course before it would be time again. Nevertheless, we should remember the process by which these events transpired when we were brought to the brink of the final events back in the late 19th century.

1. A long drawn-out war that cost the country the loss of hundreds of thousands of lives and substantial amounts of wartime spending by the federal government.[86] Today, the federal government spends

---

86  Faust, 187.

close to $1 trillion, or a third of the annual budget on military-related spending.[87]

2. A building boom in railroads and lots of speculation resulted in a huge asset bubble that eventually burst. Today, the bursting of the housing bubble has mired the economy in a three-year slump and threatens to stall any recovery.

3. The cost of the war, reconstruction efforts, over-spending, and supposition arose in high levels of debt, causing a strain on the financial system. Today, to cost of the wars in Iraq and Afghanistan as well as the ongoing cost of maintaining the military and foreign military aid is more than $1 trillion annually, which is the largest portion of the US budget deficit.[88]

4. A banking system and stock market crash caused many to lose their savings and culminated in a financial crisis. Today, most investors have yet to recover from the stock market declines in 2008.[89] Many workers are counting on pension funds for their retirement, and they are finding themselves unable to keep up with the projected future pension obligations.[90] Finally, the debt overhang for most of the developed nations is threatening the world with another round of market turmoil for both stocks and particularly bonds.[91]

---

87 "Spending Under CBO's March 2012 Baseline," Congressional Budget Office, http://www.cbo.gov/sites/default/files/cbofiles/attachments/Supplemental_byFunction.xls (accessed March 2012).

88 "Historical Debt Outstanding - Annual 2000 – 2010," Treasury Direct, http://www.treasurydirect.gov/govt/reports/pd/histdebt/histdebt_histo5.htm (accessed January 2013).

89 Nathaniel Popper, "Stock Trading is Still Falling After '08 Crisis," *New York Times*, May 6, 2012, http://www.nytimes.com/2012/05/07/business/stock-trading-remains-in-a-slide-after-08-crisis.html?pagewanted=all&_r=0 (accessed January 2013).

90 Janet McFarland, "Study warns of funding shortfalls for pensions," *The Globe and Mail*, August 21, 2012, http://www.theglobeandmail.com/report-on-business/study-warns-of-funding-shortfalls-for-pensions/article4492181/ (accessed January 2013).

91 "World Economic Outlook 2012: Coping with High Debt and Sluggish Growth," International Monetary Fund, October 2012, http://www.imf.org/external/pubs/ft/weo/2012/02/pdf/text.pdf (accessed January 2013).

5. Globally, similar events of a war and a synchronized financial crisis amplified the effects of the downturn. Today, the debt crises in Europe and Japan create great head winds against any economic recovery. In our globalized economy, problems in one region can well affect other, so an integrated debt and economic crisis could have devastating effects.

6. The economic depression resulted in great despair and decay in morality. Today, morals would be arguably already at a low point in human history, but any acceleration in the crisis could drive morality to depths yet unseen.

7. A popular movement promoted the virtues of a common day of rest and worship to restore the nation back to greatness. Today, groups like the Tea Party and the religious right wing are gaining more political power as many are unhappy with the state of the union.

There are many similarities between the events around 1888 and the events of today. Although we have not seen the recurrence of all of the events from the 1888 era yet, the trend seems difficult to ignore. Even the pestilence, in the form of the equine flu in the 1870, may now be seen in the swine flu (H1N1), bird flu (H5N1), or SARS outbreaks, which may be a precursor to a more serious outbreak. A drug-resistant tuberculosis surge has many public health officials concerned even now.[92] The global economic and social conditions are turning for the worse, setting the stage for a potential repeat of the events we have seen when the last national Sunday worship legislation was proposed.

This is certainly not a guarantee that we are, in fact, headed for the end as there is still the question of the preparedness of God's people, which is requisite prior to the passing of a national Sunday law. Nevertheless, the recent events undoubtedly raise the possibility that we are repeating the pattern from 1888 and the risks that we are not ready, again. Preparing our lives for the coming events also increases our need for a diligent work of reformation and yielding to the cleansing power of God before things escalate any further.

---

92  "'Totally Drug-Resistant' tuberculosis: a WHO consultation on the diagnostic definition and treatment options," World Health Organization Meeting Report, March 21, 22, 2012, http://www.who.int/tb/challenges/xdr/xdrconsultation/en/index.html (accessed August 2012).

One can easily argue that depressions are by nature and definition very similar events. They always involve some sort of excess in fiscal or monetary policy, creating a massive bubble. Upon bursting, it will cause a deep, economic contraction. We can wonder if the Great Depression of the 1930s was the start of another opportunity for the church to fulfill its mission. However, evidence would suggest that is was not. (This is to be discussed in the final chapter.)

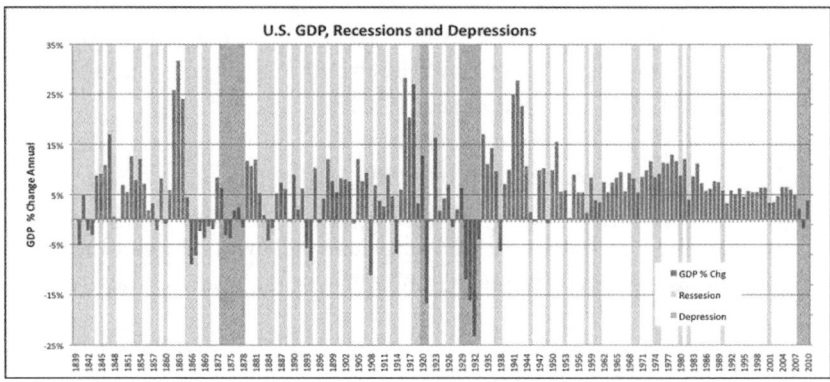

**National Bureau of Economic Analysis, MeasuringWorth.com**[93]

So this brings us to 2008 and the brewing "Greatest Depression" that the world is experiencing today. During the late 1800s, there were many and frequent recessions and economic slowdowns. Since the Great Depression of 1929–1939, recessions have become fewer and farther between as the government has exerted more financial control over the economy to engineer it to be more stable. However, this has come at a price. The cost of ever-rising debt and artificially low interest rates makes the debt affordable, but this debt-fueled economic management is not sustainable and has now come to a halt. Countries like Greece, Ireland, and Portugal are seeing the effect of rising interest rates on their mountain of debt. Their experience will soon become that of the United States.

The circumstances leading to this global crisis are very similar to the 1873 depression, but the severities are potentially much worse. The sheer number of people in the world, the astounding amount of debt, and the increasing callousness of humans toward each other is creating a perfect

---

93   "US Business Cycle Expansions and Contractions"/ "What was the U.S. GDP Then?" MeasuringWorth.com, http://www.measuringworth.com/datasets/usgdp/result.php Accessed March 2012.

storm of previously unmatched proportions. Furthermore, the spiritual condition of the Seventh-day Adventist Church, other denominations, and the world in general has set the stage for a repeat of the revival movements of the late 1800s.

> It is just as essential that the people of God in this day should bear in mind how and when they have been tested, and where their faith has failed; where they have imperiled His cause by their unbelief and also by their self-confidence. God's mercy, His sustaining providence, His never-to-be-forgotten deliverances, are to be recounted, step by step. As God's people thus review the past, they should see that the Lord is ever repeating His dealings. They should understand the warnings given, and should beware not to repeat their mistakes. Renouncing all self-dependence, they are to trust in Him to save them from again dishonoring His name. (*Testimonies for the Church*, vol. 7, 210)

Could it be that God is resetting the conditions of the world today to the same state just prior to 1888? Could it be that in His mercy, He gave his people an example, a dry run, so that this time more will be ready. Jesus pleaded with the Father, "My blood, My blood ..." when He saw that so few were ready (*Early Writings*, 38). He was prepared to wait more than another excruciating 120 years for an additional chance at the harvest; to witness two world wars, the Holocaust, genocide, communist revolutions; and children dying every day from starvation, neglect, and abuse, all the while feeling every pain that each hurting soul feels.

The trade-off must be substantial for our loving God to be willing to wait and allow the unspeakable evils that have taken place since 1888, but this time the harvest will be great—ten thousand times ten thousand (that's hundred million). Or will it be a billion or more in order to refill the ranks of the fallen angels? The "great multitude, which no man could number" is waiting to be prepared. What a privilege it will be for those in the last days to do the great work that God entrusted to them.

Is there anything we could do in this current life that surpasses the greatness of this task, the accomplishment we will feel and the joy we will share with these redeemed? What trivial matters could we forego now in order to be participants in this amazing calling? "The harvest is truly great, but the labourers are few: pray ye therefore the Lord of the harvest, that he would send forth labourers into his harvest" (Luke 10:2).

## Chapter 10

# The Food Crisis

Many people are worried about a food crisis hitting our planet, with crop failures and natural disasters everywhere, water shortages, and the US Federal Reserve printing money like crazy and devaluing the dollar, causing hyperinflation to be about ready to explode. I do believe there is a food crisis, but not what you might be thinking. No, the food crisis is not that there is too little food or that food will become very expensive, but that in the western world there is too much food.

I'm not downplaying the plight of the poor around the world who are starving, or those who are on food stamps in US, or those who are truly suffering. Nevertheless, for the majority of us, the biggest crisis is that there is too much food. We have more than we can possibly eat, we eat it all day long, at all times of the day and night, in any quantities, and we throw out more food every week from our fridge than some people may get in a month. We like to go out to eat, we order it in, we get take out, we go for coffee with friends, or we enjoy a cup in solitude; we eat to celebrate, we eat when we feel down. Clearly, one of our greatest pastimes is eating.

Some of you may be about to stop reading because you're thinking, "I don't have an eating problem; I watch what I eat; I get a bit of exercise; I dutifully eat my fruits and vegetables as well as Veja-Links—everything in moderation, right? There are bigger fish to fry." Consider this quote from E. G. White who wrote about Christ's experience of fasting for 40 days in the wilderness.

> Only by the inexpressible anguish which Christ endured, can we estimate the evil of unrestrained indulgence. *His example declares that our only hope of eternal life is through bringing the appetites and passions into subjection to the will of God.* (*Counsels on Diet and Foods*, 151, emphasis added)

Is what we eat an issue that might determine our salvation? The answer is a definite YES! Our eating habits can impact our hope of eternal life.

This is not about being vegetarian or simply being moderate in our eating; it is something far bigger. Peoples' habits are always a touchy subject, and eating is certainly among the touchiest. However, if you'll follow along, you'll see why it is so important.

**Christ's 40 Days of Fasting**

Before He started His ministry on earth, Jesus went on a 40-day fast to prepare. The purpose of the fast was to gain a victory over the most basic human needs so that not even hunger or death could cause Him to be tempted to sin.

> In man's behalf, Christ conquered by enduring the severest test. For our sake He exercised a self-control stronger than hunger or death. And in this first victory were involved other issues that enter into all our conflicts with the powers of darkness. ...

> Christ entered upon the test upon the point of appetite, and for nearly six weeks resisted temptation in behalf of man. That long fast in the wilderness was to be a lesson to fallen man for all time. Christ was not overcome by the strong temptations of the enemy, and this is encouragement for every soul who is struggling against temptation. Christ has made it possible for every member of the human family to resist temptation. All who would live godly lives may overcome as Christ overcame, by the blood of the Lamb, and the word of their testimony. That long fast of the Saviour strengthened Him to endure. *He gave evidence to man that He would begin the work of overcoming just where ruin began,—on the point of appetite.* ...

> The Redeemer of the world knew that the indulgence of appetite would bring physical debility, and so deaden the perceptive organs that sacred and eternal things would not be discerned. Christ knew that the world was given up to gluttony, and that this indulgence would pervert the moral powers. *If the indulgence of appetite was so strong upon the race that in order to break its power, the divine Son of God, in behalf of man, was required to fast nearly six weeks, what a work is before the Christian in order that he may overcome even as Christ overcame!* The strength of the temptation to indulge perverted appetite can be measured only by the inexpressible

anguish of Christ in that long fast in the wilderness. (*Counsel on Diets and Foods*, 185, 186, emphasis added)

Food is one of the most basic needs for humans and all animals. It is an instinctive need in our human nature. Christ gained this victory so that we too can rise above this need and give Him control over our human natures in order to accomplish His will.

So what does this mean for us? Why does this matter today? Does God want us to fast for 40 days like Christ? No, but there are several reasons why this is so crucial for us today as we prepare for the last days.

Initially, Christ wants us have clear minds and sound bodies so we can hear His voice and be better suited to serve Him. The relationship between our minds and the food that we eat is becoming more evident as scientific research in this area advances. How nutrition affects the brain and, in particular, the frontal lobe where much of our conscious decision making occurs is well documented. We need a proper diet, including the omega-3 fatty acid and essential amino acids, such as tryptophan to produce the needed serotonin levels for proper mental function.

The lack of proper nutrition can contribute to mental disorders and depression while, conversely, good nutrition can help the mind operate a peak mental performance.[94] For so many of us, our bodies are so clogged and our minds are numb because of the food we eat and our eating habits. High fat, high sugar diets are robbing us of normal mental function and acuity. We can barely stay awake through church. If we aren't entertained and stimulated, we can't keep our eyes open. Getting up early for prayer and personal devotions is impossible. God certainly has a higher ideal for us.

Equally important is the experience of gaining victory over our human nature through the surrendering of our will to Him. We still don't have a good grasp of what being victorious; to win a battle over our instincts to really surrender ourselves to His will. We talk about surrendering and giving our will to Him, but have we really experienced it? Many try to deny the need for any diet reform as they have lost this battle time and again, so they conclude that it is impossible to win a victory over diet, and God never intended that we should.

This translates into many other battles over sinful habits. Habits that have mastery over us, which force many to conclude that either God is not powerful enough or that He never meant for us to overcome. Since

---

[94] Neil Nedley, MD, *Depression the Way Out* (Ardmore, OK: Nedley Publishing Co., 2011), 35.

we like to believe that God is omnipotent, then it must be that He has not required us to overcome our sins. This is a faulty conclusion, of course, but one that we will necessarily come to if we haven't learned how to gain victories over our sins. It is a step-by-step process for each victory, gained only by much prayer and struggle to surrender our wills to God. Winning one victory helps us learn lessons to prepare for the next. Just as in professional sports, teams are interested in players who have had experience in winning championships to provide leadership, particularly in the playoffs, so our small victories can provide important experience and guidance for the next challenge.

Anyone who has tried to diet and lose weight knows how difficult it is to gain a victory over appetite. Perhaps this is the reason the battle ground of appetite was the first test for God's people. God's invitation is for us to work together, to figure things out, and experience victory through His power as the first assault on the enemy's territory. When we learn to be victorious in this battle, we can be ready for other victories. When we are victorious in one battle it creates a healthier body and mind through which God can communicate to us more effectively in order to face the next battle. It is a key stronghold of the enemy that Christ wants to take back and use as a launching point for many other battles to come.

Christ wants us to be victorious Christians as He overcame appetite, and we can claim that victory of ourselves if we rely on His strength. His victory can be ours if we claim His promises and submit to His will.

**Daniel and Others Tested on Appetite**

There's another reason why this issue of appetite is so important. We can go back to the Bible and think about a few individuals, starting with Daniel. The story of how Daniel and his three friends refused to eat the king's food and asked to be tested for ten days is well-known. It seems like a small thing, but it was the beginning of the work of one of the greatest prophets of the Bible and arguably one of the greatest statesmen of all time. Who else in history advised several different kings, kings from entirely different countries; in fact, kings who invaded and overthrew the previous king wanted Daniel to remain in the court as a key advisor?

Daniel's character was flawless, his integrity beyond reproach, all because he "purposed in his heart" (Daniel 1:8) to obey God in everything, starting with the very food that he would put in his mouth. He refused to eat the unhealthy foods that the king provided, and he chose to eat the foods that were approved by God.

Daniel grew up during the reign of the young King Josiah, who had rediscovered the law and ordered that the law be taught to all the people of the nation. Daniel would have been a youth growing up during the great reformation that took place in Judah at this time, and this would have been a great influence and inspiration for him, which would have helped him and his companions to remain true to God's laws, even in the palace of Nebuchadnezzar.

What an important lesson this would be for our youth today if they could also be inspired to put their trust in the Designer's plan for our diet. If they could be like Daniel who witnessed reformation among his people, who purposed to follow God, who passed the test on food, and who went on to do great things for God and his people.

Daniel was not the only Bible character that faced a test on food. John the Baptist, who was the greatest prophet (see Luke 7:28), had a strict diet from the time he was born. In fact, the angel Gabriel gave specific instruction to his father Zachariah regarding his diet. John had the privilege to prepare the way for the Messiah, and he also baptized Jesus. He lived a pure life away from the trappings of the world, following a strict diet and walking closely with God.

How about Ezekiel? God asked him to lie on his side for 390 days and eat simple barley loaves at the start of his ministry. God wanted him to understand the patience and longsuffering that He had for His people. He also wanted Ezekiel to be prepared for the powerful testimony he would be asked to give.

What about Elijah? He relied on God to feed him by ravens by the brook Cherith, in preparation for his battle against Ahab, Jezebel, and her 400 prophets of Baal. For three years he survived the famine in the land by relying solely on the provision of God.

Gideon and his 300 men took on the vast army of the Midianites. Only those who would not let even thirst stop them from advancing, were chosen to be part of the 300. Many others faced a test on the issue of appetite as a key requisite to be in God's service.

How about those who were tested on appetite and failed? Adam and Eve for starters. They lost their innocence, their home, and their relationship with God because of their infidelity on the issue of what they could eat. Esau sold his birthright for a bowl of lentils. Then there were, of course, the Israelites after the exodus from Egypt, who were chosen to be God's special people. God miraculously provided manna for them, but all they could do was complain. They wanted the fleshpots of Egypt, rather than the manna from heaven. They lost their chance to go into the Promised Land as a result.

Samson was supposed to be a Nazarene, but he didn't follow the strict diet he was supposed to and squandered his strength on a harlot and lost his freedom, his eyes, and almost his eternal life. The son's of Eli, the high priest, had uncontrolled appetites. They demanded more "offerings" from the people for their own selfish use, which led the whole nation to despise the ordinances of God. Eventually, their actions caused them act presumptuously, carrying the Ark of the Covenant into battle against the Philistines without the approval of God and lost the ark to the Philistines.

All of these people to whom God gave special missions, He first gave a test on appetite. Some endured and passed the test to go on to do some of the greatest things in the Bible. Others failed miserably and lost not only their chance to accomplish great things for God, some lost eternal life. A test on appetite was a key test that God used to measure the faithfulness of His messengers and a way to train them to be of greater use for God.

## A Test for the 144,000

If God gave a test of appetite to those in the Bible for whom He had special missions, is it any different today? Could it be that He is going use a test of appetite for whom He has a special mission in the end times? Could it be that God is looking for a people who have overcome their appetites and human natures in order to do a special work in the end times just as He did in Bible times? Is God looking for an army of followers who cannot be tempted by their appetites or passions so that even their very natures, right down to their imaginations and every thought, are in accordance to His will?

Jesus is waiting for His bride to make herself ready, clothed in the righteousness of the saints; people who have, step by step, gained victories over every besetment that could cause them to stumble; people who have had the experience of overcoming and of learning to trust in Him. He needs the 144,000 to be ready to stand in the time of trouble without an intercessor, who will stand even when everyone else is against them, and stand when it seems that even God has forsaken them. These will not be swayed by their feelings, their senses or even human instincts, but will stand on the Word of God, because they have been trained to do so. That kind of training doesn't come easily. Also, it certainly takes time. Most of us are not ready, and we would fail if severe trials came upon us at this point.

Those who exercise but little faith now, are in the greatest danger of falling under the power of satanic delusions and the decree to compel the conscience. And even if they endure the test they will be plunged into deeper distress and anguish in the time of trouble, because they have never made it a habit to trust in God. The lessons of faith which they have neglected they will be forced to learn under a terrible pressure of discouragement. ...

The "time of trouble such as never was," is soon to open upon us; and we shall need an experience which we do not now possess and which many are too indolent to obtain. It is often the case that trouble is greater in anticipation than in reality; but this is not true of the crisis before us. The most vivid presentation cannot reach the magnitude of the ordeal. In that time of trial, every soul must stand for himself before God. (*The Great Controversy*, 621)

I had the privilege to meet Pastor Fujita from Japan, whose family was one of the early Seventh-day Adventist families in Japan. He told the story of his life as a child in post World War II Japan. Food was scarce and was being rationed out by the government. The only problem was that the food was being handed out on Saturdays.

The choice was to either stand in line to get food or go to church. His mother made the faithful decision to go to church rather than to stand in line for the rations. None of her neighbors would help her, thinking that she must be getting food from the Americans since she was a Christian. They struggled greatly, but God blessed them for passing this test. Through the example of his faithful mother, Pastor Fujita has been preaching the gospel for the past fifty years.

If we had to make such a choice, could we pass the test? If we could not buy or sell, and we were hungry, would we capitulate? How about an even tougher choice: if we had a bit of food and someone else was hungry, would we give our food to them? Christ spoke of the end times, recorded in Matthew 24 and 25. In chapter 24, Jesus spoke about the signs of the end and the second advent, but He followed that with a discourse on how we as Christians should live in the end times. He said that if we give food, drink, or clothing to the poor we have done it unto Him. It sounds simple enough when we have enough to eat right now, but how about if the food appeared to be our last meal. Did Jesus give us this admonishment after the signs of the last days purposefully to give us a clue about what conditions in the world will be like as probation is about to close?

What if there was a food crisis, with natural disasters everywhere, droughts, and crop failures? What if there were laws forbidding anyone to sell food to us? Would we have the grace and strength of character to give our only bit of food to someone else and go hungry? What a powerful testimony of Christian love that would be! A time is coming when we have the chance to shine like a powerful beacon in the darkest world. When there is no charity in this world, and everyone is looking out for his or her own survival, will we as Christians reveal the character of Christ by giving all that we possess to help someone in need? Is this what Jesus had in mind when He said that if "you did it to one of the least of these My brethren, you did it to Me"? (Matthew 25:40 NKJV).

We know many will come into the church in these last days, and perhaps the mercy that we show will open the doors and hearts of many. Also, every attempt will be made to coerce our consciences, playing upon our natural sense for self preservation. Our jobs will be threatened and eventually taken away. We will be forbidden to buy or sell. Our earthly possessions will be lost. Only those who love the truth more than they love their own lives will pass the test. Only the strong in faith will survive—a faith developed, cultivated, and trained by lots of practice—and the Bible tells us that the first step in that training is often on appetite.

The book of Ezekiel tells us the cause of the destruction of Sodom. "Behold, this was the iniquity of thy sister Sodom, pride, fulness of bread, and abundance of idleness was in her and in her daughters, neither did she strengthen the hand of the poor and needy" (Ezekiel 16:49). Pride, plenty of food, and an idle lifestyle were the sins of Sodom, which are no less apparent in our society today. While this was the judgment of God that fell on Sodom and Gomorrah, we are perhaps guiltier than they. Presently, the world is polarizing ever further into the haves and the have-nots. Certainly, for many in developed countries, food is in abundance.

**Water Shortage**

The Ogallala Aquifer is a massive underground water source that lies below the Midwestern states, stretching from North Dakota and Wyoming, through Nebraska and Kansas, south to Oklahoma and northern Texas. It is the largest underground aquifer in the world; however, it is rapidly being depleted. The Ogallala Aquifer is one of the main sources of water for crop irrigation in these states, but the aquifer is being depleted at an alarming rate. Once about 240 feet deep, the aquifer is now only about 80 ft deep and falling, according to the US Agriculture Department (USDA).[95] A USDA spokesman said, "The Ogallala supply is going to run out and the Plains will become uneconomical to farm. That is beyond reasonable argument. Our goal now is to engineer a soft landing. That is all we can do."[96] Since the American plains grow about 20% of the grain and corn supply for the country, any reduction in the land that can be cultivated will have severe consequences for the US, and even more so for parts of the world that rely on US exports.

According to the US Agency for International Development (USAID), scarcity and degradation of current water sources has the potential for turning into a global water crisis. The USAID provides the following statistics about global water usage and conditions.[97]

- More than 2.8 billion people will be living in either water-scarce or water-stressed regions of the world by 2025.
- Total global water demand is doubling every 20 years.
- Freshwater ecosystems and environmental services from water resources and watersheds are increasingly at risk from human pressures including water withdrawals, dam diversions, and urban and industrial development and pollution.
- Wetland ecosystems, which serve as buffers against natural disasters and breeding grounds for fisheries, are being lost around the world at alarming rates.
- Ninety-five percent of wastewater in developing countries around the world is discharged into the environment without treatment.
- More than 1 billion people lack access to an improved water supply and more than 2 billion people lack access to improved sanitation, undermining efforts to protect public health.

---

95   Jeff Johnson, et al, "Water Conservation Policy Alternatives for the Ogallala Aquifer in Texas," http://www.aaec.ttu.edu/ceri//Published%20Papers/Tech.Reports/WaterConservationPolicyAlternatives.pdf (accessed March 2012).

96   Charles Laurence, "US farmers fear the return of the Dust Bowl," *The Telegraph*, March 7, 2011, http://www.telegraph.co.uk/earth/8359076/US-farmers-fear-the-return-of-the-Dust-Bowl.html (accessed March 2012).

97   "The Global Water Crisis: Putting the Crisis in Perspective," US Agency for International Development, http://transition.usaid.gov/our_work/cross-cutting_programs/water/global_water_crisis.html (accessed March 2012).

- More than 50 percent of the world's hospital beds are occupied by people suffering from water-related diseases.
- Nearly 2 million people—the vast majority children under age five—die from diarrhea each year.
- Seventy percent of water consumed by humans is directed to agriculture and cultivated food production, and this percentage is even higher in many developing countries.
- Ninety percent of all disaster-related deaths are water-related."

Without an adequate supply of water for irrigation, food production around the world will be diminished. With certain parts of the world already facing a shortage of food, any decrease in supply or increase in cost could have a devastating impact. The poorest nations will be impacted first as imported food will become beyond their reach. In the winter of 2011, a sharp rise in the cost of commodities caused a spike in the cost of wheat globally, rising to $350 per metric ton from a normal level of about $150.[98] The high cost of food was one of the reasons for the uprisings in Tunisia, Algeria, and Egypt. The popular uprisings were due to the anger created from people who were unable to feed their families because of the rising price of food. Such will be the impact of a water and resultant food shortage.

While there are often situations of drought, flooding, or other natural disasters that affect the production of food around the world, there is certainly a manmade element to the shortages. The first is the growing global population that continues to put great strain and demand on the production capabilities of the world.

Second, though there is an inequality in distribution of food production around the world, the bigger problem is the rising cost of food, which impacts those nations which can least afford any increase in prices. Egypt, for example, is one of the top 20 producers of wheat in the world, producing about six million metric tons per year.[99] Yet when global prices skyrocketed, wheat became unaffordable for many average Egyptians, even though their

---

[98] "Historical Basis Charts, 2010-2011" (see chart on page 13), Canadian Wheat Board, http://www.cwb.ca/public/en/farmers/producer/historical/pdf/2010-11/2010-11fpcbpccharts.pdf, (accessed January 2013).

[99] Agriculture Statistics>Grains>Wheat Production by Country, NationMaster.com, http://www.nationmaster.com/graph/agr_pro_whe-agriculture-production-wheat (accessed January 2013).

own country produced about half of the volume of wheat they consumed.[100] This is the nature of a global economy where the cost of commodities rises with demand and those willing and able to pay more to secure supply.

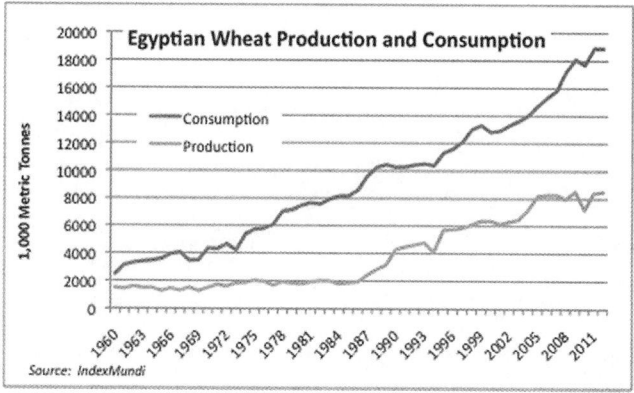

Third, the use of good crop land in America for bio-fuel is driving prices higher. As corn prices rise, they reflect higher energy prices. Approximately 40% of the US corn production is now going to ethanol production.[101]

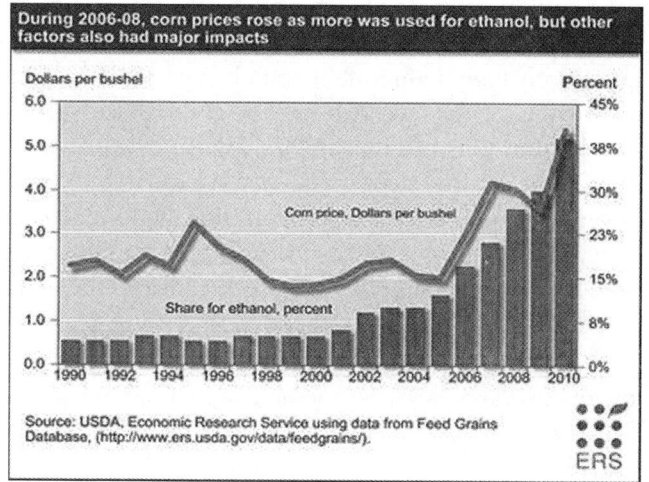

[102]

---

100 "Wheat consumptions (most recent) by country," NationMaster.com, http://www.nationmaster.com/graph/agr_gra_whe_con-agriculture-grains-wheat-consumption (accessed March 2012).

101 "Corn: Background," Economic Research Service, US Department of Agriculture http://www.ers.usda.gov/topics/crops/corn/background.aspx (accessed March 2012).

102 "Bioenergy: Findings," Economic Research Service, US Department of Agriculture,

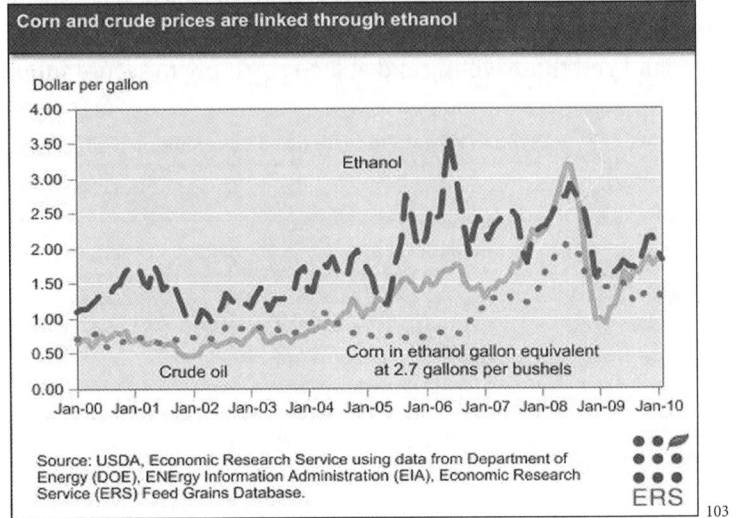
103

Corn prices have now become closely linked with energy prices, specifically, crude oil prices as demand for ethanol production continues to increase. As oil prices continue to rise, corn prices will likely rise as well. This may also put upward pressure on other grains.

Fourth, the increased numbers of people who eat a meat diet contribute to a significantly higher amount of grain being used as feed of cattle.[104] Japan, which is one of the largest buyers of grain globally, imported an estimated 25 million tons of grain in 2011, most of which was used for animal feed.[105]

Fifth, over-irrigation, pollution, urbanization, and industrialization is depleting the water supply, causing concerns for the viability of farming in many areas. These manmade problems, which added to the natural problems that occur regularly, impact food production.

---

      http://www.ers.usda.gov/topics/farm-economy/bioenergy/findings.aspx (accessed March 2012).

103  Ibid.

104  "Energy and Agriculture Top Resource Panel's Priority List for Sustainable 21st Century," United Nations Environment Programme, June 2, 2010, http://www.unep.org/Documents.Multilingual/Default.asp?DocumentID=628&ArticleID=6595&l=en (accessed March 2012).

105  "World Agricultural Supply and Demand Estimates," World Agricultural Outlook Board, US Department of Agriculture, August 10 2012, http://future.aae.wisc.edu/outlook/wasde509.pdf (accessed March 2012).

The movers had been working hard all morning, emptying our house into their truck. "Boy, you guys have a lot of stuff!" exclaimed the supervisor.

I sheepishly agreed knowing that they didn't know that I had already taken several van loads of more stuff to the new house. "Yes," I said, "I really need to get rid of some of this stuff."

By early afternoon they had finally finished loading. The supervisor looked at his clipboard and said with a quizzical look: "Where exactly are we going?"

"It's out in the country," I replied, "out about 80 kilometers northeast of the city."

Our new home was out in the Oak Ridges Moraine, the large underground aquifer north of the Greater Toronto Area providing water for more than five million people living in the cities. This important source of water sustains the many watersheds that run into Lake Ontario, purifying the water that runs through it. Very fertile farmland sits atop the moraine as well as beautiful conservation lands, river valleys, and forests. Situated among many farms and small villages was our new home. A place to be far enough from the city to avoid its encumbrances, yet close enough to work the cities with a gospel message. That's the blueprint we were given, and our experiment was to begin—a fresh beginning, but with new challenges.

My daughter announced a week before our move that she wanted to go out west to Alberta to go to university instead of going locally. My oldest had to move into a residence dorm at his university instead of living at home. My youngest was starting at a new academy.

Everything seemed to be in turmoil. We had two weeks to get things in some order before everyone had to return to school, including my wife as a professor of nursing.

We tried our best to get things settled and looked for some normalcy. We endeavored to make the house a home even as our children were off to university, living away from home for the first time. We were already looking forward to Christmas break and the following spring when everyone would be home.

One other thing that we looked forward to the next spring was planting a vegetable garden in the bit of land we had. Since we moved in mid-August, it was much too late for any gardening. So we had something else to look forward to in the next year. I wondered how much food I could grow in an acre of land.

In many of the richer countries of the world, the problem with food continues to be the over-consumption of food while there is the real potential for a true food crisis as production is not able to keep up with rising global demand. This dichotomy sets up the world for a repeat of the Arab uprising in many other parts of the world as food becomes less affordable for the masses. A battle is brewing, pitting the average wage-earner against corporations and governments as world resources become greatly constrained. Now is the time for our preparations to not only live and survive in this kind of environment but also to minister and lead others to the truth. Only the strong will survive—strong, that is, in faith and experience in living and working for God.

## Chapter 11

# Unions and Monopolies

Go to now, ye rich men, weep and howl for your miseries that shall come upon you. Your riches are corrupted, and your garments are motheaten. Your gold and silver is cankered; and the rust of them shall be a witness against you, and shall eat your flesh as it were fire. Ye have heaped treasure together for the last days. Behold, the hire of the labourers who have reaped down your fields, which is of you kept back by fraud, crieth: and the cries of them which have reaped are entered into the ears of the Lord of sabaoth. (James 5:1-4)

The trade unions will be the cause of the most terrible violence that has ever been seen among human beings. (*Manuscript Releases*, vol. 4, 23)

**Unions**

One only needs to look at Greece to get a glimpse of what happens to a nation when its economy is in a major decline and workers are unwilling to swallow the bitter pill that is needed for its cure. The labor unions have been very active in organizing protests and strikes. Even as the government of Greece agreed to further austerity measures to secure IMF funding in the winter of 2012, the masses of workers organized a two-day national strike, shutting down all government offices and many businesses. Greece has seen many protests and strikes since mid 2011 as more budget restraints and austerity measures were put in place. The Greek economy in early 2012 was falling at a 7% rate, jeopardizing their qualifications for more funding by putting its budget goals at further risk.

The unionized government workers of Greece stood to lose the most if further austerity measures where to be enacted. If the government agreed to the EU's demands for tighter budget control and deficit reduction, the government would have to accomplish this through cutbacks in wages and benefits. Entitlement benefits such as pensions would be markedly impacted. The Greeks had enjoyed very generous retirement benefits at a fairly early age, but this was to be changed. Thus, the unions mobilized the people in protests against the government and the austerity measures.

The anger of the protesters mounted when they realized that the funding that the government was seeking would largely be used to pay back the Greek government bonds held by the large European banks. So the people saw this as another bailout of the banks at their expense. From the people's viewpoint, their salaries and benefits were being cut in order to fund banks and their rich executives. In May 2012, the Greek people voted out their leaders who had agreed to the ECB and IMF bailouts in favor of a new party, which planned to try and renegotiate the arrangements. With a split decision in the voting, no effective government could be formed, so the Greeks had to go back to the polls again on June 17, 2012. In the June election the New Democracy party, that was in favor of the bailout, won by a narrow margin.[106] The bailouts were given to Greece, and protests continued in throughout the year.[107]

The people of Greece and in many countries around the Mediterranean are learning again the power of their voice and their vote. The people are trying to make their governments responsive to their needs and less so to the lobbyists and the large corporations that often fund the politicians campaigns.

While it was true that any bailout money that Greece would receive would end up in the hands of the banks; there is, of course, a flip side to that story. For many years the Greek workers have enjoyed lucrative wages and benefits, which have been funded by their government's deficit and buildup of debt.[108] While the unions protested against the seeming injustice of the austerity measures, they were the original beneficiaries of the debt that contributed greatly to the need for the latest bailout. So it is somewhat disingenuous for the unions to protest too vigorously about the bailout.

---

106  Rachel Donadio, "Supporters of Bailout Claim Victory in Greek Election," *New York Times*, June 18, 2012, http://www.nytimes.com/2012/06/18/world/europe/greek-elections.html?pagewanted=all&_r=0 (accessed December 2012).

107  Ben Brumfield, "Greek strike shuts down country ahead of cliffhanger austerity vote," CNN, November 6, 2012, http://www.cnn.com/2012/11/06/world/europe/greece-strike/index.html (accessed December 2012).

108  Landon Thomas Jr., "Patchwork Pension Plan Adds to Greek Debt Woes," *New York Times*, March 11, 2010, http://www.nytimes.com/2010/03/12/business/global/12pension.html?pagewanted=all&_r=0 (accessed March 2012).

Yet, the masses don't see the reason for the large deficits and massive debt levels is their own rich entitlements.

The recent protests in various parts of Europe were encouraged by the uprising in the North African and Arab nations earlier in 2011. The revolutions in Algeria, Egypt, and Libya fueled the spirit of protest around the world. The recent Occupy Wall Street movement was also a signal of the level of dissatisfaction of the masses of people who live on very little means and without much hope for a better future. When people have little to lose, they will take radical action and look for someone to blame and someone who will give them a handout.

Occupy Wall Street was, however, a relatively unorganized movement facilitated by the Internet and cell phones. The labor unions can be very powerful and organized when its membership feels threatened. They can mobilize quickly if pushed to action. Over the past several years since the start of the financial crisis, the labor movement has taken a step backwards. With so many companies still struggling under the effects of the global economic slowdown, many workers and unions were not interested in picking a fight with companies for better wages or benefits. In fact during 2009, there was a considerable period when there was not a single job action or strike by a major labor union in the US and there were only five total strikes for the entire year.[109] In 2010, there were only ten major strikes, still well below the recent range of 15 to 20.

With the election of President Obama, who was well supported by the labor movement, unions were expected to be more influential. However, with the economic conditions, the unions lacked the support and impetus to take on management and fight for their members who were mostly happy to have a job. Unions continued to lose political power.

In March of 2011, the state of Wisconsin passed legislation banning collective bargaining. In what became a national spectacle, the Democratic members of the state legislature refused to attend the vote so it could not be official. Some Democratic legislators even hid out of state so they could not be forced to come to the vote. In this fight, unions were being portrayed as causing much of the escalating cost of running the government, and collective bargaining was at the root of state and local budget overruns. Whether true or not, the power of the unions was on the decline.

---

109 "Major Work Stoppages in 2011," Bureau of Labor Statistics, US Department of Labor, Economic News Release, February 8, 2012, http://www.bls.gov/news.release/wkstp.nr0.htm (accessed March 2012).

# The Financial Crisis in Bible Prophecy

As the economic slowdown continued on, and more people were out of work for longer periods of time than ever before, the discontent with government and big business was on the rise. Occupy Wall Street struck a chord with the common people who found a new enemy in the 1%. The top 1% of the people who earned half the income and controlled a third of the wealth of the nation were fast becoming the villain. The 1% was portrayed as those whose influence held sway over business and government, who paid fewer taxes, and who lived in luxury at the expense of the average worker. The longer the economic conditions remain depressed, and the wider the disparity between the haves and the have-nots, the greater will be the restlessness of the common worker.

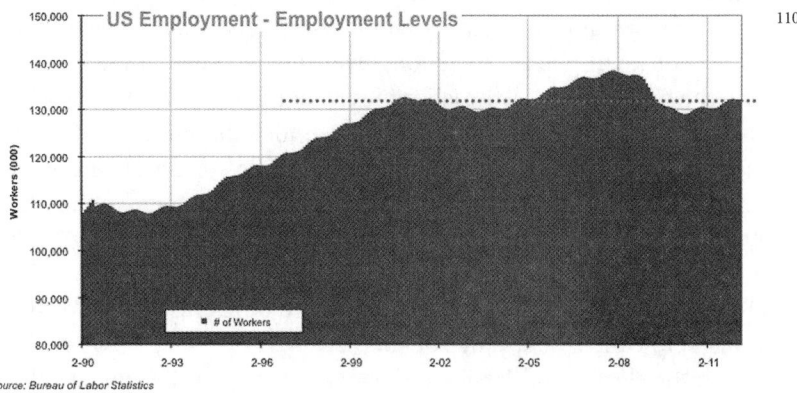

The US unemployment rate gradually came down in 2011, and the media touted this as a sign that the economy was improving. However, the reality of the situation is quite the opposite. The decline in the unemployment rate has been the result of more unemployed workers becoming discouraged and forfeiting their search for a job, dropping out of the workforce. With greater numbers falling out of the workforce, the unemployment rate has been falling. The facts are that the number of actual employed workers in the United State has fallen below the level of 2004, with only 131 million employed compared to the peak in 2007 at 137 million.[111] So not only has the number of workers not risen to keep up with population growth, but it has also fallen and stagnated so that fewer workers are

---

110 "Data Retrieval: Employment, Hours, and Earnings (CES)," Bureau of Labor Statistics, Department of Labor, http://www.bls.gov/webapps/legacy/cesbtab1.htm (accessed August 2012).

111 Ibid.

now supporting a larger and ever-growing number of people. So in spite of the positive economic indicators and rising stock market, the economic conditions are depressed, with so few being employed.

The union movement, while it looks wounded now, is starting to regain strength and support as the dissatisfaction of the people grows. Non-unionized workers are also sympathizing with the unions in protest against the 1%,[112] big business, and the government. As it was in Europe, the unions and the people of the US may not be pushed into action until austerity measures are forced upon them. Once it happens, likely due to an escalating debt crisis, unions and non-union works will stand in solidarity to protest the loss of their entitlements. Ellen White commented on the impact that the unions will have in the last days.

> The trades unions will be one of the agencies that will bring upon this earth a time of trouble such as has not been since the world began. ... The time is fast coming when the controlling power of the labor unions will be very oppressive. (*Last Day Events*, 116, 117)

> The trade unions will be the cause of the most terrible violence that has ever been seen among human beings. (*Manuscript Releases*, vol. 4, 23)

The early actions of the labor movement at the start of the twentieth century saw violent conflicts between workers and law enforcement. Great clashes between unions and the police resulted in destruction of property, injury, and death. In spite of its beginnings, the labor movement is not nearly as radical today. While there have been some localized incidents, union strikes, and protests, they have generally been orderly and non-violent; that is until recently. The protests in Greece, prompted by the unions and collaborated by the masses, brought back to mind what can happen when large groups of people are stirred into an emotional frenzy driven by anger, fear, and hatred. Even at the crucifixion of Jesus, it was the mob mentality that the priests and rulers leveraged to accomplish their desired end. The mob yelled, "Crucify him" (Mark 15:13). They also claimed that

---

[112] "Who Exactly are the 1%?" *The Economist*, January 21, 2012, http://www.economist.com/node/21543178 (accessed March 2012). The one percent are the top income earners in America who earn an average of $1.2 million in household income and own an average of $.6.9 million in assets. They are typically executives who run many of the corporations in the country.

they had no other king but Caesar, not only denouncing Jesus as their King but also denying that the God of heaven was their King.

In the mass protests in Egypt, there was a collective desire to oust President Mubarak, but within the masses of these people were mobs that carried out acts of tremendous violence against innocent people. Reporters, foreigners, and even innocent by-standers were attacked viciously by various factions found within the protests. On *60 Minutes*, a news reporter for CBS told her story of nearly being literally torn apart by a brutal mob. Such is the extent to which humans can sink when individual conscience is replaced by mob mentality. It is the darker side of humanity that a civilized society would prefer not to acknowledge; yet, it exists just under the surface. All it would take is some galvanizing event for people to become a mob.

What might be such a galvanizing event? We have seen the undercurrent of society's anger in the Occupy Wall Street movement and protests in Greece. We have seen the anger of entire nations that suffered under tyrannical rule for decades. Nonetheless, does the description of the unions as causing "a time of trouble such as not been since the world began" (Daniel 12:1) require an even more desperate populous under worse scenarios? Does it also require a group of people, who are used to ease and freedom to lose those liberties before lashing out? Will it be those who had more to lose, losing all and causing them to act out in violence? What triggers this radical union movement in the end times?

## Monopolies

Large corporations are flush with cash. Companies have been hording cash as much as possible since the financial crisis started. Apple Inc. has $97.6 billion in cash on hand. The top five US corporations had more than $276 billion in cash balances at the end of 2011,[113] and the total cash holdings for non-financial (i.e., not a bank, investment or insurance company) US corporations is $1.2 trillion. According to many analysts, this makes them good investments as they have a strong balance-sheet position. They also point to this fact as a good indication of future stock market gains since this cash will need to be deployed eventually. Companies could choose to invest their cash in more equipment, new projects, or expand

---

113 "US Corporate Cash Pile At $1.24 Trillion, Over Half Located Overseas," Global Credit Research, Moody's Investor Service Inc, March 14, 2012, http://www.moodys.com/research/Moodys-US-Corporate-Cash-Pile-At-124-Trillion-Over-Half--PR_240419 (accessed March 2012).

their operations into new regions. They could also return the money to shareholders as dividends or buy back shares, which would also help stock prices. Corporations, of course, can buy up other competitors or suppliers.

The key activity to consider is the last item. Typically, after an economic slowdown and a market decline, there will be an increase in merger and acquisitions activity, otherwise known as "M&A," particularly if some companies' stock prices held up better than others during a market down turn. The stronger company could target the weaker, whose stock prices are depressed, as an acquisition target. It could buy up the weaker company, take its market share, and become a more dominant force in that industry. The pickup of M&A activity has often been a good signal that the market will soon rebound and the economy along with it. Corporations exhibit predatory behavior when other companies are wounded and ripe for the picking. It is survival of the fittest, and to some extent this is healthy for the market and the economy. Cleaning up the financial industry of the "too big to fail" banks and other less stable competitors may have helped to set this sector on a path to recovery, rather than the constant streams of bailouts and market interventions that have occurred since the financial crisis began.

The negative aspect of M&A activities is the potential cost to workers and consumers. Often in a merger there are efficiencies created by eliminating redundant jobs for either company. The word "downsized," or the more politically correct term "right-sized," is used to describe the reason for the layoff of many workers as a result of company consolidations. The other element to control the marketing and distribution of product and most importantly for consumer is the control of prices. As companies become larger or the largest in the market place, they can become "price setters" rather than "price takers." This becomes a huge advantage for companies as they are better able to manage their profitability by setting the price at which the final goods are to be sold. Again, this can be good for corporations, but not so for consumers who face higher prices due to the lack of competition in an industry. As companies merge and become too large, they can become inefficient again; then they need to be broken up into more manageable pieces.

This is the normal course of the business cycle as economies grow and contract, and businesses are born and die. However, everything about this current business cycle suggests that it is anything, but normal. Something feels terminal about this go around as if an era is ending—all of the things we expect in normal short term cycles have not happened as they should.

Also, a greater secular change has ushered in a permanent transformation of the business and economic landscape. So in this environment the course of big business mergers and buyouts may be taking a different tone.

Over the past decade, Canadians have watched many of their natural resource companies being bought up by large foreign competitors. Companies like Alcan,[114] the giant aluminum producer; Noranda,[115] a giant mining company; and MacMillan Bloedel,[116] a forestry company—all formerly well-known Canadian companies—have all become subsidiaries of foreign firms. This trend is likely to continue around the world as resource-poor countries try to secure sources of raw materials to support their own growth. China, in particular, has been actively seeking resource companies and ventures in Canada, South America, and Africa.

It's easy to understand this trend in global business, considering the growth in countries like China and India. So how far will this trend go? We can get a clue again from the writings of Ellen White, where she wrote about what to expect in the end times.

> The work of the people of God is to prepare for the events of the future, which will soon come upon them with blinding force. In the world gigantic monopolies will be formed. Men will bind themselves together in unions that will wrap them in the folds of the enemy. A few men will combine to grasp all the means to be obtained in certain lines of business. (*Country Living*, 10)

She warned of gigantic monopolies being formed and that a few men would combine to try gain control of certain lines of business. If we look at the trends today, we can see that this is a very possible scenario. Of course, if you recognize the divine inspiration of her writing, this warning is even more potent and full of consequences. So we need to examine how this

---

114 "Our History," Rio Tinto Alcan, http://www.riotintoalcan.com/ENG/whoweare/28.asp, (accessed March 2012). Rio Tinto purchased Alcan in 2007.

115 "History: 10th anniversary," Xstrata, http://www.xstrata.com/about/history/ (accessed March 2012). In 2005, Xstrata purchased a 19% stake in Falconbridge, which was the company formed due to the merger of Noranda and Falconbridge.

116 Timothy Pritchard, "Weyerhaeuser Agrees to Buy MacMillan Bloedel for $2.45 Billion," *New York Times*, June 22, 1999 http://www.nytimes.com/1999/06/22/business/international-business-weyerhaeuser-agrees-buy-macmillan-bloedel-for-2.45.html (accessed March 2012).

might happen and what the ramifications are of such monopolies on economies and on consumers.

Looking at industries in the United States, some have very large players that have near monopolistic positions. Health insurance, for example, has a few large companies that have dominant position in certain regions. Furthermore, under the current "Obama Care" program for national health insurance, Paul Ryan, the House Republican budget chief warned that there will be a large consolidation in the health insurance industry, resulting in only a few very large, insurance companies, and pricing will be controlled by the federal government.[117] In the food and agricultural industries, a few companies control seeds and fertilizer.

In other industries there are no current monopolies, but the potential of such consolidation does exist. Industries like oil and gas production, pharmaceuticals, and financial services may be ripe for consolidation. These industries are much regulated already, and the government dictates many aspects of their businesses. In oil and gas, companies must secure many approvals and permits in order to conduct drilling, production, and distribution. While oil prices are set by the market today, the impact of rising oil and subsequently gasoline prices are certainly known to be very detrimental to the economy. Will the government intervene should oil prices go much higher and treat oil and gas like other regulated utility companies? This is a question that should be considered.

Pharmaceutical companies rely on government approvals of their drugs in order to move from research to trial and from trial to public use. During the swine flu (H1N1) pandemic concerns in 2009, the government played a more direct role in the production, distribution and use of the vaccines.[118] Many governments around the world, at the urging of the World Health Organization, took more direct measures to ensure that sufficient doses were available for their citizens. This reflects the willingness of a government to act in the instance where it deems it to be in their country's best interest.

---

117 Peter Orszag, "Cheesecake Factory Medicine," *Wall Street Journal*, August 28, 2012, http://online.wsj.com/article/SB10000872396390444358404577605233123916096.html (accessed August 2012).

118 Jesse Goodman MD, MPH, "H1N1 Preparedness: An overview of Vaccine Production and Distribution," US Department of Health and Human Services (HHS), testimony before the Committee on Energy and Commerce, Subcommittees on Health and Oversight and Investigations, US House of Representatives, November 18, 2009, http://www.hhs.gov/asl/testify/2009/11/t20091118a.html (accessed August 2012).

This is not to criticize a government for being proactive in regard to matters of public health, but we should consider its implications for times in the future when the Bible tells us of pestilence. Jesus said, "For nation shall rise against nation, and kingdom against kingdom: and there shall be famines, and pestilences, and earthquakes, in divers places. All these are the beginning of sorrows" (Matthew 24:7, 8).

The financial industry, as discussed earlier, has been in need of restructuring since the financial crisis struck in 2008. In order to deal with the issues of undercapitalized banks, bank-owned properties, toxic assets, and market manipulation in the securities industries, the government needs to allow more free-market activity to take place in the industry and let the strong survive and the weak to be culled. This would be the normal course of action for a business cycle; however, there may be a darker side to the course of action that leads to monopolies in today's world.

The key implications of monopolistic control, particularly in these key industries that provide essential products and services for daily living, are twofold. First, with monopolies comes the ability to control prices due to the lack of competition. Usually the ability to control prices results in higher prices. Monopolies can charge what they want based on their basic input costs and their desired level of profits. Without any competitors, there is little incentive to become more cost-efficient and drive prices lower or improve product quality. Even more important than the textbook implications of a monopoly is the likely connection with a hyperinflationary environment. As discussed in chapter 3, the Bible points to a hyperinflationary condition in the end times. The existence of giant monopolies in key industries would be consistent with such a condition.

The second key implication is the ability for government to influence or regulate a monopoly. To hold monopolistic control over an industry usually comes with the explicit approval of government regulators, but this comes at a cost, which is close regulation of business activities by the government or a regulatory agency. Utilities are a good example of this regulation of a monopoly. Utilities are given the authority to act as a monopoly in providing energy to consumers, but the government controls the price that the utilities can charge. The regulators may also control the way in which the company conducts business in areas such as business expansion, contracting, and hiring. The company must apply to the regulator for approval to enact any significant changes to its business. The government thus not only has a strong influence over how the business operates, but it also ensures there is no competition.

The Bible speaks of a time in the last days, when no one can buy or sell except he who has the mark of the beast on his hand or his forehead. This condition occurs as the world, reeling from many disasters, tries to enact legislation that governments believe will stem the onslaught of these calamities. It will be directed at those whom the government deems to be the cause of the calamities for their refusal to obey the dictates of the church powers, which they claim are from God. This refusal to obey is seen to be the cause of God's wrath upon the world.

> He had power to give life unto the image of the beast, that the image of the beast should both speak, and cause that as many as would not worship the image of the beast should be killed. And he causeth all, both small and great, rich and poor, free and bond, to receive a mark in their right hand, or in their foreheads: and that no man might buy or sell, save he that had the mark, or the name of the beast, or the number of his name. (Revelation 13:16, 17).

There may be many ways to control the distribution of products, particularly necessities, such as food, water, medicines, energy, shelter and transportation. Especially in times of scarcity, price controls as well as distribution controls typically have been put into place. As wars rage, famines and pestilences ravage the land and earthquakes strike in diverse places, governments may look to take control of as many elements of the economy as possible, working in conjunction with corporations and regulated monopolies to affect stability.

A further implication of gigantic monopolies being formed is the inevitable conflict with unions. With monopolies trying to control all elements of an industry, chiefly prices and costs, unions would respond with strikes. In a hyperinflationary environment where input costs, mostly for raw materials that are rising quickly, a monopoly would try to raise prices accordingly; however, can do so only to the extent that it stifles demand. At that point where demand is affected, the company would look at further cost reductions. This would be akin to corporate austerity.

We have seen the impacts of austerity measures in Greece as the country tried to wrestle with its budget problems. Major labor unions combined to force the shutdown of most government offices and businesses. The same kind of job action would likely to take place against monopolies as well. As noted, the strife from unions and monopolies is coming, resulting in the greatest tribulation that we have ever seen.

The events we have seen in the Arab world in North Africa, in Greece, in other peripheral European cities, and in China are precursors to a greater global conflict of the masses and the power that tries to control them. The climax of these events will occur when this global economic strife and defaults come to the shores of North America. When this happens, how will Americans respond?

## Chapter 12

# Spoke Like a Dragon

I beheld another beast coming up out of the earth; and he had two horns like a lamb, and he spake as a dragon. And he exerciseth all the power of the first beast before him, and causeth the earth and them which dwell therein to worship the first beast, whose deadly wound was healed. (Revelation 13:11, 12)

The ten horns which thou sawest are ten kings, which have received no kingdom as yet; but receive power as kings one hour with the beast. These have one mind, and shall give their power and strength unto the beast. These shall make war with the Lamb ... And the ten horns which thou sawest upon the beast, these shall hate the whore, and shall make her desolate and naked, and shall eat her flesh, and burn her with fire. (Revelation 17:12–16)

The description of the lamb-like beast coming out of the earth is a familiar verse for most Seventh-day Adventists, forming a key understanding of the prophetic developments in the end times. The thought that this beast represents the United States as a newly emergent world power in the late 1700s is preached by many pastors and evangelists and is well documented and found in the many writings of our church pioneers as well as our most recent theologians. The view on this prophecy as denoting the rise of the United States also includes the belief that this same country, which was established on religious and individual freedoms, will eventually change its nature and speak "as a dragon."

The prophecy further foretells that this lamb-like beast, the United States of America, will exercise "all the power of the first beast before him" (Revelation 13:12). The first beast of Revelation 13 has been identified as the power of the Roman Church or the papacy, the same power that ruled Europe during the Dark Ages and was responsible for the inquisitions and persecutions in its attempt to hold power over all peoples.

As we follow the prophecies of Revelation, chapters 14 to 16, seeing the progression of the end-time events that include the preparation of the 144,000, the finishing of the three angels' messages, the judgment taking place in heaven, and the pouring out of the seven last plagues, we come to chapter 17. Interpreting this chapter to identify the many characters and what these characters are actually doing to each other is challenging. Even in the book *Daniel and the Revelation*, by Uriah Smith, one of the preeminent books on Revelation, chapter 17 is given a relatively short review without a detailed explanation of each character.

Further, as the prophecies near the end of chapter 17 seem to be yet unfulfilled, there are many interpretations of these events, particularly verse 17, which says that the ten kings have one mind and will give their power to the beast. Some say that this is simply historic, reflecting the ten European kings in the sixth century AD who gave their power to the papacy. Others suggest that this points to a one world government, a new world order, giving rise to countless conspiracy theories. Is this verse strictly historical? Or does this verse really prophesy a singular governmental authority over the entire world? It is important to understand the connection between this verse and Daniel chapter two, where in Nebuchadnezzar's dream, the image has feet of iron and clay that never mix. If not, why not? What are the global economic trends in play today, and where are they leading? Finally, can all these things be harmonized to a consistent singular viewpoint that will help us understand what the prophecy is about to happen?

This close inspection of the 17th chapter of Revelation more fully explains these prophecies and merges them with the political and economic trends of today, providing a greater depth of understanding of the events that are taking place around us and to keep us true and focused on the issue that matters: "present truth." This chapter does not seek to set out a new or different interpretation of the prophecies on Revelation than has been previously understood. The end conclusions are the same but with more details in between now and the end. Revelation 17 not only provides important support in our understanding of last-day events, but it also helps us to understand the battles that are raging today. Therefore, a clearer understanding of this chapter is a vital part of our preparation for the end times.

The 16th chapter of the book of Revelation describes the seven last plagues, which are God's judgments poured out on the wicked inhabitants of the earth just before the second advent of Christ. The last plague poured out is a plague of hail the size of boulders that destroys much of the earth.

As John the Revelator witnessed this destruction, the angel who poured out the last plague explained the reason for these judgments. The angel opened two visions to John; the first is recorded in chapter 17, depicting the history and future of Babylon the Great, and the second is reported in chapter 18, detailing the events around the destruction of Babylon.

> There came one of the seven angels which had the seven vials, and talked with me, saying unto me, Come hither; I will shew unto thee the judgment of the great whore that sitteth upon many waters: with whom the kings of the earth have committed fornication, and the inhabitants of the earth have been made drunk with the wine of her fornication. (Revelation 17:1, 2)

The angel approached and invited John to see (understand) the judgment of the "great whore that sitteth on the many waters," which he had just witnessed. This phrase is a reference to Babylon and more specifically, the last incarnation of Babylon in the end times as evidenced by the judgment or destruction that John observed. The description says that the "whore" sits on many waters, or in other words, she controls many peoples and nations (see Revelation 17:15). The angel wanted John to understand why the severe judgments were pronounced upon Babylon, so he took John back in time to show him the actions of Babylon that earned her these judgments.

> So he carried me away in the spirit into the wilderness: and I saw a woman sit upon a scarlet coloured beast, full of names of blasphemy, having seven heads and ten horns. (Revelation 17:3)

The angel then carried John into another vision, back in time to show why Babylon had been judged. As John traveled back in time, the angel showed John a woman riding on a scarlet-colored beast, representing the Roman church. It is important to note that John said it was a woman riding on the beast, indicating that the apostate church is in control of the kingdom or political power as a beast in Bible prophecy represents a controlling world power (see Daniel 7:17, 23). In effect, it is a union of church and state. It also differentiates it from the "whore," which received the final judgments. This woman is described in verses 4 and 5.

> The woman was arrayed in purple and scarlet colour, and decked with gold and precious stones and pearls, having a golden cup

in her hand full of abominations and filthiness of her fornication: And upon her forehead was a name written, MYSTERY, BABYLON THE GREAT, THE MOTHER OF HARLOTS AND ABOMINATIONS OF THE EARTH. (Revelation 17:4, 5)

This woman, called Babylon the Great and the Mother of Harlots, is distinct her from her daughters. She was arrayed as a priestess decked in the colors of a priest, holding a cup full of evil and profaneness that she used to draw the kings of this world into illicit relationships with her.

I saw the woman drunken with the blood of the saints, and with the blood of the martyrs of Jesus: and when I saw her, I wondered with great admiration. (Revelation 17:6)

In that she was drunk with the blood of the saints adds to the evidence that this represents the papacy of the Middle Ages. John marveled at the scenes he beheld the church's persecution of fellow Christians, but in the next verse the angel asked John, "Why do you marvel?" and proceeded to show him the power behind this woman, which was none other than the dragon. Let's look at the Scripture.

The angel said unto me, wherefore didst thou marvel? I will tell thee the mystery of the woman, and of the beast that carrieth her, which hath the seven heads and ten horns. The beast that thou sawest was, and is not; and shall ascend out of the bottomless pit, and go into perdition: and they that dwell on the earth shall wonder, whose names were not written in the book of life from the foundation of the world, when they behold the beast that was, and is not, and yet is. (Revelation 17:7, 8)

The angel described the beast as having four stages: 1) *was*, 2) *is not*, 3) *shall ascend out of the bottomless pit*, and 4) *yet is* and *goes into perdition*. The angel, having shown John the Roman church during the Middle Ages (was) and when it came to an end (is not), then proceeded to explain the next two stages, where it "ascends out of the bottomless pit" and "yet is" before ultimately going "into perdition." The people of the earth will admire and seek after the beast, but the angel pinpointed that this will happen at the fourth stage of the life of this beast. In other words, the people will give their allegiance to the beast when the deadly wound of the beast is healed (see Revelation 13:3).

The beast that John saw also had seven heads and ten horns. These seven heads helped to define the history of this beast and the seven different

| Perspective within the Vision | Beast That Was | Seven-headed Beast | Historical Era |
|---|---|---|---|
| John's perspective of the time while inside the vision. | Verse 8 "The beast that thou sawest was, and is not; and shall ascend out of the bottomless pit, and go into perdition: and they that dwell on the earth shall wonder." | Verse 7 "The mystery of the woman, and of the beast that carrieth her, which hath the seven heads and ten horns." Verses 9, 10 "Seven heads are seven mountains ... there are seven kings." | Numbers equivalent to the beast head. |
| Past John saw the woman drunken with the blood of the saints. In the past from the perspective from which the angel and John are looking. | Was... ... and is not | Five are fallen | 1. Babylon 2. Medo-Persia 3. Greece 4. Pagan Rome 5. Papal Rome |
| Present This is the head or era of the beast that John and the angel are observing at this point in the prophecy. | Shall ascend out of the bottomless pit See also Revelation 11:7. Two witnesses are slain by the beast that ascends from the bottomless pit. | ... And one is ... | 6. Atheism and secular humanistic ideologies (Communism, evolutionism, humanism, etc.) born around the time of the French Revolution. |
| Future | | One is yet to come Verse 10 "The other is not yet come, and when he cometh, he must continue a short space." | 7. United States (image to the beast—Revelation 13:14) |
| The angel prophesied about the powers yet to come from the perspective of the point in the time of the vision. | Goeth into perdition Was, and is not, and yet is Was, and is not Verse 8 "They that dwell on the earth shall wonder ... when they behold the beast that was, and is not, and yet is." Verse 11 "The beast that was, and is not, even he is the eighth, and is of the seven, and goeth into perdition." | Even he is the eighth, and is of the seven, and goeth into perdition. Verses 12, 13, 16 "the ten horns which thou sawest are ten kings ... These have one mind, and shall give their power and strength unto the beast. ... These shall hate the whore." | 8. Papacy (deadly wound healed —Revelation 13:14) |

stages or rulers in its life. Thus, two different threads are used to describe the history and stages of this beast. First, the angel used a verbal description to describe the beast as it "was and is not; and yet is." Second, John saw the visible differentiation, which was the seven heads and ten horns. These two descriptions complement each other, are concurrent with each other, and reveal additional details about the beast.

Then the angel introduced his wisdom so John could understand the next part of the vision. "Here is the mind which hath wisdom. The seven heads are seven mountains, on which the woman sitteth. And they are seven kings: five are fallen, and one is, and the other is not yet come; and when he cometh, he must continue a short space" (Revelation 17:9, 10).

The seven heads represent seven kingdoms, five of which had already fallen at the point in time in the vision that John was seeing, one was currently reigning, and one was yet to come in the future. Distinguishing the various descriptions given in these verses is the key to understanding the vision and its meanings. The table on the previous page provides a graphic display of the relationships between the descriptions of the beast, the seven heads, and the historical eras they entail.

The angel, when talking about the seven heads aspect of the beast, was looking at a specific incarnation of this beast. This stage is marked by whichever of the seven heads was ruling at that point in the vision, rather than the actual time when John lived. In other words John was looking at a future incarnation of the beast. The angel indicated that it was the sixth head or king. "Five are fallen," which chronologically are Babylon, Medo-Persia, Greece, pagan Rome, and papal Rome. So the period at which John and the angel were observing the beast represented the period where the beast was not, which corresponds to the time after the beast received a deadly wound as noted in Revelation 13.

The beast, while it "is not," meaning it is not apparently visible or overtly active, is still, nevertheless, alive and moving behind the scenes, as it is said that "five are fallen, and one *is*" (Revelation 17:19, emphasis added). This corresponds to the earlier description by the angel saying that beast that "was, and is not, and yet *is* (Revelation 17:8, emphasis added). While we understand that the papacy received its deadly wound in 1798, the beast is still alive and healing. Though we understand that the papacy does not receive full power until later, this does not mean that the beast is completely dormant at this stage of its life. In fact, it is very active in a very subtle way. It is during this time when many of the new doctrines of Satan have been and will be introduced to the world, doctrines such as evolution, humanism, communism, atheism, and hedonism. In the absence of a dominant church power, such as the Roman Church was, the world was ripe for the introduction of these new theories, which have become pervasive in the current culture.

The sixth head of the beast, therefore, represents the era in which we currently live, which began in 1798 at the fall of the papal power when Berthier, a general in Napoleon's army, took the pope captive. Since that time, there has been a steady rise in a power, which would be best described as secularism or atheism. This power has been steadily growing, even though there is no distinct nation or kingdom that is visible. This power is called the "beast that ... shall ascend out of the bottomless pit" as if it were the very essence of evil. Seeing the destructive force of the many theories that have come about since this time, it is aptly described as coming out of the bottomless pit. There are six separate prophecies about the 1,260 year period in Daniel 7:25; 12:7; Revelation 11:2, 3; 12:6, 14, giving warning that the end of this period is coming. The number of times this warning is given is significant. This is not just a notice that the papal reign is ending, but a warning that a new significant era is starting,, not only at the time of the end where God begins to judge the world but also when the new beast power begins its reign.

In Revelation 11, John wrote of the "two witnesses," which prophesy 1,260 days. "I will give power unto my two witnesses, and they shall prophesy a thousand two hundred and threescore days, clothed in sackcloth" (Revelation 11:3). These two witnesses are the Old and New Testaments as identified by E. G. White in *The Great Controversy* (see page 267). The prophecy goes on to say that at the end of the 1,260 year period, the two witnesses are slain by the beast that comes out of the bottomless pit or abyss.

> When they shall have finished their testimony, the beast that ascendeth out of the bottomless pit shall make war against them, and shall overcome them, and kill them. And their dead bodies shall lie in the street of the great city, which spiritually is called Sodom and Egypt, where also our Lord was crucified. (Revelation 11:7, 8)

This was fulfilled during the French Revolution when the Bible was banned by the French government. The leaders installed the goddess of reason in place of the Bible and the God of heaven. Atheism and secular humanist philosophies were propagated as a backlash against the tyranny of the papacy, which caused the banishment of the Bible from the country.

Ellen Write wrote, "The work which the papacy had begun, atheism completed. The one withheld from the people the truth of the Bible; the other taught them to reject both the Bible and its Author" (*The Spirit of Prophecy*, vol. 4, 192). The result of abolishing the Scriptures was complete moral chaos in France, and so fearful were the results that the Bible and religion were reinstated after three-and-a-half years. However, the ideologies that began in this era continued to do its work of leading people astray from God.

Millions have been murdered by communist regimes which have their roots in the ideas of Karl Marx, who wrote his manifesto in the mid 1800s.[119] Millions more have been lost to unbelief due to the ideas of Charles Darwin, who published his first essay on the theory of evolution in 1844.[120] Millions have also been lost to the apostasy of modern secular humanism taught by philosophers, which says that man can make himself better through his own power. Millions have been lost to sin as man has invented innumerable ways to pervert the senses and fulfill his lusts and passions. Millions have been lost through indifference as man has created a multitude of ways to entertain and distract the mind from the things that are true and eternal. All of these things have largely come to the forefront of society since the beginning of the 1800s, after the power of the papacy was removed, the fifth head of the beast. These theories have now become the "ruling power" over people in this secular age and are represented by the sixth head of the beast, which is the United States as noted in the chart.

The angel then said, "the other is not yet come; and when he cometh, he must continue a short space." This "other" that "is not yet come" is represented by the seventh head of the beast. This final incarnation of the beast will be the polar opposite of the previous beast in the sense that it will be a religious regime, unlike the secular one that preceded it. This will be when the image of the beast is formed according to Revelation 13:15. This image of the beast is created when the world powers, led by the United States, join together in attempting to legislate the observance of religious

---

119 Karl Marx and Friedrich Engels, "The Manifesto of the Communist Party," February 1848, http://www.marxists.org/archive/marx/works/download/pdf/Manifesto.pdf (accessed March 2012).

120 Charles Darwin, "Sketches of 1842 and 1844," Darwin Online, http://darwin-online.org.uk/EditorialIntroductions/Freeman_Sketchesof1842and1844.html (accessed March 2012).

laws and persecute those who would oppose and stand for freedom of conscience to follow the dictates of their own beliefs.

Due to the impact of multiple crises, people will once again turn to religion for answers, for comfort, and for salvation. They will do this, not out of repentance, but out of fear of losing their worldly possessions and positions. They will turn to God to save them *in* this world, rather than *from* this world. We have already looked at this similar scenario in the chapter 9, "The Panic of 1873," when after escalating crises, the US government will seek to enact a law, proclaiming Sunday as a national day of worship and rest. It will be claimed that a national day of rest on Sunday will help bring the nation back to greatness and back into favor with God.

The proponents of this idea will stop at nothing, trampling on the freedoms guaranteed by the US Constitution to accomplish their means. It will further be claimed that those who oppose the keeping of Sunday are responsible for the calamities that are falling on the nation. In this condition the masses are ripe for the ultimate delusion that will be given to them. It will be the United States, the "lamblike beast" of Revelation 13, that will establish the image of the beast, and the world will look with amazement and be drawn to the beast. At this time the seventh kingdom, represented by the seventh head of the beast will come to power and will continue a short space. This kingdom will be comprised of ten kings, represented by the ten horns. "The ten horns which thou sawest are ten kings which have received no kingdom as yet; but receive power for one hour with the beast" (Revelation 17:12).

However, the angel makes a curious statement in the prior verse. He said, "The beast that was, and is not, even he is the eighth, and is of the seven, and goeth into perdition" (Revelation 17:11). The "beast that was, and is not," must be referring to the stage led by the sixth head since that is how the angel described it earlier—"was, and is not" when viewing the beast. The "was, and is not" is that stage after the papacy received the deadly wound and appeared to be defeated, but then it will ascend from the bottomless pit as a new and different beast (see Revelation 11:7; 17:11).

The angel said that he will be the eighth and different beast from the seven-headed beast, even though he is of the seven, as if he is distinct from the previous seven. The seven-headed beast continues its existence and morphs from the sixth stage—a secular, atheistic stage—to the seventh, the formation of the image of the beast. There will seem to be two different beasts: the seven-headed beast and the beast from the bottomless pit. This seems to be borne out by the verses in Revelation 17:16, 17.

A conflict appears to arise between the ten kings and the whore. The ten kings hate the whore and burn her with fire while they have one mind to give their power to the beast. This gives rise to the questions: Who are the ten kings? Who is the beast? Who is the whore?

Let's start by identifying the whore. Earlier in this chapter, there was a woman who was riding on a beast, which was identified as the papacy in the Middle Ages. The woman was called Babylon the Great, the Mother of Harlots. So the harlot or whore of verse 16 is one of the daughters of the woman or an apostate church that has come from the mother. The timeframes in the context of this vision would put the whore in the last stage of the seven-headed beast in which the ten horns on the seventh head are in conflict with it. This would suggest that the whore is apostate Protestantism which will be in power at the time. In particular, it would represent the religious powers of America which, even now, are increasing their hold on the government. This apostate Protestantism, which is in essence Western capitalism, aptly represents the Laodicean state of the church.

> Babylon is further declared to be "that great city, which reigneth over the kings of the earth." Revelation 17:4-6, 18. The power that for so many centuries maintained despotic sway over the monarchs of Christendom is Rome. …
>
> Babylon is said to be "the *mother* of harlots." By her *daughters* must be symbolized churches that cling to her doctrines and traditions, and follow her example of sacrificing the truth and the approval of God, in order to form an unlawful alliance with the world. (*The Great Controversy*, 382, 383)

If the whore in the text is apostate Protestantism, which controls the United States, who is the beast and who are the ten kings? We must consider these two together to properly identify these players. The ten kings are represented by the ten horns on the seven-headed beast. Each head of the beast has represented a different era in which the beast has held power. It would seem incongruent to say that the ten kings give power to the beast, which they are a part of, in other words, the seven-headed beast.

However, there is the other beast in the prophecy—"the beast that was, and is not," which "is the eighth." As mentioned earlier, this beast seems to be distinct and separate from the seven-headed beast. This beast that "was, and is not" is also described as going into perdition and as the eighth, which is also prophesied as going into perdition. This may be the link that ties these two together. So this beast from the bottomless pit may be also "the eighth." It is likely this eighth power, the beast that "was, and is not," to which the ten kings give their power. This would help identify the beast from what "was, and is not" to be the power of the papacy, which has been revived.

The United States sets up the image of the beast, taking the lead in the apostasy, but ultimately, the original beast reclaims its power with the aid of the ten kings. This is the same scenario that took place in the sixth century, when the ten European nations gave their power to the papacy, leading to the beginning of the Dark Ages. In the last days, the revival of the papacy, the beast that "was, and is not" and goes into perdition, will be the final manifestation of this beast power as we head into the close of probation.

**The Death of Globalization**

So then, who are these ten kings? For this we can turn to today's political/economic situation for clues. One major economic trend that has marked the past 30 years is globalization, the opening up of borders to trade and commerce. The movement of capital and labor between countries and continents and the industrialization of emerging markets and developing nations has been a consistent theme. We have all seen and felt the impact of globalization. Whether buying cars and stereos from Japan, fruit from South America, or fashions from Europe, we have all participated in globalization.

Many have lost jobs or have seen their businesses diminish as a result of the work being moved overseas where workers are willing to work for a fraction of the labor cost here. Many services have been outsourced to offshore centers enabled by advancements in computing and communications technology. People in countries with enormous populations seem to be working harder than those in developed nations to get education and training to participate in this global trend.

Today, it is the norm for a company to use raw materials from one continent, ship these materials to another country where parts are produced, ship to yet another country where the final product is assembled, and then ship these final goods to sell around the world. All of this is to take advantage of the low costs and expertise in these various regions to produce the best product at the lowest cost.

Globalization has become the great equalizer in the world economy, taking from richer developed nations and giving to the poorer. Western nations have not prepared well for this trend as we continue to try to maintain the status quo of our lifestyles in spite of this powerful reality. Ideally, workers and nations should have been preparing for this eventuality by getting educated, retraining, retooling factories to be more efficient, reworking contracts to ensure viability for businesses, reorganizing businesses, reshaping industries, and streamlining governments.

These would have all been important steps to prepare for globalization. Instead, we have spent the past two decades living the high life, fueled by ever-growing levels of debt, while fighting with each other to maintain our status quo. We have fooled ourselves into believing that we are still competitive globally by transforming our economy into a consumer-driven society and buying up goods to help keep up the appearance of a growing economy. We have relied on financial engineering to provide a stable, low interest rate environment in support of our debt-driven existence, but real growth as eluded the western economies.

Over the past ten years, China has emerged as an export powerhouse, utilizing their vast labor force to take production away from developed countries. India, likewise, with its massive population has taken on production and technology services away from their western competitors. Brazil is developing into a solid resource-based economy with sound financial management, having experienced their own bout with hyperinflation. Korea is becoming the next technology and industrial leader, following in the footsteps of Japan. These developing nations are taking on the leadership in the global economy in production of materials and goods, taking away value-added work from the developed nations. Globalization has rebalanced the economic wealth of the nations around the world.

As powerful and successful as globalization has been for corporations, this trend may be in danger of faltering. Several factors are conspiring against this trend to bring it to a halt, even reversing the trend. The first would be the rising cost of oil and energy products. With oil prices nearing record levels again, it is threatening the viability of globalization. Without the benefit of cheap transportation costs, producing goods by sourcing parts from around the world will cease to be economical. This may become the first obstacle for the continuation of globalization.

Second, as the developing nations standard of living rises, their cost advantage will begin to disappear. This has already been seen in Japan, where a strong yen has hurt Japanese exports. Japan has survived due to a strong technology advantage and a reputation for high quality. However, with more of a level playing field in technology and quality now than ever before, this may not be a sustainable advantage for developing nations.

Third, a cheaper currency has always been an advantage for developing countries in order to help their exports. However, with the currencies of developed nations like the US dollar and the euro weakening, countries like China are seeing this advantage erode as well.

The next set of factors is more geopolitical in nature. With rising economic stress levels, including high unemployment, austerity measures, and recession, governments will be under greater pressure to adopt protectionist trade positions for their countries. Trade unions in America are already pressuring government for tighter control over imports and accusing other nations like China of unfair trade practices. Should economic conditions worsen for any region, the likelihood of increased trade conflicts will rise along with the probability that countries will adopt policies that will restrict cross border trade. Given the importance of trade for some countries, any action by one country will certainly be met by retaliatory actions by another.

Another trend that has been growing is the increasing difference between the philosophies, religious, and political views of nations. There is, of course, the tension between communism vs. democracy. China and even Russia, where there is still the remnant of the Soviet socialist views, are often at odds with Western democracy. The tension between Christian and Muslim nations continues to grow with the escalation of sanctions against Iran[121] and Syria.[122] In addition, countries that are more fiscally conservative are increasingly wary of spendthrift nations that borrow and spend, thus debasing their currency. Countries such as Brazil, Russia, and China are already trying to adopt bilateral trade relationships with like-minded countries, avoiding the broadly used currencies like the dollar and the euro.[123] Brazil and some developing Asian nations have adopted policies to restrict capital inflows from the West in order to stem the tide of rising

---

121 "An overview of O.F.A.C. Regulations involving Sanctions against Iran," Office of Foreign Assets Control, US Department of the Treasury, January 23, 2012, http://www.treasury.gov/resource-center/sanctions/Programs/Documents/iran.pdf (accessed September 2012).

122 Barack Obama, "Executive Order 13682—Blocking Property of the Government of Syria and Prohibiting Certain Transactions with Respect to Syria," The White House Office of the Press Secretary, August 18, 2011, http://www.whitehouse.gov/the-press-office/2011/08/18/blocking-property-government-syria-and-prohibiting-certain-transactions- (accessed September 2012).

123 Jack Perkowski, "China Busy Signing Currency Deals" *Forbes*, June 26, 2012, http://www.forbes.com/sites/jackperkowski/2012/06/26/china-busy-signing-currency-deals/ (accessed August 2012).

inflationary pressures. "Hot money" coming from the developed countries are driving up asset values in these countries causing inflation that is greater than the pace of the economic growth of the country, driving their currencies higher. These developing countries are seeking to keep their costs down and their currency lower in order to maintain the competitiveness of their exports.

It has been the status of the dollar as the reserve currency of the world that has allowed the United States to enjoy its economic prosperity through debt.[124] No other nation could have amassed $16 trillion in debt without a complete collapse of their currency. Since the dollar is used for settling many financial transactions globally, the demand for the dollar remains strong. However, this status is being challenged as regions look toward other currencies to conduct trade.

Countries are looking to dump the dollar for transactions and for reserve purposes. This will likely cause the dollar's regime to weaken, and the globalization of trade will weaken as well. Without a strong dollar, US consumers will lose their purchasing power. This will have a strong negative impact on most developing countries, looking to exports as their path to economic prosperity. If the US dollar and the US consumer weaken, these nations will lose their growth engine. They will not be able to rely on exports to the US for their economic growth. To compound this problem, the eurozone is facing a long, uphill battle to climb out of its financial hole, making the hopes of export-led growth of developing nations likely to disappoint.

If global trade becomes uneconomical, impractical, and unworkable, the result will be a dramatic change in the world economy. Countries will likely look toward more regional trade and regional partners. Buying locally and doing business within a region are likely to become the future trend. Regions in close proximity and with a closer economic status will seek to do business on a more level playing field. Countries within regions will also have closer cultural and social ties and values, allowing for more trust in a business environment where there is a real lack thereof. With numerous countries potentially defaulting on debts and payments, trust may be in great demand, but short supply.

---

124 Owen F. Humpage and Margaret Jacobson, "Is the Renminbi Challenging the Dollar's Reserve Status?" Economic Trends, Cleveland Federal Reserve Bank, April 25, 2012, http://www.clevelandfed.org/research/trends/2012/0512/01intmar.cfm (accessed August 2012).

Some very likely countries and regions may prove to be natural trading partners: 1) North America (US, Canada, and Mexico); 2) South America; 3) the European Union (northern Europe) 4) the peripheral Europeans nations (like Greece, Spain, and Portugal); 5) Middle East and North Africa; 6) continental Africa; 7) Russia and Eastern Europe (almost like the old USSR); 8) India and South Asia; 9) China, and 10) Japan, Australia, and Asia Pacific. These are some likely economic blocs that represent the global economy—there are ten economic regions into which the world can naturally be divided. These could become ten kingdoms, with ten kings as prophesied in Revelation 17:12; the ten kings which have not received their kingdoms yet. While a few short years ago, the collapse of globalization would have seemed quite unlikely. Today, with the financial instability in the world, it may be only a matter of time before the world becomes fragmented and regionalized. In fact, the groundwork has already been laid, and countries are already moving toward a more regionalized structure.

The ten kings "shall hate the whore" (Revelation 17:16) and will give their power to the beast. With the economic turmoil in the world, it will be easy for the world to "hate the whore," the apostate Protestant Christianity of America that will be blamed for the faulty economic model that it will have imposed upon the world. It will be hated for it political and religious views, which claims superiority to all others. America will have set up the image to the beast, and eventually, the real beast power, the papacy, will seek to regain its power and exercise sole authority in the world. The ten kings will give ecclesiastical authority to the beast in an effort to unite the world in one religion in order to appease God, who the citizens of world believes is punishing them for the non-observance of a Sunday sabbath. The prophecy of Daniel will remain intact in that the world's kingdoms will never again be united under one civil power; however, the world will try to unite under one religious power. One group will stand in opposition to this movement—the remnant of God's true people. Against this remnant will be aimed the united powers of the ten kings and the beast.

> These shall make war with the Lamb, and the Lamb shall over come them: for he is the Lord of lords and the Kings of kings: and they that are with Him are called, and chosen, and faithful. (Revelation 17:14)

The chosen and faithful will have to endure the dragon who is furious (see Revelation 12:17), and the world who will seek to coerce obedience and worship from this remnant who chooses the biblical Sabbath over the beast power and the false Sabbath, which will be the mark of the beast. Every world government, represented by the ten kingdoms and ten kings, will seek to enact and enforce laws to accomplish their goal of universal obedience to Sunday observance in order to reinstate their economic prosperity and peace. While these governments will not be willing or able to unite in any other policy decision with the other regional governments, they will be willing to unite on this religious view. We can see the impossibility of many nations uniting and agreeing on political and fiscal agendas, as we watch the European Union struggle with its debt issues. Yet, in a state of global chaos from a devastated world economy and the fallout from disasters, the papacy will be able to take ecclesiastical authority through the galvanizing power of false miracles, signs, and wonders. This power they will use to demand that civil authorities enforce their false sabbath.

Many are awakened to the error of the apostate church and take their stand for the truth when they see the move toward the establishment of religious laws by the civil authorities. As the civil authorities attempt to impose their laws in escalating degrees of sanctions and punishment, those who are of a conscientious mind will see these actions as unchristlike and will detect the errors in a system that proclaims religious authority and compels obedience to its decree. They will see that the religion promoted by the ruling powers is not consistent with their beliefs of a loving God who gave His only Son to preserve our freedom of choice. The ranks of the true believers and followers of God will be bolstered by these conscientious souls.

Those who are looking for the establishment of a one world government, subscribing to conspiracy theories involving any number of secret societies, may not only be disappointed that no such government occurs, but they may also begin to even question prophecy. This is because the anticipated world government union doesn't occur, and the world is, in fact, becoming more fragmented. Perhaps they are waiting for signs of a one world government as a signal to get ready, which doesn't transpire so they become confused and miss the opportunity for spiritual groundwork. Preparing ourselves spiritually and helping others do so are our key responsibilities as Christians, rather than concerning ourselves with conspiracy theories.

This is not to say that there are not groups working against us, for the Bible clearly states that "we wrestle not against flesh and blood, but against principalities, against powers, [and] against spiritual wickedness in high places" (Ephesians 6:12). We need to keep vigilant; we also need to be careful not to get carried away by rumors and theories or locked into any particular views of the end time beyond what is written in the Bible, including those in this book.

Events can take many twists and turns, causing confusion and doubt, thus making it imperative that we have a strong faith in the Word of God rather than in secular theories, no matter how well founded and researched. The devil is a master at trickery and creating falsehoods that look like truth. At the end of Revelation 17, the John stated that the great city is Babylon, which stands for confusion. In the last days confusion will certainly reign as so many theories and ideas will be endorsed, and many will run to and fro looking for truth but will not find it because they have rejected the light that has been given to them.

We need to continue to study the prophecies to expand our understanding of them. Prophecies become clearer as we approach the times of fulfillment and those who vigilantly watch for their fulfillment will be given understanding by God. Our understanding must be in harmony with God's Word and consistent with the Bible's clear established doctrines around the second coming. Revelation 17 gives us a view of the events to happen as we approach the close of probation in order to give us some waymarks to see that time is closing fast.

**Most importantly, we need to realize that the battle is raging now that "the beast that was, and is not" has ascended out of the abyss and is active on this earth now!** The sixth head of the beast is waging a war on both Christians and the world today through creating disbelief in God or by addicting them to pleasures. God warned us six times that the 1,260-day period will end, ushering in a new age and a new type of warfare. The devil is swinging this world between the extremes of religious fervor in the times of the papacy and a completely secular world view as we have today, setting up for a swing back to an ultra religious state.

The pendulum is already moving in that direction. Satan is setting up for his ultimate deception by creating disasters and unrest to try to enact his laws upon the earth. We need to recognize that we must get into the fight now through consecration of self and committed service to others. When the seventh head comes to power by setting up the image to the beast, our probation will be close to an end. If we are waiting for a Sunday law or a one world government to be established before we begin our preparations, let alone active service, we will be far too late.

## Chapter 13

# Slaves and Souls of Men

The merchants of the earth shall weep and mourn over her; for no man buyeth their merchandise any more: the merchandise of gold, and silver, and precious stones, and of pearls, and fine linen, and purple, and silk, and scarlet, and all thyine wood, and all manner vessels of ivory, and all manner vessels of most precious wood, and of brass, and iron, and marble, and cinnamon, and odours, and ointments, and frankincense, and wine, and oil, and fine flour, and wheat, and beasts, and sheep, and horses, and chariots, and slaves, and souls of men. (Revelation 18:11–13)

**Slavery and the Eschaton**

Revelation 18 speaks about the final destruction of Babylon at the end of this world as the judgments of God are poured out upon the earth. "No man buyeth their merchandise anymore" is the lament for those who engaged in traffic with Babylon. All of the fine goods once offered by the city, no one will be left to buy. Of all of the items that Babylon will be trafficking, the last two are of special interest here in this chapter—slaves and the souls of men.

Is the term "slaves" simply a figurative symbol of those who are caught up in the "business" of Babylon, or is there a more literal interpretation of the term? The idea of slaves in the end times does appear more than once in the book of Revelation. In the sixth chapter when sixth seal is opened, we also encounter slaves.

> The heaven departed as a scroll when it is rolled together; and every mountain and island were moved out of their places. And the kings of the earth, and the great men, and the rich men, and the chief captains, and the mighty men, and every bondman, and every free man, hid themselves in the dens and in the rocks of the mountains. (Revelation 6:14, 15)

171

Every bondman and every free man who have not been made righteous will hide themselves from the wrath of the Lamb. Again, is "every bondman" just a symbolic term, or are there literal bondmen, in another word, "slaves," in the end time? If there is slavery in the end times, how will it manifest itself, and what might lead to the conditions in which slavery becomes common place again?

Of course there is slavery already in the world. In developing nations, slaves are an accepted part of the economy and society. In India, debt slaves work to pay off the money they or their families owe.[125] Generations of debt slaves may be working to pay off large family debts. There are also migrant workers who are working for what can only constitute slave labour.[126]

Additionally, children and women are trapped as sex slaves in many countries. This terrible underground economy exists even in rich, developed nations, even in North America.[127]

Are these the forms of slavery that these verses in Revelation are speaking of, or is it a more pervasive type of slavery, the kind that was prevalent in Bible times or even in the middle centuries? In her book *Early Writings*, E. G. White wrote about slavery in the end times. She described an environment of slavery that is reminiscent of the slavery in the 17th to 19th centuries in America in the South. The description is that of national slavery that is openly conducted and permitted by civil and religious authorities.

> His wrath burns against *this nation and especially against the religious bodies that have sanctioned this terrible traffic* and have themselves engaged in it. Such injustice, such oppression, such sufferings, are looked upon with *heartless indifference by many professed followers of the meek and lowly Jesus*. ...

---

[125] Uttar Pradesh, "Generations pay off debt through slavery," The CNN Freedom Project: Ending Modern-Day Slavery, March 8, 2011, http://thecnnfreedomproject.blogs.cnn.com/2011/03/08/generations-pay-off-debts-through-slavery/ Accessed March 2011.

[126] "Demographics," Farmworker Health Factsheet, National Center for Farm Worker Health, Inc., September 2012, http://www.ncfh.org/docs/fs-Migrant%20Demographics.pdf (accessed August 2012)/Lenard Doyle, "Slave labour that shames America," *The Independent*, December 19, 2007, http://www.independent.co.uk/news/world/americas/slave-labour-that-shames-america-765881.html (accessed January 2013).

[127] "Trafficking in Persons Report" US Department of State, June 2012, http://www.state.gov/documents/organization/192587.pdf (accessed January 2013).

Yet those who think and speak thus are at the same time holding human beings in slavery. And this is not all; they sever the ties of nature and cruelly oppress their fellow men. They can inflict most inhuman torture with the same relentless *cruelty manifested by papists and heathen toward Christ's followers* ... God's anger will not cease until He has caused *this land of light* to drink the dregs of the cup of His fury, until He has rewarded unto Babylon double. Reward her even as she rewarded you, double unto her double according to her works; in the cup which she hath filled, fill to her double. (*Early Writings*, 275, 276, emphasis added)

One could easily conclude that she must have been referring to the past as well as her era when slavery was permitted in the United States, but the next paragraph dispels that idea. It, rather, places this environment into the future at the end times.

I saw that the slave master ... will have to answer for the soul of his slave whom he has kept in ignorance; and the sins of the slave will be visited upon the master. God cannot take to heaven the slave who has been kept in ignorance and degradation, knowing nothing of God or the Bible, fearing nothing but his master's lash, and holding a lower position than the brutes. ... *the master must endure the seven last plagues* and then come up in the second resurrection and suffer the second, most awful death. Then the justice of God will be satisfied. (*Early Writings*, 276, emphasis added)

She stated that the master must endure the seven last plagues for his crime of slavery. The seven last plagues are clearly at the end of the world after the close of probation. Furthermore, she stated that the master must answer for the soul of the slave for having kept them from knowledge of God and of the Bible. She indicated that this must happen before the close of probation when souls could still have made a choice to follow God if they had been given the opportunity. This places the slavery in the time prior to the close of probation. The times of tumult precede the closing events, of which we are at the very cusp.

Also, it is clear that this is not speaking about India or other nations, but rather a professedly Christian nation. She referred to the nation as the "land of light," which would indicate that it is the very nation that had been given the favored status in receiving the light in these last days, the United

States. How does this land of freedom turn back to a state that allows slavery after having abolished slavery only about 150 years ago? How can a land that saw battles fought so hard for equality for every color, nationality, gender, and age turn back to slavery? How can the religious leaders sanction such action along with the national civil authorities? How can the people accept such an amendment to the laws of this country? We look to the Bible again for understanding.

In the 47th chapter of Genesis, the last part of the story of Joseph and the seven-year of famine is told. After the seven years of plenty, during which Joseph stored up grain, the seven years of famine came. A few years into the famine, his brothers went to Egypt to buy grain from him, and we have the familiar story of the eventual happy reunion of the sons of Jacob. Then the story goes on to tell about what happened in the later years of the famine.

> There was no bread in all the land; for the famine was very sore, so that the land of Egypt and all the land of Canaan fainted by reason of the famine. And Joseph gathered up all the money that was found in the land of Egypt, and in the land of Canaan, for the corn which they bought: and Joseph brought the money into Pharaoh's house.

> And when money failed in the land of Egypt, and in the land of Canaan, all the Egyptians came unto Joseph, and said, Give us bread: for why should we die in thy presence? for the money faileth. And Joseph said, Give your cattle; and I will give you for your cattle, if money fail. And they brought their cattle unto Joseph: and Joseph gave them bread in exchange for horses, and for the flocks, and for the cattle of the herds, and for the asses: and he fed them with bread for all their cattle for that year.

> When that year was ended, they came unto him the second year, and said unto him, We will not hide it from my lord, how that our money is spent; my lord also hath our herds of cattle; there is not ought left in the sight of my lord, but our bodies, and our lands: wherefore shall we die before thine eyes, both we and our land? buy us and our land for bread, and we and our land will be servants unto Pharaoh: and give us seed, that we may live, and not die, that the land be not desolate.

And Joseph bought all the land of Egypt for Pharaoh; for the Egyptians sold every man his field, because the famine prevailed over them: so the land became Pharaoh's. And as for the people, he removed them to cities from one end of the borders of Egypt even to the other end thereof. Only the land of the priests bought he not; for the priests had a portion assigned them of Pharaoh, and did eat their portion which Pharaoh gave them: wherefore they sold not their lands.

Then Joseph said unto the people, Behold, I have bought you this day and your land for Pharaoh: lo, here is seed for you, and ye shall sow the land. And it shall come to pass in the increase, that ye shall give the fifth part unto Pharaoh, and four parts shall be your own, for seed of the field, and for your food, and for them of your households, and for food for your little ones. And they said, Thou hast saved our lives: let us find grace in the sight of my lord, and we will be Pharaoh's servants. (Genesis 47:13–25)

**Debt Slaves**

So the story is told that, as the seven years of famine wore on, the people went to Joseph to buy grain. As their money ran out, they offered their cattle to Joseph as well in exchange for grain and bread. Then as the famine continued to last, they finally sold their land and themselves as slaves to Pharaoh. This story of Joseph and the Egyptians during the seven years of famine may be more than an interesting anecdote of the life of Joseph. It has not escaped the notice of even the public media that the seven years before the financial crisis hit in 2008, there appeared to be seven of the most prosperous years for the global economy, at least on the surface.

In these seven years of plenty everyone purchased homes and luxuries, even while amassing substantial amounts of debt, as had been discussed earlier in this book. Since the crisis hit, households have been trying to deleverage, to get out of debt, and to avoid falling into financial difficulties or even bankruptcy. In spite of their efforts, many homeowners are falling further behind. According to a CNBC report in November 2011, more than 50% of US home mortgages are now effectively underwater or in a negative equity position.[128] These homeowners cannot sell their houses and move to try and lower their costs. Other measures of debt have been

---

128 Diana Olick, "Half of US Mortgages Are Effectively Underwater," CNBC, November 8, 2011, http://www.cnbc.com/id/45209336/Half_of_US_Mortgages_Are_Effectively_Underwater, (accessed August 2012).

decreasing as consumers have pulled back on their lines of credit, loans, and credit cards. However, it has been those who are financially better off who have been able to manage this deleveraging. Meanwhile, those who have lost their jobs, or those who are forced to work only part time or at a lower-paying job, have not managed to reduce their levels of debt.

One of the most troublesome areas of increased indebtedness is in the area of student loans. The total amount of student loans in the US has now surpassed credit card debt. With nearly $870 billion in outstanding loans, student loans outstrip credit card debt of $693 billion, according to the US Federal Reserve. Furthermore, a *Los Angeles Times* reported that the amount of student loan delinquency is now about 27%.[129] The reports quoted a University of California, Berkeley study that finds only 40% to 50% of students enrolling in a university program actually graduate.

To compound the problem the employment to population ratio for the 25–29 age group remains low, currently around 74% in 2012 and down from 78% in 2002, according to the US Bureau of Labor Statistics.[130] While the government tries to make postsecondary education more affordable by making it easier for students to get loans, the number of jobs, particularly at a management level with commensurate pay for a college graduate, continues to decline. So with increasing competition for these scarce jobs, students are seeking higher levels of education, which means additional years of tuition in order to become more marketable. Universities are responding to the increasing demand for higher education by expanding their schools and programs, but higher demand means higher prices, which is basic economics.

Still, at the end of the day, there are not enough jobs to meet the demand of all of the college-educated students. To top off this problem, student loans are not forgiven, even under personal bankruptcy. As an obligation to the federal government, like taxes, there is no way to get out from under these obligations. A March 2012 report by the Federal Reserve Bank of New York indicated that 27% of all federal student loans are now more than 30 days delinquent![131] Even with interest rates at the lowest levels ever, this is a proverbial ticking time bomb.

---

129 Don Lee, "Report on college loan delinquency rate raises alarms," *Los Angeles Times*, March 5, 2012, http://articles.latimes.com/2012/mar/05/business/la-fi-student-loan-delinquencies-20120306, (accessed August 2012).

130 "Labor Force Statistics from Current Population Survey," Bureau of Labor Statistics, http://data.bls.gov/pdq/querytool.jsp?survey=ln (accessed January 2013).

131 "Student Loan Debt History," US Federal Reserve Bank of New York, http://www.newyorkfed.org/studentloandebt/ (accessed August 2012).

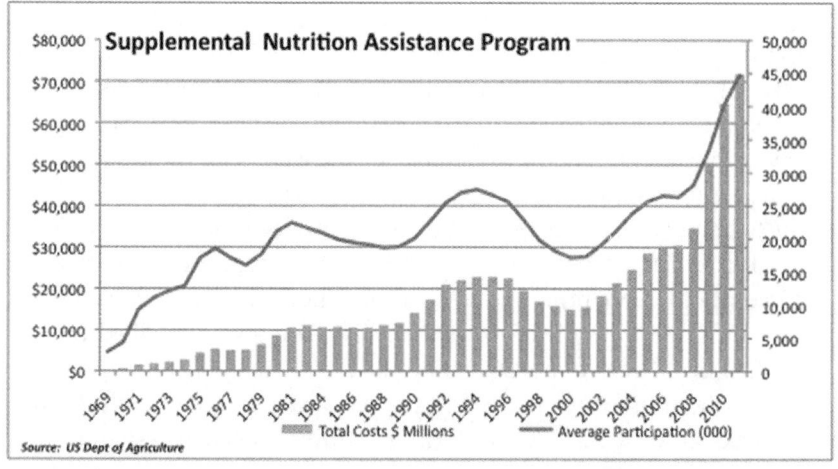

It has been more than four years since the start of the financial crisis, and many are struggling under the increased weight of debt, joblessness and despair. Usage of food stamps has climbed to a record 46.6 million people, according to the US Department of Agriculture in its monthly report (see chart).[132] Unemployment remains at a high level, unlike other periods of economic recovery after a recession. Home prices remain depressed, without any improvement on the horizon. Students are seeking more loans to get more education for jobs that just do not exist.

Like the Egyptians during the seven years of famine, people are running out of money to maintain their existence. The end of the famine or financial crisis seems to be nowhere in sight for many families. They are reaching the end of their ropes. To compound matters, if the US "defaults" on its debt, the currency becomes devalued, and hyperinflation sets in as we have seen revealed in prophecy, what will be the repercussions to those already in dire straits? Furthermore, what will be the response of those who hold the debt against those who are their debtors? The Joseph-and-the-Egyptians scenario may be played out again. Debtors may be obliged to work for their lenders as debt slaves, like other parts of the world currently have. On the other hand, those who have become so accustomed to the amenities of this world, its entertainments, and its pleasures may find that being without these comforts is unacceptable and offer themselves to the highest bidder who will buy them to maintain their lifestyles. Like some

---

132 "Supplemental Nutrition Assistance Program Participation and Costs," US Department of Agriculture, December 7, 2012, http://www.fns.usda.gov/pd/SNAPsummary.htm (accessed January 2013).

drug addicts who sell themselves to maintain their habits, those addicted to the material things of this world may get their "fix" by selling themselves, only to find that they have become a slave to a brutal master. This world continues to diverge into the haves and the have-nots, the 1% and the 99%, in terms of wealth, which may be the enabler of these events.

Governments, financial institutions, and corporations are much more prone to take action to ensure their own survival regardless of the cost. The cost will be borne by the taxpayers and the ordinary citizens of the country. The people of Greece protested to no avail as hundreds of billions of euros in bailout money was given to them. These bailouts only bailed out the banks that held Greek bonds, which would have defaulted otherwise. None of these bailout funds would benefit the people of Greece directly. Rather, the Greeks now face greater austerity measures, higher taxes, and fewer services. The hundreds of billions of euros of debt were downloaded onto their backs without any say in the matter.

Mrs. White indicated that this was national slavery with even the sanction of Christian churches. These churches would naturally represent apostate churches that would be called Babylon. A nationally approved slave trade would likely not be along the lines of race or ethnicity, given the history of the United States. Governments seem to be increasingly sensitive in being politically correct with respect to race, ethnicity, gender, and even sexual orientation. Society may find, however, that it is acceptable for an individual who borrowed significant sums of money cannot repay these debts or afford even the basics of life. They will find themselves bound by their debts to their lenders, particularly if that lender is the government of the United States. A euphemism will surely be found for the term; nevertheless, they will be debt slaves to their lender or to the government.

As the Spirit of God is gradually removed from the world, and they are left more fully to the control of Satan, as churches apostatize more fully, and as politicians seek to appease the people, the idea of a slave trade in this country may become acceptable. As events continue to escalate toward the close of probation, the situation is like to worsen and become as the vision records—a world where brutal slavery is practiced, where basic human rights are denied, and the Bible and God are kept from the slave, lest they understand the truth and be set free.

The idea of slavery in this modern age is unthinkable, but this world may be approaching an atmosphere that will make it acceptable. Various conditions are already coming into place that will facilitate this transformation. If the vision is correct, then it would be in our best interests to consider and avoid any situations that may put ourselves and our families at risk of falling victim to this tragedy.

Revelation speaks about the fall of Babylon and how the merchants mourn because no one buys her merchandise any longer: "beasts, and sheep, and horses, and chariots, and slaves, and souls of men" (Revelation 18:13). James also wrote:

> Your gold and silver is cankered; and the rust of them shall be a witness against you, and shall eat your flesh as it were fire. Ye have heaped treasure together for the last days. Behold, the hire of the labourers who have reaped down your fields, which is of you kept back by fraud, crieth: and the cries of them which have reaped are entered into the ears of the Lord of sabaoth. Ye have lived in pleasure on the earth, and been wanton; ye have nourished your hearts, as in a day of slaughter. Ye have condemned and killed the just; and he doth not resist you. (James 5:3–6)

Speaking of those who oppress their workers, holding back the hire of the labourers, James said that their cries have reached "the Lord of sabaoth." Their gold and their silver are cankered and will become a witness against them. Those who abuse their workers, perhaps even as slaves, will receive a severe judgment from God. However, it will not bring back those whom they have abased and kept from salvation. Revelation 6:15 says that "the great men, and the rich men ... every bondman, and free man" will hide themselves in the rocks and cry to the rock to fall on them to hide them from "the wrath of the Lamb" (Revelation 6:16).

We don't know how slavery will make a resurgence. The above discourse is only one plausible scenario of how it may take place. It is certain that the price of freedom is eternal vigilance. As stated by Edmund Burke, the British statesman and philosopher: "All that is necessary for the triumph of evil is that good men do nothing."[133] We must oppose any encroachment on our liberties and rights by pen and voice. As people who are given this light, our responsibility is to guard freedom as long and as far as possible, even if the prophecy eventually must come true. It is our duty to work to save as many as we can before these events come to fruition.

As parents of children, be they younger or nearly adults, our vigilance needs to be doubled. If one of our children were to become a slave, what

---

133 Martin Porter, "A study of a Web quotation," http://tartarus.org/martin/essays/burkequote.html (accessed January 2013).

would we sacrifice in order to gain their freedom? Would we not give our all to rescue them? Would it not be better to protect them from falling into such a situation?

Averting financial encumbrances and steering clear from debt may be the key means to avoid being caught in this tragedy. Steer clear of lingering around Egypt, or in other words—get out of the cities—would be the lesson we could learn from Joseph and Jacob's family. Finally, trusting in God for our every need and being trained to endure hardships will keep us from making the compromises that may lead to our captivity. These are principles that we should be following daily, not just because they may help us to keep away from becoming enslaved. God's foresight is always keen and effective, and these principles for daily living may keep us from harm's ways and from putting ourselves in danger unnecessarily.

---

My wife and I have always held the goal of having our children attend a Christian university to gain a solid education to prepare them for the workforce and to potentially find a life partner. We also had a goal to accomplish this without the need for student loans that would place an undue burden on our children while they would be trying to establish lives as independent adults. With the realization of potential dangers of indebtedness in the end times, the need to keep our students debt-free may be of even greater importance. The financial crisis put a significant dent in our preparedness, but through God's grace we are somehow managing. This has been a real test for our faith and trust in the providence of God, but it has worked to strengthen our belief.

As I look back, I see that God has always been there guiding and leading our family, even when I wasn't really listening. He was working to protect us from my own bad choices, striking the perfect balance between consequences, life lessons, spiritual growth, and answered prayers. Even those prayers that I really didn't know how to pray, God didn't leave me with only consequences of the choices I had made and the wanderings from my relationship with Him. He did, however, leave me with enough repercussion to allow me to learn the life lessons that I needed to learn, to struggle with my faith, to rethink the world around me, to change the way I looked at the world, and to help establish a new world view that would guide my thoughts. He helped me to grow in faith and trust and to seek Him more earnestly through these lessons and consequences, allowing me to have the time and space for spiritual growth to gain a better understanding of His ways and plans.

Amazingly, He has allowed our family to come through these circumstances and to still approach our dreams and aspirations that were in harmony with His principles. Our dreams of puting our kids through a Christian education are about half way accomplished, and certainly there is more work needs to be done. Day by day I grow more confident and grateful in the providence of God to get us to the end. Yet, even as we are winning this battle with God's grace, the danger remains of a relapse into a state of false security, particularly for a "recovering" Laodicean. As my children finish school so that my time and resources are freed up, what will I do with them?

## Chapter 14

## Lovers of Pleasure

This know also, that in the last days perilous times shall come. For men shall be lovers of their own selves, covetous, boasters, proud, blasphemers, disobedient to parents, unthankful, unholy, without natural affection, trucebreakers, false accusers, incontinent, fierce, despisers of those that are good, traitors, heady, highminded, lovers of pleasures more than lovers of God. (2 Timothy 3:1-4)

The topic of "fun" may be one of the most difficult to address given the very personal nature of the issue—this short word means so many different things to different people. It can be simple and innocent or decadent and perverse. The same fun activity could be uplifting or degrading, depending on situations and those involved. Fun can last for a moment, or even be found just in a thought, or fun can require vast amounts of energy and resources to acquire. Fun can be found in any situation and in any location. Our pastimes can be fun, our entertainment can be fun, our social interactions can be fun, our family life can be fun, and even our work can be fun. The word can be used in so many contexts that it almost defies description. Yet, it may be fair to say that everyone would like to have a bit of fun in their life.

The nature of fun has changed over the years, but particularly in the past century. Or it may be more correctly observed that fun has expanded and grown in that there are more ways to have fun now than ever before in human existence. What was fun for our grandparents is still fun; yet, what catches the attention of this generation is often far different. Each generation has difficulty understanding the kind of fun the next generation is having. Nevertheless, with each succeeding generation, it would seem that fun is becoming more of a right than a privilege, particularly in any affluent society.

It is inconceivable for most in today's society to live without fun. It is what most of us live for each day or look forward to at the end of a work day. A weekend without fun would simply be a disaster as fun the motivation for many. It's the reason to go to work and earn enough money to have some fun. It's the driving force for people, and, of course, it is money that gives us the ability to partake.

We train ourselves to need fun. We long to be stimulated every moment. We are "plugged in" at every opportunity. Now though social media, we can tell our "friends" and "followers," what we are doing and how much fun we are having at this very moment. It's as if our fun isn't fun unless we are telling others about it. It's like high-tech bragging. We raise our children on fun, taking them from one activity to another in order to fill up their lives with fun, lest they feel deprived of life because they didn't have fun today. Modern technology allows kids to take the fun with them, record it for later viewing, and share it with their friends. It seems our every moment, every thought, and every imagination is geared toward having fun.

Is fun wrong? If so, what would make fun wrong? Or at what point does fun become sin? Is it the specific activity? Is it the frequency or volume of fun? Is it the cost of having fun? Is it the motivation? These are difficult if not nearly impossible questions to answer since fun can be so many things to so many people. We can try to define what fun is, but that may quickly lead to a legalistic assessment. It should be easy to see that trying to judge the activity is pointless as it just results in endless debate. Yet we need some way to evaluate fun to gauge its influences and consequences.

Perhaps the only safe way to examine this idea of fun is to measure it against the yardstick of our relationship with God and our purpose for existence, particularly in the light of "present truth" and the mission we are charged with. What function does fun serve in your life? How much does it require of you? Furthermore, we need to make a distinction between what is fun and what really satisfies the soul, between what is simply a distraction and that truly adds to our sense of being.

Is our Christian experience like one stuck in the waiting room in an airport while our flight has been delayed? We look for any distraction to pass the time as we await the boarding call, visiting with fellow passengers, playing some games, or watching the airport lounge TV while glancing at the flight announcements to see if the schedule has changed. Existing without much purpose other than simply passing the time and staying out of trouble, we just wait for the plane, knowing that our ticket is secure.

The real question is: are we "lovers of pleasures, more than lovers of God" (2 Timothy 3:4)? To be able to answer this question requires an examination of the heart, which we are not capable of doing for others. Only for ourselves and only in open honesty with God can we determine which we love more. Do we love pleasure because for a time it releases our minds from the requirements of God because deep down in our hearts we find them restrictive? Do we live vicariously by the lives of those we see in media since our lives are so lifeless? How do we feel about doing God's will? Are we even taking the time to know His will? Do we have a love for souls that would make striving for their salvation our pleasure?

The love of pleasure and the love of money that facilitates the pleasure are at the core of our Laodicean experience. So ingrained is the love of pleasure in our lives that we can scarcely see that it is so. We, like the prodigal son, have received the rich blessing of God's grace, but we are spending it on the desires of our hearts. A closer look at the story of the prodigal son through the pen of E. G. White may explain in greater detail the lesson that Jesus was giving.

> The youth acknowledges no obligation to his father, and expresses no gratitude; yet he claims the privilege of a child in sharing his father's goods. ...

> With money in plenty, and liberty to do as he likes, he flatters himself that the desire of his heart is reached. ...

> The wealth which he has selfishly claimed from his father he squanders upon harlots. The treasure of his young manhood is wasted. The precious years of life, the strength of intellect, the bright visions of youth, the spiritual aspirations—all are consumed in the fires of lust. (*Christ's Object Lessons*, 199)

The prodigal son wanted the benefits of being a son without the obligations to, or the relationship with, his father. His aim was to fulfill the desires of his heart, but then E. G. White described the real prodigal.

> What a picture here of the sinner's state! Although surrounded with the blessings of His love, there is nothing that the sinner, bent on self-indulgence and sinful pleasure, desires so much as separation from God. Like the ungrateful son, he claims the good things of God as his by right. He takes them as a matter of course, and makes no return of gratitude, renders no service of love. (*Christ's Object Lessons*, 200)

We often think of the prodigal as the wayward son who lost his way, who left the church to go out into the world. The above quotation paints a different picture of the prodigal as perhaps the Christian who takes the love and blessings of God for granted in seeking after his own pleasure. The sinner is not the worldly one who knows nothing of God; he is, rather, the unfaithful Christian who claims the "good things of God as his by right," but "renders no service of love." We know the world today is bent on having fun; even we in the church are caught up in fun. "Good, clean fun," we might argue. Nevertheless, we are with the world in being lovers of pleasure more than lovers of God. Our daily choices reveal this fact. We spend more time and effort in having fun and enjoying the pleasures of this world than in seeking God and seeking to save the lost. Here we see the true condition of the prodigal and, by extension, our true condition.

> The man who separates from God that he may serve himself, is the slave of mammon. The mind that God created for the companionship of angels has become degraded to the service of that which is earthly and bestial. This is the end to which self-serving tends. If you have chosen such a life, you know that you are spending money for that which is not bread, and labor for that which satisfieth not. There come to you hours when you realize your degradation. (*Christ's Object Lessons*, 200)

We have become slaves to money and degraded by the life of pleasure that we seek. We, like the prodigal son, have received an abundance of blessings from our Father; yet, we neither acknowledge His goodness nor our responsibility toward Him. We believe ourselves to be "rich, and increased with goods, and have need of nothing" (Revelation 3:17). We often do not see our true state of being until our situation changes. Similarly, for the young prodigal his joy was turned to sorrow. A great famine arises and the prodigal finds himself out of money, out of work, and out of friends. Mrs. White further wrote:

> The youth who has boasted of his liberty, now finds himself a slave. He is in the worst of bondage—"holden with the cords of his sins." (Proverbs 5:22.) ... Where now is his riotous joy? Stilling his conscience, benumbing his sensibilities, he thought himself happy; but now, with money spent, with hunger unsatisfied, with pride humbled, with his moral nature dwarfed, with his will weak

and untrustworthy, with his finer feelings seemingly dead, he is the most wretched of mortals. (*Christ's Object Lessons*, 200)

The prodigal was trying to still his conscience and numb his senses though pleasure. Likewise, we have quieted our conscience or drowned it out by the constant barrage of media. Debased by our desire for pleasure, we have no ability to extricate ourselves from this trap. Yet God is still working on us and for us. The parable shows that God had a plan for returning the prodigal son to both his senses and to his father. Additionally, Mrs. White wrote:

> The love of God still yearns over the one who has chosen to separate from Him, and *He sets in operation influences to bring him back to the Father's house*. The prodigal son in his wretchedness "came to himself." The deceptive power that Satan had exercised over him was broken. He saw that his suffering was the result of his own folly, and he said, "How many hired servants of my father's have bread enough and to spare, and I perish with hunger! I will arise and go to my father." Miserable as he was, the prodigal found hope in the conviction of his father's love. It was that love which was drawing him toward home. So it is the assurance of God's love that constrains the sinner to return to God. "The goodness of God leadeth thee to repentance." Romans 2:4. A golden chain, the mercy and compassion of divine love, is passed around every imperiled soul. The Lord declares, "I have loved thee with an everlasting love; therefore with loving-kindness have I drawn thee." Jeremiah 31:3. (*Christ's Object Lessons*, 202, emphasis added)

It is God's love that draws us back to Him, but He allowed the prodigal to be put into a situation that broke the power of Satan over him. God set "in operation influences to bring him back to the Father's house." God permitted a financial crisis in the land to win back the prodigal's senses, so he could see through the deception of the enemy and think about the love and the goodness of his Father.

Once again, God's method of restoration is again revealed in the parable. Similar to the Israelites who had returned from Babylon, God sent a famine, an economic crisis, to awaken His people from the stupor caused by their love of money and pleasure. Since our attention has been drawn by our love of money, of pleasure, and of ease, the removal of these things will allow us to return our focus and trust to God because we have no power fix our lives. Even as we are convicted of our need to repent from our lives of pleasure-seeking, we have no ability to change our hearts. Our hearts are desperately wicked, and we cannot find our own way back to the Father. No acts of piety will free our hearts from the grip that Satan has on them through the pleasures of this world. Only by pleading to God and allowing His Spirit to change us can we be made a son again.

One of the great tragedies of this generation is the loss of our individual freedoms and the decline of the free society. Along with this tragedy is the decline of a free market society that provides equal opportunities to every person with an idea and the willingness to work hard. This loss of freedoms and opportunities comes from our lackadaisical attitude toward the government and the political process. Freedoms are being eroded and wealth is being stolen from right under our noses; yet, most people are blissfully unaware of what is happening. Many have been so medicated by entertainment and pleasure-seeking that they are oblivious to these losses.

Since 9/11 there has been a steady erosion of rights in the United States, starting with the passing of the Patriot Act, which expanded the powers of the government to defend the country against terrorism. These expanded powers allow the government to encroach on the civil rights of its citizens. According to the New York Civil Liberties Union,[134] there are eight areas in which civil rights have been degraded since 9/11, include the following:

- First Amendment right to freedom of speech—the government can define those who engage in nonviolent civil disobedience as terrorists.

- First Amendment right to freedom of association—the government can now monitor the activities of any religious or political group.

- Fourth Amendment right to freedom from unreasonable search and seizures—the government can conduct searches of your home or workplace without reasonable cause.

---

134 "Eroding Liberty," New York Bill of Rights Defense Campaign, New York Civil Liberties Union, http://www.nyclu.org/pdfs/eroding_liberty.pdf (accessed April 2012).

- Fifth Amendment right to due process—the government can detain anyone they classify as a threat to security without a formal charge.

- Sixth Amendment right to legal representation and a speedy trial—the government can hold people indefinitely without charge, be denied access to an attorney, and without trial.

- Eighth Amendment right to freedom from cruel and unusual punishments—the government can place individuals in solitary confinement without charge and without access to their families.

- Fourteenth Amendment right to equal protection under the law—the government can monitor individuals because of their race, religion, or nationality.

This has been continuing since 9/11; yet, most Americans are unaware of these erosions of liberty. The few who are aware have done little to take action against these incursions.

Likewise, there has been steady erosion in American's wealth and financial freedoms by a stealthy yet deliberate effort to maintain a financial system that is broken. Since the start of the financial crisis, the US Treasury and the US Federal Reserve have undertaken the task of stabilizing financial institutions and corporations at the expense of America's citizens. The bailouts, deficit spending by the Treasury, and the zero interest rate policy (ZIRP) by the Fed are resulting in a de facto taxation of the people without any representation. The bailouts have propped up banks at the expense of taxpayers, still allowing banks to earn record profits and bonuses. The taxpayers have received no benefit from this additional tax.

While the bailed out banks would argue that the financial system has been saved and financial Armageddon avoided, this intervention was done without direct consultation and representation of the people to consider such a costly program. People were basically told that this must be done, or we will have the destruction of the financial system and economic chaos. There was little talk about any other alternative programs. Also, ZIRP resulted in punishing savers who diligently put their money into the banking system for retirement or other needs. Savers gain no benefit from putting their money into a bank because they continue to lose purchasing power as inflation steadily decreases the value of their savings. ZIRP forces savers to invest their money in riskier assets in order to stay ahead of inflation.

Financial institutions benefit from ZIRP by being able to borrow at essentially zero interest rates while they can earn great rates of return from lending or investing in longer-term assets that pay higher interest rates.

The constitution is changed and individual rights are trampled while the people tune into *American Idol* to vote for their favorite singer. The Federal Reserve System steals money literally right out of people's pockets, and the people go out for a night of shopping or dinner. Wall Street looses trillions of dollars, destroys the value of homes, then gets bailed out and pays themselves large bonuses; all the while, people are planning their next renovation project. The media tells them that all is well in the economy, and so they continue to live their lives carelessly, in spite of the disaster that is brewing.

The average citizen has become too distracted to take notice, too busy to take action, and too jaded to think anything can be done. So they tune out the things that are important, that impact their lives, and tune into their favorite show or the "game" or any number of diversions. The government handouts enable and ensure that this destructive behavior remains in place, giving people just enough to keep them on the hook of pleasures and pastimes.

Our constant need for pleasure-seeking is not only keeping us from developing a deeper relationship with God, but it is also allowing those with power to change the rules. This sets us up for a time in the very near future when human rights will be trampled, religious freedoms will be taken, and even slavery will be accepted again. Furthermore, when God's severe reproof is given, His means of bringing His people back to their senses is put in operation, and the world is in turmoil, the pleasure-seeking crowd will be depressed and angered by the loss of their favorite gratifications.

When they are told that this is the result of a small group of people who will not conform to the laws of the land, their ire will be turned toward God's true commandment-keeping people. They will fail to see that these new laws are unconscionable and immoral. Their desire will be to regain their worldly wealth and their worldly pleasures. The natural outcome will be the oppression of all peoples who are seen as obstacles. "Whose end is destruction, whose God is their belly, and whose glory is in their shame, who mind earthly things" (Philippians 3:19). In such a world, spiraling out of control and persecuted by the pleasure-seeking crowd, how can we find the fortitude to stand for truth? Where can we train today to meet the tests that are sure to come tomorrow?

## Chapter 15

# Joseph and His Two Coats

The story of Joseph has many points of instruction some of which we have already studied. There is another part of the story of Joseph that would be instructional and inspirational to those of us living in the time of the end. In a happier time for Joseph during his younger years, he was the beloved of his father Jacob. The family of Jacob was quite the dysfunctional family with siblings from four different mothers, two who were wives and two who were concubines. The older brothers appeared to be constantly in competition with each other. They also seemed to possess more than a few nasty character traits. In spite of Jacob being a godly man, his sons appeared to be out of control, except Joseph and Benjamin, who were the sons of Rachel, Jacob's true love. Whether he did so intentionally or not, it was obvious to all of the family that Joseph was the favored of the father, and this gave rise to hard feelings from his brothers. Of course Joseph's dreams did not help the situation.

We should be familiar with the story: Jacob gave Joseph a coat of many colors to express his love and favor toward Joseph. There are, nonetheless, questions. Why did Jacob give this coat to Joseph? Why is it recorded in the Bible? Is it just an interesting anecdote, a sideline to the story to help thicken the plot? Was it simply the object that became the focal point of the anger of his brothers? Or did God use the situation as another lesson for us to help us understand His ways? This was yet another one of my mental queries that long went unanswered until recently.

Joseph did not see how his position of favor affected his brothers. The Bible gives the impression that he was oblivious to their feelings of animosity toward him. He spoke of his dreams, wondering aloud about their meanings, not realizing that it further alienated him from them. Perhaps he did know, so he deliberately pushed their buttons, knowing that his father favored him. Regardless of which condition was true, it was also true that he did not perceive any danger to himself when he went to visit his brothers one afternoon on an errand for his father. So it was that Joseph, the beloved of his father, was on a journey to search for his brothers. Full of confidence and feelings of superiority, he didn't understand the danger he was in.

Dressed in his coat of many colors, which represented the love of his father, he arrived at the place where his brothers were keeping the sheep. Seeing Joseph and his colorful coat, his brothers' anger was fired up. They suddenly seized him, ripped the coat from him, and threw him into a pit, intending to kill him; perhaps they were uncertain as to how to do it or who would be the one to carry out the act. Joseph did not understand what was happening to him, or why his brothers were treating him so. He appealed to their sense of right and to their relationship, but his brothers would not hear him. The brothers were persuaded by the oldest, Reuben, to spare his life; instead, they sold him as a slave to a caravan going to Egypt. So it was that his brothers persecuted Joseph for his favored status with the father, raising false accusations against him. Note the point that it was ultimately the sorrow that his brothers felt for persecuting their brother Joseph that caused them to repent and become changed men.

Joseph didn't understand why this was happening to him. He did not know why God was "punishing" him. It was a sore trial. Yet, Joseph determined in his heart to serve God. God acknowledged that determination and blessed Joseph. He upheld Joseph with the right hand of His righteousness. God had a purpose for Joseph and for the trials that he faced.

As we know, Joseph was bought by Potiphar as a slave. God's blessing was on Joseph, and Potiphar recognized this. Joseph gained the trust of Potiphar, who then put Joseph in charge of all of his wealth. Because of God's blessing on Joseph, Potiphar and his house was blessed as well. So it is that the determination to obey God has a wide-reaching benefit for many others. Nevertheless, the next great test was soon to come upon him.

Joseph not only caught the eye of Potiphar but also of his wife. Joseph was a young man and in the prime of his life. His life of service likely made him fit and healthy, and his character would have been attractive. Potiphar's wife took notice of Joseph, and she tried to seduce him. Joseph did not respond to her advances. She likely tried repeatedly to convince Joseph to take her offer, perhaps even reminding him that he was a slave and that he must obey her wishes. Yet, Joseph would not yield to temptation. In the climactic occasion, Joseph was alone with Potiphar's wife, and she made a final attempt to tempt Joseph. She demanded that Joseph obey her wishes, and she to hold of Joseph's coat to pull him closer to her. E. G. Write wrote of this occasion.

Few temptations are more dangerous or more fatal to young men than the temptation to sensuality, and none if yielded to will prove so decidedly ruinous to soul and body for time and eternity. The welfare of his entire future is suspended upon the decision of a moment. *Joseph calmly casts his eyes to heaven for help, slips off his loose outer garment, leaving it in the hand of his tempter,* and while his eye is lighted with determined resolve in the place of unholy passion, he exclaims, "How can I do this great wickedness, and sin against God?" The victory is gained; he flees from the enchanter; he is saved. (*Manuscript Releases*, vol. 4, 221, emphasis added)

Joseph certainly understood the situation that he was in. Potiphar's wife was demanding that he, as a slave, obey her demands. He knew his refusal would enrage her and would have severe consequences. The harlot woman was trying by all means at her disposal to get Joseph to enter into sin, but Joseph would not. Joseph had learned by his early trials to trust in God and place his life in God's hands. Joseph did not try to debate her or try to negotiate his way out of the situation.

Joseph did not regard his early position as something of any value compared to his relationship with God. He did not enter into any conversation or negotiation to try to save himself, but rather, he left consequences in God's hands. Unlike Eve, who fell into the trap of conversing with the devil, Joseph rebuked Potiphar's wife and walked away. This example of Joseph is one for us to learn in dealing with the temptations that will surely come our way to entice us to keep our earthly possessions and positions. He calmly looked up to heaven to gain strength, and he let go of his coat, leaving it in the hands of the temptress.

"How ... can I do this great wickedness, and sin against God?" he exclaimed, looking directly at her.

With her sin exposed and called out, she retaliated against Joseph, falsely accusing him of trying to make advances at her. With his wife making such accusations, Potiphar had no choice but to send Joseph to prison, though the fact that he spared Joseph's life indicates that Potiphar understood the situation.

Consider the symbolism of the two coats and their meaning. The first time Joseph had a coat, he was at home in the favor of his father. The coat was a token of the love and favor of his father; yet, it was perceived by his brothers as a sign of Joseph's superiority over them. Joseph was naïve to the feelings of his brothers and exacerbated the situation by telling his dreams.

The coat became a symbol of Joseph's status and position with his father and was hated by his brothers.

When his brothers turned on Joseph, they stripped him of his coat, symbolically taking from him all of the wealth he had as a son of Jacob. Joseph did not know why this was happening to him. Like Job, he did not understand that a greater plan was being played out. He could not see God's wonderful providence working to preserve his family, to restore the relationship with his brothers, and to form in him a Christ-like character. All he saw was his world being torn from him, and the darkness of uncertainty was being cast over him. Nevertheless, Joseph resolved to follow God and maintain his faith in Him. He learned to have an unflinching trust in God as he began to see that God was working in his life. So much so that when Potiphar's wife tempted him, he had no inclination to fall. She grabbed his outer garment to take from him either his virtue or his position.

When his coat of many colors was taken from him, he had no choice and no understanding of the events. Yet, unlike this first time his garment was taken from him by his brothers, when Potiphar's wife grabbed his coat, Joseph knew exactly the consequences of what would take place. Joseph had full knowledge of the decision that faced him. He willingly let go of the garment, fully knowing that he faced hardship and possibly death, but hewas undaunted by either outcome. He made the decision in a heartbeat, although it was a determination forged through perseverance and trust in God over many earlier trials. He looked to heaven and calmly let go of the coat, leaving it in her tempting hand.

God, in His great mercy and understanding of our characters, may be preparing us for a time when we must make a similar decision, a decision between our virtue and our possessions. A time will come when we will be faced with a choice to comply with those who will force our compliance with manmade laws or to face the repercussion of following God's commandments. Our choice will be to either follow the world and its temptations or give up our possessions and positions to leave all in order to follow God. The decisions we make now will affect the decisions we make then and will have eternal ramifications.

A law will be urged upon us to worship on a spurious Sabbath day, a false day, instead of the true and holy Sabbath. This will be done in stages; with each step the pressure to comply will escalate. Just like Potiphar's wife pressed her advances toward Joseph with greater force at each rejection, our opponents will increase theirs. If we compromise on the first step, the next step will become harder to resist, making it easier to fall. Only as we stand firm from before the trial even starts, can we hope to be victorious in the trial. Only as we have put all of our worldly possessions and our positions on the altar of sacrifice today, can we hope to be able to make the right decisions when the challenges come tomorrow.

So it is that God may be placing in our path a crisis by which we will learn to let go of the world and cling to Him. Just like the first time Joseph lost his garment at the hands of his brothers, God may be working to strip us of our worldly possessions in order that we may learn to trust Him. This financial crisis may be the means that God uses to cure us of the love of money and the love of pleasure so we may be ready to stand for God when the final trials come.

When all earthly support is cut off, we need to have a firm experience in leaning on God for our every need, to have the faith to carry on for Him. This is accomplished by our passing through the financial crisis today. Furthermore, the crisis is necessary as a means to activate God's people to put their all into the gospel work now. This is the dual purpose of the economic calamity we are living in today. These two functions of the ordeal are necessary as it is not sufficient for Christians to make ourselves ready for the time of trouble, but we need to prepare others to be ready as well. So how much more urgent is our need to get ready when the salvation of so many others will be dependent upon our work? Ultimately, it is this work of serving God and seeking to save the lost that will befit us to meet the last trials.

Joseph worked as a servant for many years, learning humility and trust, obedience and faith in God. As a servant he had no possessions to lose, which made his decision simpler. All he had were his virtue and character, which could not be taken from him by force. How much simpler will our decision be for Christ if we have laid our all on the altar and have given it to the Lord? How much easier will it be when a choice will be demanded of us if all we have in this world is a Christ-like character and His robe of righteousness?

## Chapter 16

# The Law of the Medes and Persians Which Altereth Not

Then these men assembled, and found Daniel praying and making supplication before his God. Then they came near, and spake before the king concerning the king's decree; Hast thou not signed a decree, that every man that shall ask a petition of any God or man within thirty days, save of thee, O king, shall be cast into the den of lions? The king answered and said, The thing is true, according to the law of the Medes and Persians, which altereth not. (Daniel 6:11, 12)

The future does look foreboding with many storm clouds hanging over our heads. With such uncertainty in front of us, how can we find the courage to move forward for ourselves, let alone put ourselves wholeheartedly into the work of spreading the gospel? It could be easy to become discouraged, fall into despair, or worse yet, give up on the hope of eternal life. While we know that the second coming of Christ is imminent, it may be difficult for our hearts to see past the daily obstacles that stand in our way. The Bible is our source of strength for such times as these, and we can turn to it for one more story that gives us inspiration and confidence in God's providence.

We turn to a very familiar story in the Bible, the story of Daniel in the lions' den. One thing has always frustrated me about this story in Daniel, chapter 6, and it would be the line that is included in the verse at the beginning of the chapter: "the law of the Medes and Persians, which altereth not." Even from my youth, this concept bothered me as it seemed so incongruent to all of the other kings in ancient history. Why could the king not change the law? He was the king! Every other king seemed to do as he pleased whether he was a Pharaoh, an Assyrian king, or Babylon monarch. Even the kings of Judah or Israel often did as they pleased if they dared to rebel against God. Ahab killed the prophets of God. Herod had no second thoughts about wiping out an entire town's infants. Heathen kings took life or gave rewards as they pleased, and yet this one king, who ruled the most powerful nation on the earth, could not change his mind to save his dear friend. This seemed preposterous to me. What kind of king was he?

To irritate me more, this "rule" is found in the story of Esther as well when Ahasuerus was tricked by Haman to make a decree so that the Jews would be killed. Ahasuerus didn't actually rescind that law at Queen Esther's request. He made another law that allowed the Jews to defend themselves. "Odd, very odd," I thought to myself for a long time. Was it just another curious anecdote or oddity reported in the Bible? Why is that phrase recorded four times, once in the book of Esther and three times in the book of Daniel? Did God have a point to make? Was He repeating it to make sure we understand?

The king involved in the story of Daniel in the lions' den was King Darius the Mede. Darius was the king who marched against the city of Babylon, "breached" its walls and destroyed King Belshazzar the grandson of Nebuchadnezzar. A brilliant military strategist, Cyrus diverted the waters of the great river Euphrates that flowed though the city of Babylon. The Euphrates provided the inhabitants an abundance of fresh water, allowing them to last through even a prolonged siege of the city. By diverting the water of the river, the Median army marched right into the city on the dry riverbed and captured it without a long, drawn-out siege.

Once the city of Babylon was conquered, Darius was installed as the king of that realm. Darius found Daniel to be a great statesman and made him chief of all of the princes of the land. The jealousy of the other princes caused them to lay a plot to take the life of Daniel. To trap him, they took advantage of the fact once it was enacted, that the king could not change a law. As the familiar story goes, the princes convinced Darius that a law should be made that no one could make a petition to any god or man other than Darius for thirty days. Once Daniel was caught by this law, there was no way for Darius to free Daniel. The king desperately looked for a means to absolve Daniel, but no loophole could be found. The law of the Medes and Persians could not be altered!

Fortunately for Daniel, God protected him in the lions' den, sending His angel to shut the mouth of the lions. It should not be overlooked that Darius told Daniel, "Thy God whom thou serveth continually, He will deliver thee" (Daniel 6:16). Daniel's faith was so "infectious" that even this heathen king believed in God's power to deliver.

"The law of the Medes and Persian, which alters not"—what is there to learn from this? King Darius of Media was the uncle of King Cyrus the Great, who was the king of the Persia. Cyrus gave control of all lands that

Darius conquered to the control of his uncle. There were two monarchs who controlled the empire of the Medes and Persians. Is was around this same time of the story of the lions' den, 537 BC,[135] that King Cyrus of Persia made the first decree that the Jews could return to their country and rebuild the temple that Nebuchadnezzar had destroyed.

Shortly after this time Daniel had his vision that is recorded in Daniel, chapters 9 and 10, which gave the prophecy of the seventy weeks, when the prophecy was to start, and the 2,300-day prophecy of Daniel 8. Daniel was praying earnestly for God to fulfill the prophecy of Jeremiah (Jeremiah 25:11), the promise to restore the nation of Israel and the city of Jerusalem. Perhaps this was the real reason why the devil wanted the other princes to stop Daniel from praying to God. E. G. White stated:

> The deliverance of Daniel from the den of lions had been used of God to create a favorable impression upon the mind of Cyrus the Great. The sterling qualities of the man of God as a statesman of farseeing ability led the Persian ruler to show him marked respect and to honor his judgment. (*Prophets and Kings*, 557)

Cyrus was considering a decision about allowing the Jews to return to Jerusalem. Of course the devil didn't want the Jews to leave Babylon to rebuild the temple and Jerusalem, for without Jerusalem, there could be no fulfillment of the prophecies of the Messiah. "The effectual fervent prayer of a righteous man availeth much" (James 5:16), and Daniel was righteous and much beloved in heaven. The intercessory prayers of Daniel may have been an important part of the battle over the mind of Cyrus to win the freedom of the Jewish people from Babylon.

So it was in the year 536 BC[136] after King Cyrus' decree that the Jews began to return to rebuild the temple and establish self government based on their Mosaic laws, including the rites and services of the temple. Ezra, the scribe educated in the Mosaic laws, was one of the principle characters who returned to the ruined city of Jerusalem. He, along with the prophets Haggai and Zechariah and the priest Zerubbabel, left Babylon and returned to Jerusalem. In the seventh month after their return, they gathered

---

135 Francis D. Nichol, ed., "Main Events of the Persian Empire and Judea," *Seventh-day Adventist Bible Commentary*, vol. 3 (Washington, DC: The Review and Herald Publish Association, 1957), 325.

136 *Seventh-day Adventist Bible Commentary*, vol. 3, 325.

at the ruins of the temple and repaired the altar of sacrifice and offered burnt offerings, reinstating the worship services.

The return of the Jews and the reinstatement of the worship services were not celebrated by everyone in the region. As discussed in chapter 7, "The Bride, the Builders, and the Crisis," the Samaritans that lived in the area were not pleased with the return of the Jews. They sought to halt the temple's reconstruction and the reestablishment of the government of the Jewish people.

> Then the people of the land weakened the hands of the people of Judah, and troubled them in building, and hired counsellors against them, to frustrate their purpose, all the days of Cyrus king of Persia, even until the reign of Darius king of Persia. (Ezra 4:4, 5)

After many years of attempting to obstruct the building of the temple, the Samaritans took a different tact. A new king, Darius of Persia (different from Darius the Mede) sat on the throne in Persia in 522 BC. They appealed to Tatnai, governor of the region, questioning the right of the Jews to rebuild the temple. That Samaritans questioned the validity of the authority claimed by the Israelites to rebuild the temple and suggested that the king verify the decree, hoping that no such authority had been given or perhaps that the decree would not be found. The governor Tatnai sent a letter to the king Darius of Persia. The letter said:

> Be it known unto the king, that we went into the province of Judea, to the house of the great God, which is builded with great stones, and timber is laid in the walls, and this work goeth fast on, and prospereth in their hands. Then asked we those elders, and said unto them thus, Who commanded you to build this house, and to make up these walls? ... Now therefore, if it seem good to the king, let there be search made in the king's treasure house, which is there at Babylon, whether it be so, that a decree was made of Cyrus the king to build this house of God at Jerusalem, and let the king send his pleasure to us concerning this matter. (Ezra 5:8, 9, 17)

When Darius received this letter from Governor Tatnai, he enacted a search of the scrolls to find if the Jews did have authority to rebuild the temple. Ezra 6 records the details of this act.

Then Darius the king made a decree, and search was made in the house of the rolls, where the treasures were laid up in Babylon. And there was found at Achmetha, in the palace that is in the province of the Medes, a roll, and therein was a record thus written: In the first year of Cyrus the king the same Cyrus the king made a decree concerning the house of God at Jerusalem, Let the house be builded, the place where they offered sacrifices, and let the foundations thereof be strongly laid; the height thereof threescore cubits, and the breadth thereof threescore cubits; with three rows of great stones, and a row of new timber: and let the expenses be given out of the king's house: and also let the golden and silver vessels of the house of God, which Nebuchadnezzar took forth out of the temple which is at Jerusalem, and brought unto Babylon, be restored, and brought again unto the temple which is at Jerusalem, every one to his place, and place them in the house of God. (Ezra 6:1–5)

So a scroll was found in the province of the Medes confirming that King Cyrus had indeed made a decree that the Jews could return to Jerusalem and rebuild the temple. Also, the temple artifacts should be returned to the Jews to be put back into the temple. Thus, Darius wrote back to Governor Tatnai: "Let the work of this house of God alone; let the governor of the Jews and the elders of the Jews build this house of God in his place." (Ezra 6:7). Why did Darius order the governor to let the work of this house of God alone? It was because "the laws of the Medes and Persians ... altereth not"! King Cyrus had made this decree in the first year of his reign and this decree could not be altered. The very same policy that forced Daniel to face the lions' den and that made it necessary for the Jews to defend themselves in the days of Queen Esther was now working in the favor of the Jews to allow them to continue building the house of God.

Who could have known? God, of course. The same God who shut the mouth of the lions, established Esther as a queen, and kept the three Hebrew worthies safe in the fiery furnace also made sure that decades later the kingdom controlling the destiny of the children of Israel operated on laws and decrees rather than the whims of a monarch. This same government held even its kings accountable to their own laws and decrees. Furthermore, these laws were well documented and were carefully maintained with some form of organization so that they could be found and reviewed by future kings and rulers. With the kingdom of Persia in control of the destiny of Israel, God was able to fulfill His purpose in restoring the temple and the city of Jerusalem. He also made sure that His purposes could not be interfered or tampered with by future kings as long as Persia was in power.

When Darius the king of Persia, found the decree of Cyrus, he not only upheld the decree according to the laws of the Medes and Persians, but he also made his own decree to support the Jews, adding to the decree of Cyrus. "Moreover I make a decree what ye shall do to the elders of these Jews for the building of this house of God: that of the king's goods, even of the tribute beyond the river, forthwith expenses be given unto these men, that they be not hindered" (Ezra 6:8).

In addition, King Darius of Persia also provided for the funding of the construction work. He gave bullocks and rams and lambs for the burnt offering as well. One of the amazing parts of the story is that King Darius, the king of the "heathen" nation of Persia, asked that when the Jews offered sacrifices to Jehovah, that they would also pray to the God of heaven for himself and his sons.

> That which they have need of, both young bullocks, and rams, and lambs, for the burnt offerings of the God of heaven, wheat, salt, wine, and oil, according to the appointment of the priests which are at Jerusalem, let it be given them day by day without fail: that they may offer sacrifices of sweet savours unto the God of heaven, and pray for the life of the king, and of his sons. (Ezra 6:9, 10)

The influence of Daniel and other Jewish leaders like Ezra and Nehemiah was profound in that many of the Persian kings acknowledged the God of heaven and reverenced Him. The details of the decree show that Darius had a good understanding of the temple services and what was required for its performance. These kings showed more regard for the God of heaven than many of the kings of Israel.

Having lost this round of the fight, the devil was not about to quit and give up his attempts at stopping Jerusalem from being rebuilt. When Satan first tempted Christ in the wilderness, Jesus answered, "It is written …" (Matthew 4:4). In the second temptation Satan attempted to turn the tables by using the same words: "Cast thyself down: for it is written, He shall give his angels charge concerning thee" (Matthew 4:6).

Satan had tried to use this tactic once before. Having been thwarted by the fact that "the laws of the Medes and Persians … altereth not," he tried to use the records against the Jews the second time around. The temple had been completed, and the Jews were starting to rebuild the walls of the city of Jerusalem. While there was no direct mention in the decrees of either Cyrus or Darius about building the walls of the city, there may have been an implied permission to do so.

The governors of the region "beyond the river" (Ezra 4:17) in Judea, at the urging of the Samaritans, wrote a letter to then King Artaxerxes that these people, the Jews, were a rebellious people, and if they were permitted to rebuild the wall, they would revolt against the king. They did not question the authority given to the Jews to build the walls,[137] but rather tried to use their past history as recorded carefully in the archives of Babylon and Persia. These governors accused the Jews of planning sedition and claimed that if the walls were built that they would not pay tribute to the king of Persia. So the governors asked the king to review the history of the Jews to see the kind of people they were because it was written in their books.

> Therefore have we sent and certified the king; That search may be made in the book of the records of thy fathers: so shalt thou find in the book of the records, and know that this city is a rebellious city, and hurtful unto kings and provinces, and that they have moved sedition within the same of old time: for which cause was this city destroyed. We certify the king that, if this city be builded again, and the walls thereof set up, by this means thou shalt have no portion on this side the river. (Ezra 4:14, 15)

Artaxerxes I Longimanus was the king of Persia at this time, the son of Xerxes, which is literally what his name means. Xerxes was also known as Ahasuerus, the very same king who married Esther and made her queen. There was certainly a connection between Xerxes and the Jewish people, but it is unknown how Artaxerxes felt about the Jews at the time the report came to him from the governors on the other side of the river. Artaxerxes did search the scrolls and found that the report of his governors was accurate, and that the previous kings of Judah were rebellious.

> I commanded, and search hath been made, and it is found that this city of old time hath made insurrection against kings, and that rebellion and sedition have been made therein. There have been

---

137 Angel Manuel Rodriguez, "The 70 Weeks and 457 B.C.," (paper for Biblical Research Institute, Silver Spring, MD, April 1994).

mighty kings also over Jerusalem, which have ruled over all countries beyond the river; and toll, tribute, and custom, was paid unto them. Give ye now commandment to cause these men to cease, and that this city be not builded, until another commandment shall be given from me." (Ezra 4:19–21)

Artaxerxes gave the command to force the Jews to stop building the temple and the walls of the city. The order was that it was to stop and not to recommence until he specifically gave the order to start again. The next mention of Artaxerxes is in the book of Ezra, chapter 7, in the scene where Ezra went back to Jerusalem with a letter, a decree from King Artaxerxes, allowing the Jews to restart the work of building the temple. The decree stated:

Artaxerxes, king of kings, unto Ezra the priest, a scribe of the law of the God of heaven, perfect peace, and at such a time. I make a decree, that all they of the people of Israel, and of his priests and Levites, in my realm, which are minded of their own freewill to go up to Jerusalem, go with thee. Forasmuch as thou art sent of the king, and of his seven counsellors, to enquire concerning Judah and Jerusalem, according to the law of thy God which is in thine hand; And to carry the silver and gold, which the king and his counsellors have freely offered unto the God of Israel, whose habitation is in Jerusalem, And all the silver and gold that thou canst find in all the province of Babylon, with the freewill offering of the people, and of the priests, offering willingly for the house of their God which is in Jerusalem. (Ezra 7:12–16)

The king had quite a change of heart between his first decree to stop the work of rebuilding and the decree he sent with Ezra. He not only permitted the work to continue, but he also sent his freewill offerings of silver and gold. This was directed from both the king and his seven counselors. Why the change of heart? Was it because he had reexamined the scrolls of the decrees of Cyrus and Darius? No. The answer would seem to be found in verse 23.

Whatsoever is commanded by the God of heaven, let it be diligently done for the house of the God of heaven: for why should there be wrath against the realm of the king and his sons? (Ezra 7:23)

Artaxerxes decreed that whatsoever is commanded by the God of heaven should be done because he did not want to have the wrath of God against him or his sons for having stopped the work of building His house and his city. It would seem that Artaxerxes had quickly developed a very keen respect, even a fear, for the God of heaven. How did this happen?

While the answer is not recorded in Scripture, it may be reasonable to postulate that as the king studied the history books and scrolls, he did learn that Jerusalem and its kings had been rebellious. He may have learned that Jehoiakim, the king of Judah, did evil in the sight of the Lord and was taken captive by Nebuchadnezzar to Babylon. He may have seen then that two more kings were put in place, Jehoiachin and Zedekiah, who both did evil in the sight of the Lord. Zedekiah then rebelled against Nebuchadnezzar. Zedekiah even led the priests and the people to pollute the house of the Lord, and because of this rebellion, the Lord allowed Nebuchadnezzar destroyed the city and burn the temple (see 2 Kings 24, 25). This would have confirmed the warnings by his governors about the dangers of allowing the Jews to rebuild Jerusalem.

Given how meticulous the Persians were about recordkeeping and history, it may be that the king and his seven counselors continued to study the history books about these people. Artaxerxes' command to cease the building of the temple indicated that he intended to study the issue further, for he said that this stoppage was "until" he made another commandment. The king may have read the history of the Jews in Babylon and about a young man named Daniel who became an advisor to not only Nebuchadnezzar but also Darius the Mede. He may have read the prophecy that Daniel made in interpreting the dream of Nebuchadnezzar, foretelling of the rise of the Medo-Persian Empire to a world power, a prophecy that had obviously come true.

Artaxerxes would also have read that the Greeks were the next in line to be a world power, according to the prophecy that was painfully obvious as his father Xerxes had already fought many battles with Greece by that time. Xerxes would have already suffered a terrible defeat at Themopylea at the hands of King Leonidas and his 300 Spartans.[138] So Artaxerxes had a front row seat in watching the prophecies of Daniel unfold, confirming the power of his God to tell the future.

---

138 "Greek and Roman Materials," Diodorus Siculus, Library, http://www.perseus.tufts.edu/hopper/text?doc=Diod.+11.4 (accessed December 2012). Doidorus Siculus was a Greek historian who lived around 30 BC.

Reading on he may have discovered the attempt by Nebuchadnezzar to coerce all peoples to worship his statue, but three young Hebrew men defied him. When King Nebuchadnezzar threw these three men into a fiery furnace to execute them, they were unharmed. Thus, the king made a decree that everyone should worship the God of Shadrach, Meshach, and Abednego or face severe punishment! These kings certainly loved to make decrees!

Continuing to read the history of the Jews in Babylon, Artaxerxes would have come to the decree of Darius the Mede who also commanded that no one could ask a petition to any God or man for thirty days. He would have read the outcome of this decree, which was yet another decree, "that in every dominion of my kingdom, men should tremble and fear before the God of Daniel" (Daniel 6:26) Artaxerxes would also likely have read that even Cyrus the Great, in his decree to rebuild the temple, identified the Lord God of heaven as the God who had given Cyrus and the Persian nation rulership over all the kingdoms of the earth.

Such evidence may have caused Artaxerxes to have a change of heart regarding the stoppage of the building of the temple and the walls of Jerusalem. Perhaps he began to fear going against the God of heaven who is all powerful and who gives kingdoms to whom He pleases and can take away kingdoms from those who oppose Him. He may have been so fearful of the wrath of such a powerful God that he and his counselors gave offerings of gold and silver to help build His temple and His city of Jerusalem. In Artaxerxes' decree of 457 BC, he mentioned four times that the house of God was in Jerusalem, inextricably tying the temple to the city so that no one could think to stop the work of building the temple or the walls.

Lastly, Artaxerxes mentioned in his decree that Ezra should teach all the people who were "beyond the river" the laws of God and judge them according to these laws (Ezra 7:25). The king had knowledge of the laws of God, of which Ezra, a priest and a scribe, was an expert. Having been given such an understanding of the laws of God, which had been handed down to Moses, would the king not have learned from Ezra of the great exodus of the Jewish nation from Egypt? This exodus culminated with ten plagues, the last of which was the death of the firstborn of each family.

So neither Artaxerxes nor his sons wanted to incur the wrath of God by halting the building of God's house, thus thwarting Satan's plan to use the history of the Jewish nation against them. In studying the history of the Jewish nation, Artaxerxes would have seen the wonderful workings of

God in favor of His people and how this was meant to be a blessing to all peoples, even his own nation.

"The law of the Medes and Persians, which altereth not"! A powerful statement testifies to the providence of God in caring for not only His people but also in providing for the salvation of the world. God put into place many events to ensure that the rebuilding of the temple and the city of Jerusalem would occur exactly as He had proclaimed through his prophets, for the temple and the city would be central to the works of the Messiah.

This begs yet other questions. Why was God in such a rush to build the temple and the city of Jerusalem in 457 BC? This was 454 years before the birth of Christ, certainly more than enough time to build the temple and the city. Why did God push His people to complete the building in spite of hardships and challenges? Why did He reprove His people so sternly through famines and financial crises when they slackened their pace in the building of His house? The answers are quite evident by looking at history. The Greeks were coming to power.

The temple was completed in 515 BC, while the city walls of Jerusalem were completed in 444 BC, just three years after the decree of Artaxerxes.[139] The building apparently went much more smoothly after the decree and the warning of severe consequences for anyone who caused opposition to the work. With the completion of the temple and the city, the people were instructed in the Mosaic laws and learned to worship the true God of heaven. The laws were strictly enforced, for the Jews feared that Jerusalem would be destroyed again if they disobeyed.

This strict observance, combined with national pride, eventually became a religious culture deeply ingrained in legalism where observance of the law was deemed to be the way to salvation. Into this culture of pharisaical observance of the law came Christ to show "the way, the truth and the life" (John 14:6). However, in the centuries between the completion of Jerusalem and the advent of Christ, two world powers were to arise. The first one came to power 120 years after the completion of Jerusalem when Alexander the Great led the army of Greece to conquer the world.

The Greek belief system had its basis in its philosophers and gods, and the people were always searching for enlightenment. Philosophers such as Socrates and Plato established the Greek mindset, and they worshiped false gods such as Apollo and Zeus. There was no room in the Greek psyche for

---

139 *Seventh-day Adventist Bible Commentary*, vol. 3, 326, 7.

a God of the universe who was Creator and Savior. Simple faith in a loving Creator was an idea scorned by the Greeks as unintellectual. Neither was there a support of such religion as the Jews held nor was there help politically or financially. Furthermore, it was necessary for the Jewish faith and culture founded on the laws of God to be well established in order to withstand the years of oppression that was to follow at the hands of the Greeks and the Romans. The time of relative peace under the protection of the Persians was beneficial for the Jewish people to reacquaint themselves with God of their fathers and His way.

> A mighty king shall stand up, that shall rule with great dominion, and do according to his will. And when he shall stand up, his kingdom shall be broken and shall be divided toward the four winds of heaven; and not to his posterity, nor according to his dominion which he ruled: for his kingdom shall be plucked up, even for others beside those. (Daniel 11:3, 4)

Daniel prophesied about the rise of Alexander the Great who would come to power in 323 BC after the fall of the Persian Empire as a global power. Judea, under the control of Greece for the next 150 years, would be ruled by the ever-changing political powers that represented the time of Greek rule. From Alexander, to his four generals, to the Ptolemies and Seleucids in Egypt and Syria, to Antiochus IV Epiphanes, there was constant turmoil throughout the region, and the Jewish religious services were corrupted by these powers.

Then, in the second century BC, a new power came into power, which brought some stability but no less turmoil in the religious order of the Jews. "The robbers of thy people shall exalt themselves to establish the vision" (Daniel 11:14). Daniel introduced the Romans as the next power, which would have power over Judea and control the Jewish people. "He that cometh against him shall do according to his own will, and none shall stand before him: and he shall stand in the glorious land which by his hand shall be consumed" (Daniel 11:16). By 65 BC, Syria and Egypt were under the control of the Roman Empire, and its reach also covered Palestine.

"Then shall stand up in his estate a raiser of taxes in the glory of the kingdom: but within a few days he shall be destroyed, neither in anger nor in battle" (Daniel 11:20). Here, Daniel spoke about the raiser of taxes, Augustus Caesar, who was the ruler at the time of Christ's birth. His decree to take a census of all the people caused Mary and Joseph to go to their hometown of Bethlehem where Christ was born in a manger, thus fulfilling prophecy.

God's providential leading and perfect timing were both essential in ensuring that all of His plans were carried out in the fullness of time, even as it was executed by human hands. Any slippage in this timing and His plans may not have succeeded. We have the benefit of hindsight and historical records to see these great workings of God. In accordance with the 70 week-prophecy of Daniel chapter 9, Messiah the Prince was born, and He began his ministry exactly 483 years, or 69 prophetic weeks, after the decree of Artaxerxes. Jesus was dedicated in the temple, and at the age of 12, He questioned the learned elders and rabbis on the Scriptures at the temple.

At the start of His ministry, He cleansed the temple to signify His purpose in ministry. He healed all manner of diseases and infirmities, blessed the children, and taught about the kingdom of heaven. He rode triumphantly into Jerusalem in the last week of His ministry and wept over the city. Then in the midst of the week, or three and one-half years after beginning His ministry, the Messiah was sacrificed, making an end of sins and finishing the transgression and to make reconciliation for iniquity.

After another three and one-half years at the stoning of Stephen outside the gate of Jerusalem, the 70 weeks provided to the Jewish nation were finished. The temple and Jerusalem were closely linked with the ministry of Christ, marking the importance of its completion. The completion was necessary at the time of the Persians and the favorable treatment of the Jews. God worked through people, rulers, and kings to make the prophecies about Jerusalem come true at times working with great urgency.

These events all transpired in the early years of the 2,300-day prophetic period. Rolling forward 2,300 years into the future, which would be at the end of this prophetic period, God was moving again to put conditions into place, this time to draw the Christian church out of Babylon and prepare them for His second coming.[140] God was moving powerfully to bring about these final events in preparation for the second advent.

From 1844 onward, there were great revivals and powerful movements that could have launched the last-day events, but God could not bring them to fruition due to the church's lack of willingness and its unprepared state. In 1903, Ellen White said that sadly, it was too late. She had a vision which, she wrote about and entitled "What Might Have Been." This vision

---

140 See a discussion of these events in chapter 7, "The Bride, The Builders, and the Crisis"; and in chapter 9, "The Panic of 1873."

showed what might have happened in the church, and the revival and reformation that still needs to take place in the church before we are prepared to do the final work as the latter rain is poured out. In waking from her vision, she was disappointed to find out that it was only what might have been and not actual.

To the Battle Creek Church—

One day at noon I was writing of the work that might have been done at the last General Conference if the men in positions of trust had followed the will and way of God. Those who have had great light have not walked in the light. The meeting was closed, and the break was not made. Men did not humble themselves before the Lord as they should have done, and the Holy Spirit was not imparted.

I had written thus far when I lost consciousness, and I seemed to be witnessing a scene in Battle Creek.

We were assembled in the auditorium of the Tabernacle. Prayer was offered, a hymn was sung, and prayer was again offered. Most earnest supplication was made to God. The meeting was marked by the presence of the Holy Spirit. The work went deep, and some present were weeping aloud.

One arose from his bowed position and said that in the past he had not been in union with certain ones and had felt no love for them, but that now he saw himself as he was. With great solemnity he repeated the message to the Laodicean church: "'Because thou sayest, I am rich, and increased with goods, and have need of nothing.' In my self-sufficiency this is just the way I felt," he said. "'And knowest not that thou art wretched, and miserable, and poor, and blind, and naked.' I now see that this is my condition. My eyes are opened. My spirit has been hard and unjust. I thought myself righteous, but my heart is broken, and I see my need of the precious counsel of the One who has searched me through and through. Oh, how gracious and compassionate and loving are the words, 'I counsel thee to buy of Me gold tried in the fire, that thou mayest be rich; and white raiment, that thou mayest be clothed, and that the shame of thy nakedness do not appear; and anoint thine eyes with eyesalve, that thou mayest see." Revelation 3:17, 18.

The speaker turned to those who had been praying, and said: "We have something to do. We must confess our sins, and humble our hearts before God." He made heartbroken confessions and then stepped up to several of the brethren, one after another, and extended his hand, asking forgiveness. Those to whom he spoke sprang to their feet, making confession and asking forgiveness, and they fell upon one another's necks, weeping. The spirit of confession spread through the entire congregation. It was a Pentecostal season. God's praises were sung, and far into the night, until nearly morning, the work was carried on.

The following words were often repeated, with clear distinctness: "As many as I love, I rebuke and chasten: be zealous therefore, and repent. Behold, I stand at the door, and knock: if any man hear My voice, and open the door, I will come in to him, and will sup with him, and he with Me." Verses 19, 20.

No one seemed to be too proud to make heartfelt confession, and those who led in this work were the ones who had influence, but had not before had courage to confess their sins.

There was rejoicing such as never before had been heard in the Tabernacle.

Then I aroused from my unconsciousness, and for a while could not think where I was. My pen was still in my hand. The words were spoken to me: "*This might have been.* All this the Lord was waiting to do for His people. All heaven was waiting to be gracious." I thought of where we might have been had thorough work been done at the last General Conference, and agony of disappointment came over me as I realized that what I had witnessed was not a reality.

God's way is always the right and the prudent way. He always brings honor to His name. Man's only security against rash, ambitious movements is to keep the heart in harmony with Christ Jesus. Man's wisdom is untrustworthy. Man is fickle, filled with self-esteem, pride, and selfishness. Let the workers doing God's service trust wholly in the Lord. Then the leaders will reveal that they are willing to be led, not by human wisdom, which is as useless to lean upon as is a broken reed, but by the wisdom of the Lord, who has said: "If any of you lack wisdom, let him ask of God, that giveth to all men liberally, and upbraideth not; and it shall be given him. But let him ask in faith, nothing wavering." James 1:5, 6. (*Testimonies to the Church*, vol. 8, 104–106)

For nearly 60 years, from 1844 to 1903, God was working with the church to bring about the conversion and reformation needed before the latter rain, the time of trouble, and the second coming of Christ. The unfaithfulness of the church in preparing themselves was at the heart of this failure. Just as in the time of Daniel, Ezra, and Nehemiah, God's providence was shown in moving time and again to prepare His people to complete the building of the temple and the city, but just like the Israelites at the borders of Canaan, we wouldn't go in. As in the time of Daniel to Haggai, God had His mighty messenger, Ellen White, to speak through to the people directly. However, unlike the Jews at the time of Daniel, we failed to heed the call. But is there something we can learn from our failure in taking advantage of God's providence?

Certainly, we can learn many spiritual lessons from the 1888 experience, but perhaps there is an important historical lesson as well. Why did God work so hard to try to bring about the end of this world in the late nineteenth century around the time of Mrs. White? We learned from Ezra's and Nehemiah's experiences that God wanted to finish building the temple and the city because He knew that the Greeks and Romans would be coming into power. God also knew that these kingdoms would not be supportive of the work that needed to be done. Could there be a parallel in modern history?

The next 80 years that would pass from the turn of the twentieth century would be the bloodiest in the history of the world. Starting with the World War I (WWI) in 1914, wars and rumors of wars dominated world events. WWI saw 16 million casualties, including soldiers and civilians. As WWI was raging, the Russian Revolution was also taking place in 1917, which saw nine million dead. Another eight million people died due to the Holodomor and Soviet Famines from 1932 to 1933.[141] The Chinese

---

141 "Soviet Policy and the Ukrainian Genocide of 1932-33," Ukrainian Genocide Famine Foundation, USA Inc. http://ukrainiangenocide.org/dsovietpolicyandukrainiangenocide.html (accessed August 2012).

Communist Revolution began in 1926 lasting until 1949 and the famine that resulted took more than 40 million lives.[142] The 1930s saw the rise of Adolf Hitler in Germany, during their period of great economic collapse. The Nazis under Hitler executed six million Jews, but also not to be forgotten are the many others who died at their hands, including their own political dissenters, Russian POWs, Polish and Soviet citizens, the handicapped and mixed-race children, amounting to 17 million in total.[143]

World War II (WWII) broke out in 1939, embroiling most nations and resulting casualties of about 66 million people.[144] Deaths during WWII in Germany and the USSR accounted for more than 10% of their respective populations.[145] The fall of Burma to the Japanese during WWII also resulted in the Bengal famine, which resulted in four million deaths.[146]

Following WWII, the Korean War[147] resulted in three million deaths between 1950 and 1953., followed by the Vietnam War,[148] which took six million lives. Three million died in the killing fields of Cambodia.[149] Genocide in Rwanda[150] saw a million deaths. Three million died in the

---

142 Richard Louis Walker, *The Human Cost of Communism in China*, Senate Committee Print (Washington, DC: US Government Printing Office, 1971), iv.

143 Brzezinski, Zbigniew, *Out of Control: Global Turmoil on the Eve of the Twenty-first Century* (New York: Touchstone, 1995), 10, 11.

144 "Source List and Detailed Death Tolls for the Primary Megadeaths of the Twentieth Century: Second World War," http://necrometrics.com/20c5m.htm#Second (accessed August 2012).

145 "World War II casualties," Wikipedia: The Free Encyclopedia, http://en.wikipedia.org/wiki/World_War_II_casualties (accessed August 2012).

146 Dr. Gideon Polya interview by Robyn Williams, "Bengali Famine," Radio National, February 21, 1999, http://www.abc.net.au/radionational/programs/ockhamsrazor/bengali-famine/3556698#transcript (accessed August 2012).

147 "Death Tolls for the Major Wars and Atrocities of the Twentieth Century," Korean War, http://necrometrics.com/20c1m.htm#Ko (accessed August 2012).

148 Ibid., Vietnam War, http://necrometrics.com/20c1m.htm#Vietnam (accessed August 2012).

149 R. J. Rummel, "Statistics of Democide: Genocide and Mass Murder Since 1900" http://www.hawaii.edu/powerkills/NOTE5.HTM (accessed August 2012).

150 "Rwanda: How the Genocide Happened," BBC News, December 18, 2008, http://news.bbc.co.uk/2/hi/1288230.stm (accessed August 2012).

Sudan[151] and five million in the Congo.[152] Incalculable losses of humanity in the past century were due to these and many more wars, genocides, and the famines that resulted from wars and revolutions. How it must have pained God to have to see so many people die horrible deaths when it could have been prevented. How difficult it must have been to for God to make the decision to put a stop to the events that would lead to His second coming, knowing that all of these deaths would occur!

The impact on the gospel work because of these armed conflicts and political turmoil of the past century is that the work was stymied. The fighting, border closings, the denial of religious freedoms, and the horrendous death tolls have made it nearly impossible to finish the gospel commission to preach to the whole world. The world, in large portions and over long periods of time throughout the twentieth century, has been inaccessible to gospel workers. Even though nothing is impossible for God, He still works through His human agents and relies on governments and leaders to pave the way for His messengers.

While God has had His workers in every part of the world, the conditions that have prevailed universally have been an insurmountable obstacle for a mass communication of the gospel. The global wars in the first half of the century had rendered the gospel work impossible to conduct on a worldwide scale. Then in the second half of the century, the Cold War with the USSR and the closure of China due to the Communist regime sequestered a third of the world population from the Bible. Jesus said that we would hear of wars and rumors of wars (Matthew 24:6). In the twentieth century, this is precisely the order of events: WWI and WWII, then the Cold War. Wars and rumors of wars!

In the past two decades a change has occurred, starting with the fall of communism in the USSR. Since 1989, all of the countries that formed the Soviet bloc are now open to the work the work of the gospel. China has become more moderate, realizing that they need the rest of the world in order to complete its industrial revolution. By opening to commerce, China is also now more accessible to the world and to the church. While

---

151   Brad Phillips, Matt Chancy, "Three Million Dead and Counting, Mr. President," Persecution Project Foundation, September 1, 2011, http://persecutionproject.org/general/million-dead-counting-president/ (accessed January 2013).

152   Joe Bavier, "Congo war-driven crisis kills 45,000 a month: study" Reuters, January 22, 2008, http://www.reuters.com/article/2008/01/22/us-congo-democratic-death-idUSL2280201220080122 (accessed January 2013).

armed conflicts continue in the world, there is relatively more peace now than ever before in the past century.

The revolutions in the Middle East and the Arab Spring that started in Tunisia in 2011 are opening up North Africa and the Middle East. Though it is far from being a "walk in the park" to preach the gospel in Islamic countries, the political landscape is changing and doors appear to be opening, even if just a crack.

With the death of Kim Jong-Il, North Korea has decided to allow the United Nations to provide food assistance to the country. This is perhaps an indication that the new leader, Kim Jong-Un, the son of Jong-Il, is perhaps more open to change than his father. In the past century since Ellen White lamented that it was too late for the latter rain to fall, never before has the world been a more receptive place for the message of the gospel, the three angels' messages, the Sabbath, and the second coming of Christ as it is now! Our opportunity may be here to once again walk up to the Jordan and cross over into Canaan!

## Chapter 17

# Approaching the Jordan Again

As they that bare the ark were come unto Jordan, and the feet of the priests that bare the ark were dipped in the brim of the water, for Jordan overfloweth all his banks all the time of harvest. (Joshua 3:15)

When the Israelites came to the Jordan to cross it for the second time, the river was swollen and overflowing because it was the time of the harvest. The priests were to walk up to the river with the Ark of the Covenant and dip their feet in the water. As soon as they stepped into the water with faith, the waters parted and they walked on dry ground.

God has now brought us near to the borders of the Promised Land once again, murmuring and complaining, ungrateful, unrepentant, and unmindful of the time and place that we find ourselves in. We have failed to become the light of the world as God had asked us to be. As faint as it may be, we have this hope that we can cross over even though we are so woefully unprepared. As we approach the banks of the Jordan once more, God once again, has sent a financial crisis into this world to arouse His people to action and to set the stage for the final battles to begin. He will never again see His work make a retreat from the frontlines. He will prepare His people in a trial by fire to purify them to be ready to finish the great commission. He has given more light to us than ever before, and the experiences of the past should guide our actions now.

> It is just as essential that the people of God in this day should bear in mind how and when they have been tested, and where their faith has failed; where they have imperiled His cause by their unbelief and also by their self-confidence. God's mercy, His sustaining providence, His never-to-be-forgotten deliverances, are to be recounted, step by step. *As God's people thus review the past, they should see that the Lord is ever repeating His dealings.* They should understand the warnings given, and should beware not to repeat

their mistakes. Renouncing all self-dependence, they are to trust in Him to save them from again dishonoring His name. In every victory that Satan gains, souls are imperiled. Some become the subjects of his temptations, never to recover themselves. Then let those who have made mistakes walk carefully, at every step praying: "Hold up my goings in Thy paths, that my footsteps slip not." Psalm 17:5. (*Testimonies to the Church*, vol. 7, 210, emphasis added)

God has been giving us example after example, lesson after lesson, and warning after warning. If we can't see the events that are before us, it is only because we choose not to see. We often murmur and complain about the things that have happened to us rather than to try to see the way that God was trying to lead us. When we recognize the providence of God, we will see that he has so lovingly and carefully guided our way and that we have fallen only when we choose to disregard the grace He has given us.

For some, there is no need to press the point further about the financial crisis as they are fully immersed in its impacts. So many are just barely hanging on to hope or languishing in despair because of the calamities that the crisis has already placed upon them. It may be hard to see God's grace in their trials or any sign of providence in their tribulations. To these I would say that God does have a plan and is working on your behalf even now, even through the surrounding darkness and uncertainty.

Though we may plead for deliverance, or even just to see the light at the end of the tunnel, it may be that it is more needful for us to ask for grace to endure and to learn to trust God than for us to receive the resolution or a mere sign that it may be near. We are preparing for a time when all we will have to rely on for our very existence are His promises and our faith in Him. If we humble ourselves, move forward in faith, seek to serve God, and honor Him with our lives, we will have made the wise purchase of the gold tried in the fire. We will become prepared to be part of the remnant that vindicates His name.

Still, many have not felt the weight of the financial crisis and do not sense the urgency of the situation and the impending disasters that await us. God has ever repeated His dealings with His people so that none can mistake the messages that He conveys. Through the experiences of Joseph, the children of Israel, Daniel, the exiles from Babylon, and many others, He has been trying to show us the pattern of things to come. From the prophetic writings of Daniel, Isaiah, Habakkuk, and John, as well as the writings of E. G. White, we are given specific details so we can understand the events soon to unfold. Through our daily experiences, we can see God's leading and providences working in our lives.

Through these lights we can have clearer understanding of the events that are happening around us today. We could just wait to act until it begins to impact our lives. We could prepare by carefully stockpiling resources to try to make ourselves comfortable for the bumpy ride ahead. Or we can respond by committing our time and resources to seize the opportunity that God is presenting to us to finish the work.

Twice in the Old Testament God required a numbering of his people. In the book of Numbers, Moses called for warriors from each and every tribe to come forward and be accounted in preparation for the battle.

> Take ye the sum of all the congregation of the children of Israel, after their families, by the house of their fathers, with the number of their names, every male by their polls; From twenty years old and upward, all that are able to go forth to war in Israel: thou and Aaron shall number them by their armies. And with you there shall be a man of every tribe; every one head of the house of his fathers.
>
> And these are the names of the men that shall stand with you: of the tribe of Reuben; Elizur the son of Shedeur. Of Simeon; Shelumiel the son of Zurishaddai. Of Judah; Nahshon the son of Amminadab. Of Issachar; Nethaneel the son of Zuar. Of Zebulun; Eliab the son of Helon. Of the children of Joseph: of Ephraim; Elishama the son of Ammihud: of Manasseh; Gamaliel the son of Pedahzur. Of Benjamin; Abidan the son of Gideoni. Of Dan; Ahiezer the son of Ammishaddai. Of Asher; Pagiel the son of Ocran. Of Gad; Eliasaph the son of Deuel. Of Naphtali; Ahira the son of Enan. These were the renowned of the congregation, princes of the tribes of their fathers, heads of thousands in Israel. (Numbers 1:2-16)

Again in the book of Nehemiah, God called His people out from Babylon to rebuild Jerusalem and the temple.

> Now these are the children of the province that went up out of the captivity, of those which had been carried away, whom Nebuchadnezzar the king of Babylon had carried away unto Babylon, and came again unto Jerusalem and Judah, every one unto

his city; which came with Zerubbabel: Jeshua, Nehemiah, Seraiah, Reelaiah, Mordecai, Bilshan, Mispar, Bigvai, Rehum, Baanah. The number of the men of the people of Israel: The children of Parosh, two thousand an hundred seventy and two. (Ezra 2:1–3)

God was calling out His people, asking who would stand for Him. He made it very personal, calling each family out by name and recording their numbers. This will happen one more time. God is calling for people who will stand for Him in battle, for those who will build His temple and His city. They are called the 144,000.

Saying, Hurt not the earth, neither the sea, nor the trees, till we have sealed the servants of our God in their foreheads. And I heard the number of them which were sealed: and there were sealed an hundred and forty and four thousand of all the tribes of the children of Israel.

Of the tribe of Judah were sealed twelve thousand. Of the tribe of Reuben were sealed twelve thousand. Of the tribe of Gad were sealed twelve thousand.

Of the tribe of Aser were sealed twelve thousand. Of the tribe of Nepthalim were sealed twelve thousand. Of the tribe of Manasses were sealed twelve thousand.

Of the tribe of Simeon were sealed twelve thousand. Of the tribe of Levi were sealed twelve thousand. Of the tribe of Issachar were sealed twelve thousand.

Of the tribe of Zabulon were sealed twelve thousand. Of the tribe of Joseph were sealed twelve thousand. Of the tribe of Benjamin were sealed twelve thousand. (Revelation 7:3–8)

God is looking for a people who will represent Him and do His battle, and the battle does not lie in the time of great tribulation after the close of probation. The battle does not start when the death decree is passed. The battle does not begin when Sunday laws are passed. We cannot join the battle when the latter rain begins to fall. The battle starts today so we can be ready to receive the latter rain. We cannot receive the latter rain unless we take up the battle today!

> "I saw that many were neglecting the preparation so needful and were looking to the time of "refreshing" and the "latter rain" to fit them to stand in the day of the Lord and to live in His sight. Oh, how many I saw in the time of trouble without a shelter! They had neglected the needful preparation; therefore they could not receive the refreshing that all must have to fit them to live in the sight of a holy God. ... *I saw that none could share the "refreshing" unless they obtain the victory over every besetment, over pride, selfishness, love of the world, and over every wrong word and action.* We should, therefore, be drawing nearer and nearer to the Lord and be earnestly seeking that preparation necessary to enable us to stand in the battle in the day of the Lord. Let all remember that God is holy and that none but holy beings can ever dwell in His presence. (*Early Writings*, 71, emphasis added)

The financial crisis is deepening and intensifying even as leaders try to fix it, mask its effects, or deflect if from our view. Countries are in debt well beyond their ability to manage. Demographics in the developed world are a ticking time bomb as more people retire and fewer are born. The solutions that governments are employing will only make the crisis worse in the future. Even more so, the Bible points to greater calamities than the world has ever faced. There is an enemy at work trying to bind in darkness and despair anyone who doesn't know the protection of a Savior and the providence of His love for us. The financial crisis was a wake-up call for me, and it is God's wake up call to His people to take a stand, to purify themselves, to be ready to receive and benefit from the latter rain. It is a call to arms for the remnant of God's people to serve the King of kings, to prepare our households for the trials ahead, and to put in motion plans to minister and reach the people with the gospel of Christ. The financial crisis is an escalation of end-time events that lead to His second coming. They are events that have been put into motion that will ultimately fulfill the long-awaited Bible prophecies.

# TIDINGS OUT OF THE Northeast

## Marc Alden Swearingen

$14.95 | RP1033
ISBN: 978-1-933291-02-4
Pages: 272, paperback

As humanity speeds toward the second coming of Christ, precious few are truly prepared for Him. Indeed, even many Christians don't know what Bible prophecy really has to say about their role in the last days, giving Satan a powerful inroad to create confusion and faithlessness on the part of God's people.

That's why this detailed study into the verses of Daniel 11, one of the most confusing yet powerful prophetic chapters in the Bible, was written. Step by step, the author first leads you through key passages in Daniel and Revelation that will lay the pivotal groundwork needed to grasp the events of Daniel 11. Then with scholarly, but easy-to-understand detail, he takes you on an exciting historical journey that has staggering implications for you and your loved ones today.

If you have ever been intimidated by the book of Daniel, you no longer need to be. Now you can boldly lead others to a truer understanding of earth's final events and the role that God's people will play in the very end of days.

Don't go another day without diving into the mysteries found on these pages. It's an awesome resource for your study library.

## VISIT WWW.REMNANTPUBLICATIONS.COM OR CALL (800) 423-1319 TO ORDER.

# The REMNANT STUDY BIBLE
## WITH E. G. WHITE COMMENTS

**KJV** — Available in the classic King James and the New King James versions. Also in Large Print — **NKJV**

## POWER-PACKED FEATURES INCLUDE:

- Two-color printing, plus words of Christ in red letters
- 20 topical studies chained throughout the Bible with index to chains
- Thousands of helpful end-of-verse Scripture cross-references and notes
- Full-color section featuring Bible timeline, furniture and cleansing of the sanctuary, and prophetic symbols
- How-to-use section, brief biography of E. G. White, Bible symbols and their meanings, parables and miracles of Jesus Christ, read-your-Bible-through-in-a-year guide, how sin began, and more
- Extensive concordance, 8-page section of color maps, 2 ribbon markers, wider margins, plus much more!

### Prices starting at $49.95
### Get the last study Bible you'll ever need!

### Visit www.RemnantPublications.com or call (800) 423-1319 to order.